LITTLE LIVES
of
THE GREAT SAINTS

By
John O'Kane Murray, M.A., M.D.

Author of
Popular History of the Catholic Church in the United States,
Prose and Poetry of Ireland,
Lives of the Catholic Heroes and Heroines of America
and *Lessons in English Literature.*

"Let all thy works, O Lo.
thee: and let thy saints bless thee. They
shall speak of the glory of thy kingdom:
and shall tell of thy power: To make thy
might known to the sons of men: and the
glory of the magnificence of thy
kingdom."
—Psalm 144:10-12

TAN BOOKS AND PUBLISHERS, INC.
Rockford, Illinois 61105

IN SPEM VITAE AETERNAE

Imprimatur.

John Card. McCloskey
Archbp. of New York

June 2d 1880.

Originally published in 1880 by P. J. Kenedy & Sons, New York, New York.

Reprinted in 1977 by Marian Publications, South Bend, Indiana.

Library of Congress Catalog Card No.: 82-50593

ISBN: 0-89555-190-X

Printed and bound in the United States of America.

TAN BOOKS AND PUBLISHERS, INC.
P.O. Box 424
Rockford, Illinois 61105

1985

Prayer
Before Reading

COME, Holy Spirit, fill the hearts of Thy faithful and enkindle in them the fire of Thy love.

℣. Send forth Thy spirit and they shall be created.

℟. And Thou shalt renew the face of the earth.

Let Us Pray.

O God, Who didst instruct the hearts of the faithful by the light of the Holy Spirit, grant us by the same Spirit to have a right judgment in all things and ever to rejoice in His consolation. Through Christ our Lord. Amen.

THE ANGELIC SALUTATION
—

Hail Mary, full of grace, the Lord is with thee, blessed art thou among women and blessed is the fruit of thy womb, JESUS. Holy Mary, Mother of God, pray for us sinners, now and at the hour of our death. AMEN

•

Our Lady of Perpetual Help
Pray For Us

PREFACE.

THIS little volume contains thirty-one **Lives** arranged in the order of time. It begins with the Most Blessed Virgin, and ends with Saint Alphonsus Liguori. It is a month of Great Saints.

Each Life will be found short enough, I believe, to read at a sitting. Each is complete in itself. It has been my earnest endeavor to make every point as plain and interesting as possible by means of abundant notes—literary, historical, theological, descriptive, and geographical.

We live in a busy, enquiring age. But there is little leisure and less inclination for the perusal of large books. I have kept this fact in mind, and I venture to hope that no reader will feel weary over any portion of the *Little Lives*.

Biography has become very popular, and justly so. In no field of literature can wisdom and entertainment be gleaned more pleasantly than in reading the lives of truly illustrious men and women. But far above all the other children of Adam are the great Saints of the Catholic Church, in whose bright and virtuous careers we behold redeemed humanity soaring to the pinnacle of immortal glory.

In the preparation of this simple work, I have consulted none but the most approved and trustworthy sources of information. I have used no doubtful material. I am especially indebted to the writings of Ratisbonne, Montalembert, Butler, Baunard, Orsini, Camus, Gueranger, De Ligny, Jocelin, Vaughan, Weninger, Ormsby, Thébaud, Vetromile and many others.

I return my warm thanks to the learned and venerable Father A. J. Thébaud, S. J., of New York, for aid and light on several obscure points; and to the Rev. Father Maurice Ronayne, S. J., of the College of St. Francis Xavier, New York, who has been so kind and courteous as to read the advance sheets, and to give me suggestions and his valuable opinion of the work.

And now if there is one wish I would like to record here it is, that the *Little Lives* may fall into the hands of many young people, and that the perusal of it may increase their love of virtue, and their faith in the Catholic Church — the Guardian of Truth, and the Mother of the Great Saints.

JOHN O'KANE MURRAY.

BROOKLYN, N. Y.

January, 1880

CONTENTS

Contents.

LITTLE LIVES

OF

THE GREAT SAINTS.

THE MOST BLESSED VIRGIN MARY,

MOTHER OF GOD AND QUEEN OF SAINTS AND ANGELS

"Ave Maria! Thou whose name,
All but adoring love may claim."

"Bright Mother of our Maker, hail!
Thou Virgin ever blest,
The Ocean's Star by which we sail
And gain the port of rest!"

IT brings us back to the dawn of ages. It is the saddest event recounted in history. Tears cluster around the very words. Our first parents fell, and were driven out of the

lovely garden of Paradise.⁴   True happiness departed for other spheres.   Sin came.   The beauty
of the world was blighted, but the human race
was not left hopeless.   The serpent, in time, would
be crushed; and a woman, it was promised, would
repair the evil done by woman.⁵

This much we learn in the third chapter of that
Sacred Book which goes back to the beginning,
and fails not to carry us with mysterious grandeur
to the consummation of ages.

But in the meantime long centuries rolled by.
The Deluge nearly swept mankind out of exist-

⁴ The Arabian traditions place the terrestrial Paradise in that fair
valley of Damascus which the Eastern poets call the emerald of the
desert.   This idea is justified by its admirable situation, its beauty,
and its fertility; and a learned commentator on Genesis has not
hesitated to set down this fair site as that of the Garden of Eden;
although the names of the Euphrates and the Tigris indicate a position somewhat different.   In support of this Arab tradition, there is
shown, about half a day's journey from Damascus, a lofty mountain
of white marble shaded with beautiful trees, and therein is a cavern
pointed out as the abode of Adam, of Abel, and of Cain.   There also
is seen the sepulchre of Abel, which is much respected by the Turks.
The spot whereon the fratricide was committed is marked by four
pillars.—*Abbé Orsini.*

⁵ As soon as God communicated to fallen man His decree of
redemption, and promised that "the seed of the woman would
crush the head of the serpent," the Church was born, at least in
design.   Mankind was to be regenerated, born again; and those
who should comply with the conditions of reconciliation would
form a society united anew with the Creator.—*Father Thébaud
S. J.*

ence. Great empires arose, flourished, and decayed. The world was far from becoming better.
God was almost forgotten; but at length, unseen,
the glorious light of the bright day of promise
began to dawn on this sin-dimmed earth.

At Nazareth,[6] a city of Galilee,[7] there lived a
good, humble man of the race of David, named
Joachim. His wife was Anne. They had walked

[6] Nazareth, the place where the great work of the redemption of
man commenced, where the reconciliation of man with God had
its beginning, where the earth was declared to be at peace with
God, and where justice and peace kissed each other, is a city or
village of 3,000 inhabitants, 2,500 of which are Catholics. It is
handsomely located on an elevation of the western side of one of
the most beautiful valleys of Syria, and the land surrounding it is
in a fine state of cultivation—all laid out in gardens, orchards, and
luxuriant fields.—*Vetromile.*

Nazareth is about 65 miles north of Jerusalem. The houses
are mostly of stone, well built and flat-roofed. The population
has a more prosperous appearance than in any other part of the
country, and the women of Nazareth are famous for their beauty
—*Am. Cyclopædia.*

[7] Galilee was a division of northern Palestine, bordering on
the Mediterranean, and bounded on the east by the river Jordan.
Palestine, or the Holy Land, extends along the eastern shores of
the Mediterranean a distance of 175 miles from north to south.
It is from 50 to 90 miles wide; corresponds in latitude with the
State of Alabama: and embraces an area of about 13,500 square
miles. In ancient times it was a very fertile region—"a land
flowing with milk and honey." It is a country of hills and valleys, being traversed by two ranges of mountains. Of these Le-
banon is the highest, and Carmel, perhaps, the most noted. The
prophet Elias dwelt on Mount Carmel; it is on the sea-coast.

in the ways of virtue, but heaven had not blessed
them with children.

The goodness of Joachim and Anne, however,
was not left unrewarded. Twenty years passed
away, and on the 8th of September a wonderful
child was sent to cheer their old age. The promised Virgin, who was to repair the primitive fault,
was born; and she came into the world clothed
with inexpressible purity and beauty. On the
ninth day, according to custom, the *Babe Immaculate*[8] received the name of MARY.[9]

"And assuredly," says St. Bernard, "the Mother
of God could not have a name more appropriate,
or more expressive of her high dignity. Mary is
in fact, that fair and luminous star which shines
over the vast and stormy sea of this world."

> "Mary, sweet name revered above,
> And oh, how dear below!
> In it are hope and holy love,
> And blessings from it flow!"

The child's understanding, like the day in some

---

[8] The Immaculate Conception of the Most Blessed Virgin is a
truth of faith. It is thus expressed by the Church:

"We define that the Blessed Virgin Mary in the first moment
of her conception, by the singular grace and privilege of Almighty
God, and in virtue of the merits of Jesus Christ, the Saviour
of the human race, was preserved free from every stain of original
sin."—*Pius IX., Bulla Dogmat.*

[9] Mary means, in the Syriac language, *lady, sovereign,* or *mistress,*
and in Hebrew *star of the sea.—Orsini.*

favored regions, had scarcely a dawn. It shone out clearly from her earliest years. Her precocious virtue and the wisdom of her words, at a period of life when other children still enjoy but a purely physical existence, made the parents judge that the time of separation was come; and when Joachim had offered to the Lord, for the third time since the birth of his daughter, the first-fruits of his small inheritance, the husband and wife, grateful and resigned, set out for Jerusalem, in order to deposit within the sacred precincts of the Temple the treasure which they had received from the Holy One of Israel.

The ancient capital of Judea[10] was soon reached, and for the first time Mary passed through its ponderous gates and beheld its frowning battlements. The pious parents presented their child

[10]Jerusalem is the holy city of the Jews and Christians. It is 33 miles east of the Mediterranean and 15 miles west of the Dead Sea. Its elevation above the Mediterranean is over 2,000 feet. The population is about 20,000; but it is conjectured that in the days of our Blessed Redeemer it had a population of perhaps 200,000. The country around Jerusalem is rocky and not very fertile. The streets of the city are narrow, winding, dirty, and badly paved. The principal and broadest street is about 15 feet wide. Some are only 5 or 6 feet wide. The houses are usually two or three stories high, and built of heavy masonry. The siege of Jerusalem by Titus in the year 70 is one of the most memorable in history. It ended in the complete destruction of the city. In this siege, according to Josephus, 1,100,000 Jews perished. — *Am. Cyclo.*

in the great Temple[11] of the Lord of Hosts. She was received by the priest with the usual ceremonies, and then placed among the consecrated virgins, who occupied a portion of the sacred edifice set apart especially for themselves.[12]

Mary spent the best years of her young life in the Temple. It was the precious time of prepa- ration. The future Virgin-Mother was well edu- cated, but in those days domestic duties were wisely looked upon as important branches of edu- cation. She arose daily with the lark, thought of the holy presence of God, and dressed herself with the greatest modesty.

"Her toilet," writes the Abbé Orsini, "was ex- tremely simple, and occupied but little time. She

[11] The Temple into which Mary was about to enter had an event- ful history. Solomon built the first Temple, and made it the glory of the East. But the demon of destruction came, and its splen- dor passed away like a vision of the night. It finally arose from its ruins under Zorobabel, who built it sword in hand, notwith- standing the active opposition of many hostile nations. The second Temple, however, with all its unheard-of magnificence, was as in- ferior to the first in grandeur as in sanctity.—*Orsini.*

Josephus tells us that the exterior front of the Temple was so thickly covered with plates of gold that, when day began to ap- pear, it was no less dazzling than the rays of the rising sun. As for the other sides, where there was no gold, the stones were so white that, at a distance, the superb structure looked like a mountain crown- ed with snow.

[12]Mary was then about three years of age. The Church cele- brates the feast of the Presentation of the Blessed Virgin on the 21st of November.

wore neither bracelets of pearl, nor chains of gold inlaid with silver, nor purple tunics, such as were worn by the daughters of the princes of her race. A robe of celestial blue, a white tunic, confined at the waist by a cincture with flowing ends, a long veil, simply but gracefully arranged so as completely to cover the face when necessary—these, with a kind of shoe corresponding to the robe, composed the oriental costume of Mary.''

Each day had its hours for the exercises of religion. The voice of prayer and the hymn of praise were wafted aloft from the pure lips of the young Virgin.

We are told that Mary was somewhat above the middle stature. Her lovely face was the mirror of her most pure and beautiful soul, and her person was physical perfection itself. She was the most exquisite work of nature. St. Denis the Areopagite, who saw the Blessed Virgin, assures us that she was of dazzling beauty.''

She excelled in embroidery and all the accomplishments of her time. She had a perfect understanding of Holy Scripture. But of her physical, mental, and moral gifts this heavenly Girl made no parade. She spoke little, and always to the

[13] It is neither climate, nor food, nor bodily exercise which forms human beauty; it is the moral sentiment of virtue, which cannot subsist without religion. The beauty of the countenance is the true index of the soul.—*Bernardine de St. Pierre.*

purpose.   Virtue and good sense regulated her
thoughts, words, and actions.

Thus Mary passed silently along the way of
life like some fair star gliding through the silver-
lined clouds.   Thanks to her Immaculate Conception, she possessed a sweet and natural inclination
to virtue; and her shining deeds were like the
wreath of snow which silently falls on the moun-
tain-top, adding purity to purity and whiteness to
whiteness, till it rears itself into a shining cone
which attracts the rays of the sun and dazzles the
eye of man.

The Blessed Mary had spent nine years in the
retirement of the Temple, when the first dark
cloud obscured her young life.   Joachim, her beloved father, fell dangerously ill; and she came
home just in time to pray at his bedside and to receive his last blessing.[14]   But still another affliction
was at hand.   A short time after, St. Anne blessed her dear daughter and died in peace.   Mary was
now an orphan, but she bore her sorrow in silence
and patience.

[14] Some pious authors have thought that, at the moment when
Joachim extended his hands to bless his child, a revelation from
on high suddenly disclosed to him the glorious destiny awaiting
her; the joy of the elect diffused itself over his venerable countenance, his arms fell by his side, he bowed his head, and died.
—*Orsini.*

It must be remembered that Mary's seclusion in the Temple was
not monastic.

It is the opinion of several distinguished writers that it was at this period, when her path was darkened by the clouds of sadness and desolation, that the holy young Virgin made her vow of perpetual virginity, and offered, for ever and forever, the purest of pure hearts to God.

But while Mary was always to remain *the* Immaculate Virgin, it was manifested to her, as a decree of Heaven, that she should enter the marriage state. The choice was made. The divine will pointed out Joseph; and it is said that Mary received the solemn assurance from on high that this man of many merits would be to her only a protector, a worthy companion, and the honored guardian of her angelic chastity. The marriage ceremony[15] was performed in Jerusalem, and at the end of a week, St. Joseph and his beautiful bride retired to the birthplace of both, the town of Nazareth.

Blessed was the humble home of Mary and Joseph. It was guarded by angels. It was full of peace, purity, and happiness. While he attended

[15] It took place on the 8th of September. The Angelic Doctor, St. Thomas Aquinas, is of the opinion that it was immediately after the celebration of their marriage that St. Joseph and the Most Blessed Virgin, by mutual consent, made their vow of perpetual chastity. It may, perhaps, be asked, "Can this marriage of two persons, vowed to virginity, be considered a true one?" Most certainly. St. Augustine says that it is *the consent of the parties* which constitutes the marriage tie.

his workshop, she joyfully made the round of her
daily duties. With her own delicate hands she
prepared the meals, and ground the wheat and bar-
ley, which she then baked in the form of thin, round
cakes. And, wrapt in her white veil, this illustrious
Virgin might often be seen as, with graceful modesty,
she went on her way to draw water in a neighboring fountain.

But the dawn of a mighty event drew near—an
event so extraordinary that it was announced by
Gabriel, one of the four bright angels who always stand before Almighty God in the Court of
Heaven.

"The Angel Gabriel," says the Holy Book, "was
sent from God into a city of Galilee, called Nazareth,
to a Virgin espoused to a man whose name was Joseph, of the house of David; and the Virgin's name
was Mary.

"And the angel being come in,"[16] said to her:

---

[16] The Sanctuary of the Annunciation is built on the same site
and occupies precisely the very identical spot on which stood the
house of the Blessed Virgin, *which was transported by the angels to
Italy.* The present house in Nazareth is of the same dimensions,
and an exact copy of the real one now at Loretto. A granite pillar, suspended from the vault, marks the place where the Blessed
Virgin stood when she received the Angelic Salutation; and an
other about three feet distant, points out the spot occupied by the
Archangel Gabriel in delivering to her the message sent from
Heaven. This Sanctuary is enclosed in a large, fine church,
called the Church of the Annunciation, the interior of which is

' Hail, full of grace, the Lord is with **thee. Bless-**
ed art thou among women.'"

"Who having heard, was troubled at his saying,
and thought with herself what manner of salutation
this might be.

"And the angel said to her: 'Fear not, Mary,
for thou hast found grace with God. Behold thou
shalt conceive in thy womb, and shalt bring forth
a Son; and thou shalt call His name Jesus. He
shall be great, and shall be called the Son of the
Most High, and the Lord God shall give unto Him
the throne of His father David ; and He shall reign
in the house of Jacob for ever, and of His kingdom
there shall be no end.'

"And Mary said to the angel: 'How shall this
be done, because I know not man ?'

"And the angel answering, said to her: 'The
Holy Ghost shall come upon thee, and the power

covered with fine and rich silk damask, which hangs all around the
walls.— *Vetromile.*

[17] Is it not, in truth, a subject for pity, and a clear proof that
heresy and prejudice blind the intellect and stupefy the religious
side of man's nature, when we come to think that the holiest of
virgins and the purest of women—a woman to whom the great
Archangel Gabriel said: "Hail, full of grace, the Lord is with
thee: blessed art thou among women"—is *now* regarded by Protestants as nothing more than a *common woman?* What folly and
blasphemy in people who pretend to have the Bible under their
very noses seven days in the week! This is to have eyes and see
not,

of the Most High shall overshadow thee. **And,** therefore, the Holy who shalt be born of thee shall be called the Son of God.   And behold thy cousin Elizabeth, she also hath conceived a son[18] in her old age; and this is the sixth month with her that is called barren.   For no work shall be impossible with God.'

"And Mary said: 'Behold the handmaid of the Lord, be it done to me according to thy word.' "

Even towards an angel of heaven how wise is Mary's conduct, how beautiful her words! Had the great saints and philosophers of all time been engaged for years in framing an answer to the wonderful announcement of Gabriel, we feel sure they would have tried in vain to compose anything that so bears the shining seal of force, beauty, brevity, wisdom, and humility as the immortal words that issued from the lips of the Blessed Virgin—"Behold the handmaid of the Lord, be it done to me according to thy word."

On hearing those precious words the angel disappeared, and JESUS CHRIST *became man* in the womb of the Immaculate Mother.[19]

---

[18] St. John the Baptist.

[19] According to Father Drexelius, the mystery of the Incarnation took place on the 25th of March, on a Friday evening —*Orsini.*
The house visited by the Angel Gabriel, and in which Mary gave her consent to become the Mother of God, is now at the city of Loretto, in Italy. It is commonly known as the "Holy House

Soon after this, the Most Holy Mary went to pay a visit to her cousin, St. Elizabeth, who lived in a city in the hill-country of Judea.

"And she entered into the house of Zachary," writes St. Luke, "and saluted Elizabeth. And it came to pass that when Elizabeth heard the salutation of Mary, the infant[20] leaped in her womb. And Elizabeth was filled with the Holy Ghost; and she cried out with a loud voice, saying:

"'Blessed art thou among women, and blessed is the fruit of thy womb. And whence is this to me that the mother of my Lord should come to me? For behold as soon as the voice of thy salutation sounded in my ears, the infant in my womb leaped for joy. And blessed art thou that hast believed, because those things shall be

of Loretto." This precious Sanctuary in which God became man, "was transported by the angels," writes Rev. Dr. Vetromile, "first from Galilee to Dalmatia in 1291; thence to Italy, near Recanati, in 1294; and finally, in 1295, to the spot where it now remains. This house is 30 feet long, 15 wide, and 18 high; it is built of ebony and small bricks, and is covered by a kind of wooden roof overlaid, I think, with tiles. There is a window apparently opening on the loft; but it seems to have communicated with the roof and another window through which the Archangel Gabriel appeared to her. This holy house is now covered externally with fine marble, and upon this Sanctuary a large and splendid church has been erected. An immense number of pilgrims continually visit this Sanctuary."—*Travels,* vol. ii.

Loretto has a population of about 5,000.

[20]St. John the Baptist.

accomplished that were spoken to thee by the Lord.'"

On hearing these prophetic words, Mary pronounc̊ ed that inspired and beautiful poem called the *Magnificat:*

"My soul doth magnify the Lord; and my spirit hath rejoiced in God my Saviour.

"Because He hath regarded the humility of His handmaid; for behold from henceforth all generations shall call me blessed."[21]

[21]Thus the inspired words of Mary herself proclaim that "all generations "—that is, all generations that from that time to the end of the world will believe in the Redeemer to be born of her —shall call her blessed.   But it is in the Catholic Church *alone* that, generation after generation, this sacred prophecy is fulfilled. Protestants, however, to borrow the words of Archbishop Gibbons, "are careful to exclude themselves from the *generations* that were destined to call her blessed; for, in speaking of her, they almost invariably withhold from her the title of *blessed*, preferring to call her *the Virgin*, or *Mary the Virgin* or the *Mother of Jesus*. And while Protestant churches will resound with the praises of Sarah and Rebecca and Rachel, of Miriam and Ruth, of Esther and Judith, of the *Old Testament*, and of Elizabeth and Anna, of Magdalen and Martha of the *New*, the name of MARY, THE MOTHER OF JESUS, is uttered with bated breath, lest the sound of her name should make the preacher liable to the charge of superstition."

On this important subject of honoring the Most Holy Virgin, we have only to examine both sides of the question, by recalling to mind who honor her and who do not; and no person of religious principles and sound common sense will long hesitate as to the side on which he should range himself.

Who honor Mary?

" Because He that is mighty hath done **great** things to me; and Holy is His name.

" And His mercy is from generation unto generation, to them that hear Him.

" He hath shown might in His arm; He **hath** scattered the proud in conceit of their heart.

(1) Almighty God honored her for ever by preserving her **from** original sin, and by sending her an archangel to announce the coming of the world's Redeemer.

(2) Jesus Christ, the Son of God, bestowed upon her **a glory** everlasting by becoming *her* Son.

(3) Mary herself, inspired by the Holy Ghost, declares that "all generations shall call her blessed."

(4) The Archangel Gabriel styles her "full of grace " and "blessed among women."

(5) St. Elizabeth, mother of the great St. John the Baptist, inspired by the Holy Ghost, styles her " blessed among women " and " the mother of my Lord."

(6) The Catholic Church," the pillar of truth," honors her, age after age, above all creatures, and styles her the "Queen of Saints," the "Queen of Angels," and the "Mother of God.'

Who dishonor Mary by refusing to honor her ? The fanatical followers of Luther, Calvin, Knox, Henry VIII., John Wesley, and other so-called Christians. To them we look not for the truth. " You change," said the great Bossuet to Protestants, " and that which changes is not the truth." No Protestant ever saw the Blessed Mary, and Protestants, therefore, can speak of her not from the depth of knowledge and affection, but from the abundance of their ignorance and malignity.

Who, then, can hesitate, even for a moment, to range himself under the banner of the Most Blessed Virgin, and on the side of God, the Bible, the Archangel Gabriel, St. Elizabeth, and the Holy Catholic Church?

" He hath put down the mighty from their seat, and hath exalted the humble.

" He hath filled the hungry with good things; and the rich He hath sent away empty.

" He hath received Israel His servant, being mindful of His mercy, as He spoke to our fathers —to Abraham and his seed for ever." [22]

Mary remained three months in her cousin's country-house, which was in a fertile valley near the city of Ain. She then returned home. But now we find ourselves on the threshold of a mighty event.

"It came to pass, " writes St. Luke, " that in those days there went out a decree from Cæsar Augustus, that the whole world should be enrolled. This enrolling was first made by Cyrinus, the Governor of Syria. And all went to be enrolled—every one into his own city.

" And Joseph also went up from Galilee out of the city of Nazareth into Judea, to the city of David, which is called Bethlehem[23]—because he was of the house and family of David—to be enrolled with Mary his espoused wife, who was with child.

"And it came to pass, that when they were there, her days were accomplished, that she

[22]This sublime canticle makes the Most Blessed Mary the *first* Catholic poet, as it is the *first* Christian poem.

[23] King David was born in Bethlehem

should be delivered. And she brought forth her first-born Son, [24] and wrapped Him up in swaddling clothes, and laid Him in a manger, because there was no room for them in the inn. [25]

" And there was in the same country shep-

[24]According to Baronius, our Saviour was born on a Friday.

[25]Bethlehem, at a distance, presents a fine and imposing appearance ; but in the interior it is just like the rest of the towns of Palestine.   I remarked, however, a cheerful appearance amongst the Bethlehemites, and I saw them several times laughing, and their children playing and enjoying themselves—*a thing that I had never observed in any other part of Palestine.* Bethlehem contains about 2,500 inhabitants, and they are almost all Christians and Catholics. . . . The subterranean church—which is the place of the Nativity of our Saviour—is entered by two spiral staircases of fifteen steps each, one belonging to the Latins, the other to the Armenians and Greeks.   This most noted Sanctuary is irregular, because it occupies the irregular site of the *stable.*   It is hewn out of the rock, and is a little over thirty-seven feet in length, eleven broad, and nine high.   The floor, the place where our Saviour was born, and the site of the manger, are cased with beautiful marble, the work of St. Helena ; but the walls and ceiling are covered with fine tapestry—now falling into rags—and nobody dares to repair or replace them for fear of the jealousy of the schismatics. No light penetrates from the outside ; but the Crypt is illuminated by the thirty-two lamps sent by different princes, which burn day and night.   At the further extremity on the east side is the spot where the Blessed Virgin brought forth the Redeemer of the world.   This spot is marked by a circle of marble covered with jasper, and circular plate of silver surrounded by rays of the same material, around which are written the following words : " HIC DE VIRGINE MARIA JESUS CHRISTUS NATUS EST "— Here Jesus Christ was born of the Virgin Mary.—*Vetromile, Travels,* 1869.

herds watching, and keeping the night-watches
over their flocks.   And behold an angel of the Lord
stood by them, and the brightness of God shone
round about them; and they feared with a great fear
and the angel said to them:

" 'Fear not, for behold I bring you good tidings
of great joy, that shall be to all the people; for this
day is born to you a SAVIOUR, who is Christ the
Lord, in the city of David.   And this shall be a
sign unto you—you shall find the Infant wrapped
in swaddling clothes, and laid in a manger.'

" And suddenly there was with the angel a multitude of the heavenly army, praising God, and
saying : 'GLORY TO GOD IN THE HIGHEST; AND ON
EARTH PEACE TO MEN OF GOOD WILL.'

" And it came to pass, after the angels departed
from them into heaven, the shepherds said one to
another : 'Let us go over to Bethlehem, and let us
see this word that is come to pass, which the Lord
hath showed to us.'

" And they came with haste; and they found
Mary and Joseph, and the Infant lying in the manger. And seeing, they understood of the word that
had been spoken to them concerning this child.
And all that heard wondered at those things that
were told them by the shepherds.

" But Mary kept all these words pondering *them*
in heart.   And the shepherds returned, glorifying and praising God, for all the things

they had heard and seen, as it was told unto them."

> "What lovely Infant can this be
> That in the little crib I see?
> So sweetly on the straw it lies—
> It must have come from Paradise.
>
> Who is that Lady kneeling by,
> And gazing on so tenderly?
> Oh! that is Mary ever blest—
> How full of joy her holy breast!
>
> What man is that who seems to smile,
> And look so blissful all the while?
> 'Tis holy Joseph, good and true—
> The Infant makes him happy too."

On the eighth day after His birth, the Son of God was circumcised, and named Jesus, in accordance with the command of His heavenly Father.[26] Doubtless many of the good, simple people came daily to adore the wonderful Babe in the manger.

[26]The priest enquired of the holy spouses what name they intended to give the circumcised Child. Our sweet Lady, always attentive to the respect which she bore to St. Joseph, requested him to mention it. Turning toward her with veneration, the saint intimated that so sweet a name should be pronounced by her lips—when, by a divine impulse, Mary and Joseph said at the same moment: "*Jesus is His name.*" "In this you are of one mind," replied the priest, "and great is the name you give to the Infant." While in the act of writing it, he was touched by a great interior tenderness, saying to them: "I assure you that I believe this Child will be a great prophet of the Lord."— *Cité Mystique de Dieu.*

But a miracle of greater celebrity soon brought
the first converts of the Gentile world[27] to the
same lowly crib. "The shepherds of Judea, had
led the way," writes Orsini; "it was for kings and
sages to follow."

"Now, when Jesus was born in Bethlehem of
Juda, in the days of King Herod," writes St.
Matthew, "behold, there came wise men[28] from
the East to Jerusalem, saying: 'Where is He
that is born King of the Jews? For we have
seen His star in the East, and are come to adore him.'

"And King Herod hearing this was troubled,
and all Jerusalem with him. And assembling together all the chief priests and the Scribes of the
people, he enquired of them where Christ should
be born. But they said to him: 'In Bethlehem
of Juda. For so it is written by the prophet':

"*And thou Bethlehem the land of Juda art not
the least among the princes of Juda; for out of thee
shall come forth the Ruler that shall rule my people
Israel.*

"Then Herod, privately calling the wise men,
learned diligently of them the time of the star
which appeared to them; and sending them into
Bethlehem, said: 'Go and diligently enquire after the

[27] That is, all nations except the Jews.
[28] The Magi, or wise men, according to tradition, were kings, and
three in number. Their country, it seems, was Persia, and their
names—Gaspar, Melchior, and Baltassar.

Child; and when you have found Him, bring me word again, that I also may come and adore Him. Who having heard the king, went their way; and behold the star which they had seen in the East, went before them, until it came and stood over where the Child was.

"And seeing the star,[29] they rejoiced with exceeding great joy. And entering into the house they found the Child with Mary His Mother, and falling down they adored Him. And opening their treasures, they offered Him gifts—gold, frankincense, and myrrh. And having received an answer in sleep that they should not return to Herod, they went back another way into their country."

Forty days after the birth of our Lord, the Most Blessed Virgin prepared to return to Jerusalem in order to fulfil the law of Moses, which pre-

---

[29] As to the nature of this wonderful star, it is useless to add conjecture to conjecture. Science knows nothing about it; and it has not pleased God to gratify our curiosity on the point. It is in accordance with reason, however, to assume that the star which guided the Magi was not one of those immense suns— commonly called stars—that light up the firmament, but some small luminous body provided for the occasion. The learned Father De Ligny, S. J., is of the opinion that it "was not a real star, but a meteor more brilliant than stars usually are, inasmuch as its lustre was not eclipsed by the brightness of daylight" "A new star," says the great St. Augustine, "appeared at the birth of Him whose death was to obscure the ancient sun."

scribed the purification of mothers and the redemption of the first-born. This law, it is true, applied not to Mary. Though she was the mother of the Redeemer, she was still the purest of virgins. But like Christ Himself she wished "to fulfil all justice." "For the sake of example," writes Bossuet, "she willingly submitted to a law which was in no way binding on her, because the secret of her virginal maternity was unknown."

Scarcely had Mary, Joseph, and the Holy Infant entered the Temple for the purpose of making the necessary offering [30] when Simeon, a venerable old man, followed. He had been anxiously "waiting for the consolation of Israel." "And he received an answer from the Holy Ghost," says St. Luke," that he should not see death before he had seen Christ of the Lord."

When Simeon saw the Divine Child, he took Him in his arms, and blessed God, exclaiming:

"Now Thou dost dismiss Thy servant, O Lord, according to Thy word, in peace. Because my eyes have seen Thy salvation, which Thou hast prepared before the face of all people—a light to the revelation of the Gentiles, and the glory of Thy people Israel."

The Most Holy Virgin and St. Joseph "wondered at those things which were spoken con-

---

[30] The offering was two doves for sacrifice.

cerning Him. And Simeon blessed them," continues the Evangelist, "and said to Mary His Mother: 'Behold this CHILD is set for the fall and for the resurrection of many in Israel, and for a sign which shall be contradicted. And thy own soul a sword shall pierce, that out of many hearts thoughts may be revealed.' "

The Holy Family returned to Nazareth, but their stay there was to be short. One night an ángel appeared to St. Joseph in his sleep. "Arise," whispered the messenger of Heaven, "and take the Child and His Mother, and fly into Egypt, and be there until I tell thee. For it will come to pass that Herod[31] will seek the Child to destroy him."

The Holy Virgin and St. Joseph asked the blessing of the Divine Child, which He bestowed in a manner not to be mistaken. Then, gathering their humble garments, they departed a little after midnight, making use of the same beast of burden[32] which they had brought from Nazareth to Bethlehem.[33] The soft moonlight illumined the dreary earth, and guided the lone, silent march of the blessed travelers. "The

[31]Three Herods are mentioned in the New Testament. This Herod, surnamed the Great, was the first of his family who reigned in Judea.

[32] An ass, which in Palestine is a beautiful animal.

[33] "Cité Mystique de Dieu."

weather was still cold," [34] says St. Bonaventure,
"and while crossing Palestine, the Holy Family
had to choose the wildest and least frequented
roads."

The poor but illustrious fugitives hastily passed
over hill, and plain, and valley, and often by the
secluded den of the murderous robber. Then
came the perilous desert. On leaving the city
of Gaza, whose decaying towers re-echoed the
hoarse murmur of the waves, they saw before
them only immense wastes of sand, dreary, desolate, and frightful in their wild nakedness. A
scorching wind agitated the desert, and a fiery
sky seemed to change the very face of nature.
At length, after a long and painful journey of
about four hundred and twenty miles, the Holy
Family reached the outskirts of the pagan but
historic land of Egypt. [35]

As the weary travelers entered the gate of the
famous city of Heliopolis [36] a majestic tree under
which they passed bowed down to the earth in
honor of the God of nature. Near this city was

---

[34] It was about the middle of February.

[35] In the "Cité Mystique de Dieu" it is stated that the journey
was over six hundred miles, and occupied more than fifty days.
According to the same work, when Jesus entered Egypt " the idols
fell with a loud noise, the temples sank into ruins and the altars
were overthrown."

[36] Heliopolis signifies *the city of the sun.*

a pretty village, shaded with lofty sycamores, and having the only fountain of fresh water in Egypt. There, in a poor habitation, the Holy Family found rest and safety; at last they were free from the power and malignity of Herod.

But now came a time of toil, exile, and extreme poverty. "As they were poor," writes the great St. Basil, "it is clear that they had to work very hard in order to procure the necessaries of life, and even these—were they always able to obtain them?" "It often happened," says Landolph of Saxony, " that the Child Jesus, pressed by hunger, asked His Mother for bread when she had none to give Him." [37]

When the infant Saviour was a year old, He first broke silence, and spoke in a distinct voice to his faithful foster-father. " My father, " said the little Jesus, as He rested in his Mother's arms, " I am come from heaven to be the light of the world, and as a good shepherd, to seek and to know my sheep, and to give them the food of eternal life. I desire that you may both become

[37] The following paragraph relates to the early experiences of the Holy Family in Egypt : "St. Joseph having received payment for certain work, he made a little bedstead, entirely of wood, for the Mother, and a cradle for the Infant. For himself he prepared no other bed than the earth. Nor was there any furniture in the house, till, by the sweat of his brow, he earned money to purchase some necessary articles. "—*Cité Mystique de Dieu.*

children of the light, since you are so near to its Source." [38]

Soon after this He said to the Most Holy Virgin: "My Mother, you will clothe me in a long tunic of a plain color. I will wear none but it. It shall grow with me, and it shall be for this that they will cast lots after my death." This sweet Mother did as she was desired, and spun, wove and made the seamless tunic, which lasted the Son of God during His mortal life. [39]

Even to this day tradition recalls the memorable sojourn of the Holy Family in the land of the Pharaos. The majestic sycamore, in whose grateful shade Mary loved to sit with the Divine Child on her knee, is still pointed out, after the lapse of over eighteen centuries. [40]

[38] " Cité Mystique de Dieu."

[39] The Queen of Heaven provided wool of the natural color, of which she spun and made a little tunic—all of one piece. Then she wove it on a frame. There was mystery in making this tunic without seam. On the prayer of our Blessed Lady, it changed its natural hue into another, between a violet and silver color, very perfect, so that the shade could not be distinguished.—*Cité Mystique de Dieu.*

[40] It is called the "Tree of the Virgin Mother," and it is situated in the village of Matarieh—the same in which the Holy Family lived —a few miles distant from Cairo, and in the immediate neighborhood of the ancient Heliopolis, whose site is now occupied only by a few scattered ruins and a picturesque monolith over seventy feet high. Near this monolith is the village of Matarieh, now a heap of houses in a state of ruin, presenting the most wretched appear-

After the Holy Family had spent about seven years in Egypt, an angel appeared to St. Joseph in his sleep. " Arise, " said he, " and take the Child and his Mother, and go into the land of Israel. For they are dead, that sought the life of the Child." The guardian of Jesus and Mary did as he was commanded. "And coming, " says the Holy Book," he dwelt in a city called Nazareth, that it might be fulfilled which was said by the prophets—'that he shall be called a Nazarite. ' "

Again the Holy Family were in their humble home, and again it was a life of cheerful toil, lighted up by the sacred presence of the Holy Child.

ance, but surrounded, however, by large and well-cultivated gardens, in the centre of which rises, with an imposing appearance, the great tree of the Blessed Virgin—an old sycamore. It is very large. Seven men could hardly span the lower part of its truuk. Its age is unknown, but by the concentric circles which a section of one of its largest branches, which has been detached from the trunk for some years past, presents, we may conclude that it has withstood the storms of centuries. The present Viceroy of Egypt, at the time of the inauguration of the Suez Canal, presented this sycamore to France, in accordance with the desire expressed by the Empress Eugénie, who went to see it. She had it surrounded with an elegant railing, and appointed two guardians to protect it and take care of the lilies and geraniums which she caused to be planted around it. These guardians are still paid by France. This tree is held in great veneration not only by the Christians but even by the Arabs. Natives and foreigners gather its leaves, to which they attribute healing virtues.—*The Ave Maria,* 1878.

The Most Blessed Virgin and St. Joseph observed faithfully the law of their fathers, and went
every year to Jerusalem in order to celebrate the
Passover.   When Jesus was twelve years old, they
made the journey as usual.   It took the pilgrims
four days to reach the Holy City, then filled with
countless multitudes.⁴¹

When the festival was over, Mary and Joseph
set out for home, while Christ remained in Jerusalem ; " and, " says St. Luke, " His parents knew
it not.⁴²   And thinking that He was in the company, they came a day's journey, and sought Him
among their kinsfolks and acquaintance; and not
finding Him, they returned to Jerusalem, seeking
Him.

" And it came to pass, that after three days they
found Him in the Temple, sitting in the midst of
the doctors, hearing them and asking them questions.   And all that heard Him were astonished at
His wisdom and His answers."

It was thus the Divine Boy was occupied when
His Mother made her way through the doctors,

---

⁴¹ According to Josephus, the festival of the Passover gathered
to Jerusalem about 2,500,000 persons.

⁴² They " knew it not," because, according to St. Epiphanius, the
men went in troops, separated from the women.   It is easy to
understand that Mary and Joseph, thus separated, might each think
that Jesus was with the other.   It was only in the evening, however, when the travelers assembled together, that the truth became
known.

with a look of mingled joy, wonder, and tender reproach. "Son!" said she mildly, "why hast Thou done so to us? Behold, Thy father and I have sought thee sorrowing." The answer was dry and mysterious: "How is it that you sought me? Did you not know that I must be about my Father's business?"

Mary and Joseph were silent. It seemed that at the moment they failed to grasp the drift of His reply. But " He went down with them," continues the Evangelist, "and came to Nazareth, and was subject to them. And His Mother kept all these words in her heart. And Jesus advanced in wisdom, and age, and grace with God and men."

For many years the life of the Holy Family is lost to the gaze of the world. It is unknown to history. But this was doubtless the time in which Mary spent her best and brightest days. Life is not happiest when it rolls on with the noise of the winter torrent ; its most precious hours are those which glide gently by like the calm current of some silvery stream.

But the clouds began to gather. St. Joseph grew very feeble during the last years of his life. He was assailed by a long and severe illness ; and finally, at the urgent request of our Blessed Lady, he ceased working. "I will now labor for you, " said this heavenly Woman, " in testimony of my gratitude, and as long as the Lord shall give us life."

Thus Mary toiled with more than heroic devotion for the support of Christ and St. Joseph. God so willed it, in order that her merits and virtues might reach the sublime pinnacle of perfection, and shine as an example which may well put the children of Adam to shame.

At this time the Immaculate Virgin was thirty-three years of age, and, according to Mary of Agreda, her holy form retained all its natural perfections. Her pure and beautiful countenance was the admiration of the angels. It was the mirror of her own peerless soul.

Our Blessed Redeemer had just reached His twenty-sixth year when the Angel of Death called away the noble St. Joseph. The head of the Holy Family was no more. His end was happy. Jesus and Mary consoled his last moments. "The great ones of Galilee," says Orsini, "died not thus. More show and greater ostentation attended their departure ; but, at the final moment they had not the glorious prospects of the carpenter of Nazareth."

Christ worked His first miracle at the request of His holy Mother. It was at the historic wedding of Cana. "They have no wine," said the sweet, thoughtful Lady. There was a moment's hesitation, as His "hour had not yet come;" but

He said to the waiters, "Fill the water-pots with water." It was done. "Draw out now," said the same divine lips; and the delicious wine astonished even the chief steward.

During the public career of our Lord, we can well imagine that Mary's angelic breast was filled with mingled joy and anxiety. She followed His blessed footsteps. She listened to His words of life and power. She bore with matchless fortitude the trials of that busy, troubled period.

"Loving Jesus more than ever mother loved her child," writes Orsini, "yet never did she intrude into His presence when, by so doing, she might interfere with the duties of His regenerating mission. Never once did she speak to Him of her fatigue, her fears, her melancholy forebodings, or her personal wants."

But the sublime end came, and Mary stood upon Calvary. Our unworthy pen may not describe that touching and sacred scene.

> "Under the world s redeeming wood
> The most afflicted Mother stood,
> Mingling her tears with her Son's blood.

> "As that streamed down from every part,
> Of all His wounds she felt the smart—
> What pierced His body, pierced her heart [43]

[43] The Fathers and great Doctors of the Church place the sufferings of the Most Blessed Virgin on Calvary above those of all the martyrs.—*Orsini.*

"Oh! worse than Jewish heart that could,
Unmoved behold the double flood
Of Mary's tears and Jesus' blood.

.   .   .   .   .

"Great Queen of sorrows! in thy train
Let me a mourner's place obtain,
With tears to cleanse all sinful stain." [44]

"Behold thy Mother," said the dear, dying Lord to St. John. A moment passed, He bowed His holy head, the earth trembled, rocks were rent, and the REDEMPTION of the world was accomplished!

Forty days after Christ's Ascension into heaven, we find the Immaculate Virgin at prayer in the "upper chamber," where, in the company of the Apostles, she received the Holy Ghost. She was the luminous pillar that guided the march of the infant Church. To her the Evangelists came for light;[45] the Apostles for unction, courage, and con-

[44] *Stabat Mater.*

[45] The Church styles her " Queen of Evangelists." Who other than Mary, and likewise who better than she, could have made known the mystery of the Incarnation, of the Annunciation; the promise of the angel; the visit of St. Elizabeth; the hymn with which God that day inspired her; the manger at Bethlehem; the adoration of the angels, of the shepherds, and of the Magi; the presentation in the Temple; canticle of Simeon; the flight into Egypt; and the finding of the child Jesus amid the doctors?—of all these Mary alone held the secret. "She had kept them, pondering them *in her heart*," remarks the Evangelist who has related them, as if by these words he sought to indicate whence the knowledge thereof had been so directly and faithfully transmitted to him —*Abbé Baunard.*

stancy; the afflicted for spiritual consolation; and all
went away praising and blessing the ever-blessed
Mary.

St. John the Evangelist, her adopted son, took
this sweet Holy Mother under his protection.
They lived in Jerusalem.[46] But of this period history knows next to nothing. It is hidden with
God. It would, indeed, be inspiring to penetrate
into the last years of Mary's Immaculate life, in
order to study closely that lofty ideal of human
perfection. But the true sign and special excel-
lence of that matchless perfection is to remain hidden; and, for the world, its hidden obscurity is the
best example and the highest instruction.

The traditions of the early Church, however,
have preserved the remembrance of the Mother
of God's manners and personal appearance in her
last years. "In every action," says Nicephorus, [47]
"she evinced gravity, dignity, and honor. She
spoke little, and only when it was necessary. To
others she willingly listened. She was gentle,
humble, and affable, rendering to every one the
respect they deserved. She ignored laughter,

[46] Some writers represent the Most Blessed Virgin as residing
at Ephesus; but, at present, that opinion seems to be abandoned.
"According to impartial and severe truth," says Baunard,
"Mary lived and died in Jerusalem."—*Life of the Apostle St.
John.*

[47] Nicephorus was a Greek monk and historian of the fourteenth
century.

trouble, and anger; but she was horrified at **wick-edness.** Her eyes were brilliant, but dimmed and hollowed from weeping. Her hands were blood-less and transparent; and all her features were sharpened by constant suffering." St. Denis the Areopagite, who witnessed the death of the Most Blessed Virgin, tells us that even then she was still strikingly beautiful.

At length there came a day, lovely and solemn, when the peerless soul of Mary winged its flight to heaven. The end is thus recounted by Nice-phorus:

"In those days an angel was sent to Mary by her Son, in order to warn her that the time was near to return to Him, as an angel had formerly given her notice that God was to come to her.

"Having learned through him that her day was at hand, her heart was filled with very great joy; and, having made it known to her friends and to her relatives, she prepared herself for her final pas-sage. Then, soon after, she was forced to take to her bed in the dwelling she occupied upon Mount Sion.

"There was St. John, who had sheltered her, and with him all the illustrious Christians living in Jerusalem, who were attached to Mary either by relationship, by veneration, or by friend-ship.

"Then Mary gave orders to the Virgin Disci-

ple, and to the others assisting, to distribute her
two tunics to those of the widows in her vicinity
who towards her had testified the most affection.

"Hearing her speak in that manner, all shed
abundant tears over the solitude wherein they
would be left by the departure of Mary.

"Finally, her Divine Son descended from heaven, with the countless army of holy angels, to receive that soul so entirely celestial.

"The Apostles, likewise, had assembled from
all parts, and Mary, seeing them gathered around
her with lighted torches, bade them adieu with
great gladness, giving thanks to her Son.

"Then she fell back, dying, upon her bed, joining her hands gravely and religiously, and de-
cently disposing her venerable body—purer than
the sun. 'Be it done to me according to thy word,'
she whispered, and at once seemed to fall
asleep.

"And thus surrounded by all those who were
most dear to her, did she yield up her blessed
soul."

Her precious body was laid in the tomb, but
there it was not to repose. It was too pure to
feel the cold breath decay. It soon rejoined
the glorified soul, and nothing more remained of
Mary in this world. Crowned in the heights of
Heaven was she—

"Who so above
All mothers shone—
The Mother of
The Blessed One."

"Mary, so beautiful and bright,
More lovely than the morning light,
I pray to thee, look down on me,
Sweet Star that shines o'er life's dark sea."[48]

[48]Devotion to the Most Blessed Virgin is as old as the Church. A glance at its history in Europe would carry us into the lives of all great and good Catholics, and through all that is most beautiful in poetry, oratory, painting, and architecture. It is the same in the New World. The great Columbus so loved the Immaculate Mother that before setting forth on that immortal voyage in which the size of the world's map was doubled, he had his own ship blessed, and named the *Holy Mary*. He called the second island he discovered after the Queen of Heaven. With a banner of the Blessed Virgin borne before him, the swift and hardy genius of Cortes conquered the vast pagan empire of Mexico. The bold and chivalrous Champlain carried the name of Mary through the gigantic forests of Canada. The pious and gallant De Maisonneuve—chaste knight of the seventeenth century—founded Ville Marie, or the town of Mary, now the flourishing commercial city of Montreal. Centuries ago the Jesuit Fathers—glorious pioneers of the Faith—made her sweet name known in the wigwams of the red man from the shores of the Great Lakes to the Gulf of Mexico. On discovering the Mississippi, Father Marquette, S. J., called it the Immaculate Conception. The fair and holy Margaret Bourgeois founded the first religious order in the New World, and happily named it the "Sisters of the Congregation of Our Lady." It was on the feast of the Annunciation that the Catholic Pilgrim Fathers took formal possession of Maryland. The first town in that State was named St. Mary's. The two oldest Catholic seats of learning in Maryland are called after

the Mother of God. To-day over one dozen Catholic colleges in the United States bear the name of Mary. The Seminary of our Lady of Angels stands like a sentinel of Truth near Niagara's mighty fall, and the University of Notre Dame is a growing fortress of Faith and knowledge in the great West. Laval, Canada's Catholic university, proclaims to the world that it is under the protection of the Immaculate Virgin ; and the most magnificent church in the Dominion glories in the name of Notre Dame. In May, 1846, the bishops of this Republic, assembled in the Sixth Council of Baltimore, solemnly decreed that " THE MOST BLESS- ED VIRGIN CONCEIVED WITHOUT SIN IS CHOSEN AS THE PATRON- ESS OF THE UNITED STATES. " The Catholics of our country pos- sess in the *Ave Maria*, founded by the venerable Father Sorin, C. S. C., the only periodical in America, and perhaps in the world, wholly devoted to Mary. Her bright name is borne by twenty of our cathedrals. In short, countless towns and cities from the majestic St. Lawrence to the great Rio de la Plata have reared splendid churches under her name and protection · and from the historic rock of Quebec to the distant shores of Chili, the pealing sound of the Angelus bell wafts her praises on high and calls the faithful to prayer.

SAINT JOSEPH,

*THE SPOUSE OF THE MOST BLESSED VIRGIN, THE FOS-
TER-FATHER OF JESUS CHRIST AND PATRON OF THE
UNIVERSAL CHURCH.*[1]

DIED A. D. 22.[2]

T. JOSEPH, whose glory is as old as
Christianity and as wide as the world, was
nobly descended from the ancient patri-
archs and the greatest of the Kings of Juda. His
life has not been written by men. The Holy Spirit
himself has recounted the principal actions in his
career.

He was born at Nazareth, but reverses of for-
tune, in which we can trace the hand of God, led
him to Jerusalem. The Divine Redeemer was
about to visit this sin-stained world. In the natural order of things, He would require a pro-

[1] The great and holy Pius IX. proclaimed St. Joseph " *Patron
of the Universal Church*" shortly after the Council of the Vatican.

[2] This date is founded on the account given by the Venerable
Mary of Agreda in her celebrated work called "Cité Mystique de
Dieu," wherein it is stated that St. Joseph, at the date of his holy
death, was sixty years of age, a little more than twenty-seven
of which he had spent in the society of the Most Blessed Virgin.

[3] Joseph is from the Hebrew, and signifies *he shall add.*

tector and the Most Holy Mary would need a virtuous companion. But who could be found worthy of those lofty distinctions? There was one. It was Joseph.

When thirty-three years of age, he was espous-ed to the Most Blessed Virgin.[4] He was then, it is said, well made, agreeable in person, and with a countenance which beamed with inexpressible modesty and goodness. At the age of twelve he had made a vow of chastity, and his life was as pure as a lily.

St. Joseph seems for a time to have been un-acquainted with the fact that the Holy Spirit had accomplished the mystery of the Incarnation in his Immaculate Spouse. He was aware of his own chaste conduct towards her; but many an anxious thought crossed his upright mind on find-ing that, in spite of the holiness of her life, he

---

[4] Others aspired to that honor, but the divine will was mani-fested by a miracle. The various suitors deposited their wands in the Temple over night, and next morning the rod of the just Joseph, like that of Aaron, was found to have budded forth into leaves and flowers. The painters do not forget this beautiful in-cident.

Writing of this, Mary of Agreda says: "All were engaged in prayer when they saw blossoms bud forth from the rod borne by Joseph, and at the same instant a beautiful dove was seen to descend and alight on the head of the saint." According to the same authority, he was related to the Immaculate Virgin in the third degree.

might well be assured that she was about to become a mother.*

He was, however, as the Holy Book styles him,
"a just man," and, of course, possessed of all
the virtues, especially mildness and charity. So
after carefully weighing the whole affair in his
mind, he determined to leave our Blessed Lady
without saying a word. He neither accused nor
condemned. He committed the matter to God,
and God mercifully sent an angel from heaven to
clear away his doubts, and to reveal to him the
adorable mystery of the Incarnation.

"But while he thought on these things," says
the first of the Evangelists, "behold, the angel of
the Lord appeared to him in *his sleep*, saying:
"Joseph, son of David, fear not to take unto thee
Mary thy wife; for that which is conceived in her is
of the Holy Ghost.

"' And she shall bring forth a Son; and thou
shalt call his name Jesus; for He shall save His
people from their sins.'

---

* Mary had not informed him of anything. There were two
causes for her silence: (1) her confidence in God, in whose care
for her reputation she reposed entire confidence; (2) her prudence
—an occurrence of this nature could not be credited on her report. Heaven must speak to make it credible.—*De Ligny.*

Undoubtedly God could have shortened these sufferings of
Joseph by sooner revealing to him the mystery of Mary's preg-
nancy; but his virtue would not then have been put to test.
—*Bossuet.*

"Now all this was done that the word might be fulfilled, which the Lord spoke by the prophet, saying:

" 'Behold a Virgin shall be with child, and shall bring forth a Son, and they shall call his name Emmanuel, which being interpreted is *God with us.*'

"And Joseph, rising from his sleep, did as the angel of the Lord had commanded him."

The humble house of Joseph, we are told, consisted of but three chambers. One of these was his own bed-room. Another he used as a workshop.* The third contained a small bed which was made by our saint. Here the Blessed Virgin slept and made her abode. It might in truth be called the apartment of the Queen of Heaven.

These holy personages kept no servant. Mary did her own work. Their nourishment was very frugal; but they partook of it every day together. St. Joseph sometimes ate flesh-meat, the Most Holy Virgin never. Their usual diet consisted of

*From St. Matthew it appears that he was a carpenter. St. Ambrose says he was a carpenter; but St. Hilary asserts that he wrought in iron as a smith. Mary of Agreda speaks of his trade as that of a carpenter. Butler thinks it probable that he worked both in wood and iron ; and St. Justin favors this opinion by saying: "He and Jesus made ploughs and yokes for oxen."

At the Nazareth of to-day a "little chapel is erected on the site of the workshop of St. Joseph. In this chapel an old wall is to be seen which is believed to have formed a part of St. Joseph's house."

fish, fruits, bread and cooked vegetables, taken
with great moderation, and varied according to circumstances.[7]

The journey to Bethlehem and the birth of the
infant God in a stable are wonderful events known
to every one in our day. But St. Joseph was the
first man to witness them. How tenderly he saw
and adored the new-born Saviour of the world!
How faithfully he acquitted himself of the double
charge of educating Jesus and guarding His Blessed
Mother!

"He was truly," says St. Bernard, "the faithful
and prudent servant whom the Lord appointed
master over His household—His foster-father, the
comfort and support of His Mother, and His most
faithful co-operator in the execution of His deepest
counsels on earth."

"What a happiness," continues the same great doctor, "not only to see Jesus Christ, but also to bear
Him, to carry Him in his arms, to lead Him from
place to place, to embrace and caress Him, to feed
Him, and to be a witness of all the sublime secrets
which were concealed from the princes of this
world!"

We would be ungrateful to this illustrious saint
if we did not remember that it is to him, as an instrument of God, that we are indebted for the

[7] "Cité Mystique de Dieu."

preservation of the Divine Infant from the fiendish malignity of King Herod.

"An angel of the Lord," says St. Matthew,
"appeared in sleep to Joseph, saying: 'Arise and
take the Child and His Mother, and fly into Egypt;
and be there until I shall tell thee. For it will
come to pass that Herod will seek the Child to
destroy Him.'

"Who rising up, took the Child and His Mother
by night, and retired into Egypt.

"And He was there until the death of Herod,
that it might be fulfilled which the Lord spoke by
the prophet, saying: 'Out of Egypt have I called
my Son.'"

There is a tradition, handed down by the
Fathers of the Church, that upon the Holy
Family's entering the land of Egypt, the presence of the Child Jesus had the miraculous effect
of striking all the pagan oracles of that superstitious country dumb. The statues of the gods
trembled, and in many places fell to the ground.

The Holy Family fixed their abode at Heliopolis. On entering this famous city, they passed
under a stately sycamore-tree, which gracefully
bent down its branches as an act of homage to
the Son of God. It stands to this day, a relic
of venerable antiquity.[8] Thus the city of the

---

[8] It is asserted that its leaves afterwards cured many diseases.
Of this renowned tree a learned traveler writes : "I took the

sun,* in accordance with its name, saw the true
Sun of Grace and Justice.

Several years passed away, and Joseph was
commanded to leave the land of the Pharaos.

"Now Herod being dead," writes St. Matthew,
"behold an angel of the Lord appeared in sleep to
Joseph in Egypt, saying:

" 'Arise and take the Child and His Mother,
and go into the land of Israel; for they are dead
who sought the life of the Child.'

"Who rising up, took the Child and His Mother, and came into the land of Israel.

"But hearing that Archelaus reigned in Judea
in the room of Herod his father, he was afraid to

road for Heliopolis, which is about three miles east of Cairo.
. . . We arrived at the Garden of Matarieh, where there is a
famous sycamore-tree which, as a time-honored tradition says,
had the honor of sheltering the Holy Family in their flight into
Egypt. It is a noble and venerable-looking tree. I knelt on
that spot which had been sanctified by the sacred presence of the
Holy Family. I prayed there, meditating on the great mystery
of the flight into Egypt. I kissed the ground consecrated by the
feet of our Redeemer, and, gathering some limbs and leaves of
this holy tree, I mounted my donkey, and in a short time was on
the site where Heliopolis once stood."—*Rev. Dr. Vetromile, Travels,* 1869.

⁹ Heliopolis signifies *city of the sun.* At present there is
nothing to indicate its ruins "except an obelisk, seventy feet
high, which stands alone on a pedestal six feet two inches in dia-
meter. This obelisk was erected by Ositarsen, 1750 years before
Christ. It is the oldest monument of its kind in existence."—*Dr.
Vetromile.*

go thither; and being warned in sleep, he retired into the parts of Galilee.

"And he came and dwelt in a city called Nazareth, that it might be fulfilled which was said by the prophets—that he shall be called a Nazarene."

St. Joseph was a strict observer of the law of Moses, and, in conformity to its directions, he went yearly to Jerusalem to celebrate the Passover. When our Saviour had reached the age of twelve years, He accompanied His parents to the Holy City. After performing the usual ceremonies of the Feast, the Blessed Virgin and St. Joseph directed their steps homeward.

But the Divine Boy "remained in Jerusalem, and His parents knew it not.

"And thinking he was in the company, they came a day's journey, and sought him among their kinsfolks and acquaintance.

"And not finding Him, they returned into Jerusalem, seeking Him.

"And it came to pass that after three days they found Him in the Temple, sitting in the midst of the doctors, hearing them and asking them questions.

"And all who heard Him were astonished at His wisdom and His answers.

"And seeing *Him*, they wondered. And His Mother said to Him: ' Son, why hast Thou done

so to us ?   Behold, Thy father and I have sought
Thee sorrowing. '

"And He said to them: ' How is it that you
sought me?   Did you not know that I must be
about the things that are my Father's ? '

"And they understood not the word that He
spoke unto them.

"And He went down with them, and came to
Nazareth, and was subject to them.   And His
Mother kept all these words in her heart.

"And Jesus advanced in wisdom and age, and
grace with God and men." [10]

How full of rich, suggestive thought is the last
sentence of the Evangelist, "And Jesus advanced
in wisdom and age, and grace with God and men"!
What a bright and precious example for the young,
what a stimulus even for the old—to advance during this short and fleeting life " in wisdom and age,
and grace before God and men"!

The Holy Book makes no further mention of St.
Joseph; but we are not destitute of valuable information, from approved sources, in relation to
the last years of his pure, simple, and beautiful
life." [11]

The cares, travels, and ceaseless fatigues which

[10] St. Luke, chap. ii.

[11] For the remainder of this sketch we follow in substance the account of St. Joseph's last years as given by the **Venerable Mary of
Agreda** in her "Cité Mystique de Dieu. "

the great Saint had undergone for the support of the Most Holy Virgin and the Divine Child soon told on his delicate constitution. Long before old age his health began to fail. It seems that during the last eight years of his life he ceased working on account of his growing infirmities, and at the urgent request of the Immaculate Mother herself.

"I beg of you to cease from this incessant toil and repose yourself," said the Blessed Mary to our Saint one day. "I will now labor for you, in testimony of my gratitude, and as long as the Lord shall give us life."

For some time St. Joseph hesitated but at length her sweet arguments prevailed. He was thus relieved from labor, and for the rest of his days he gave himself to the practice of virtue and the contemplation of those sublime mysteries of which he had been a happy witness. With the Son of God and His Blessed Mother so near, it is not astonishing to learn that our Saint arrived at so high a degree of sanctity that next to his Immaculate Spouse—who stands alone among mere creatures—he surpassed all men.

Thus God graciously conducted His servant Joseph along the royal road of suffering. It was, no doubt, to increase his merits and his crown—before his power of gaining merits had ceased—that in the last years of his life he was visited by certain maladies exceedingly acute ; maladies which

caused great debility, and racked his feeble body
with excessive pain.

> "But when his last hour drew nigh,
>   Oh! full of joy was his breast;
> Seeing Jesus and Mary close by,
>   As he tranquilly slumbered to rest."

During the nine days that preceded the death
of St. Joseph, he was tenderly watched day and
night by Christ and the Most Blessed Virgin.[12]
It was so arranged that one or the other was
always present at his bedside. Three times daily
the angels chanted celestial music for the holy
patient. Thus cheered and fortified, the precious
end came, and with his head supported on the
bosom of the Son of God, and a last benediction
from the Divine Lips brightening the path to
eternity, this glorious guardian of the Holy
Family, at the age of sixty years and some days,
bade adieu to the toils and hardships of this
world.[13]

[12] During the three last years of St. Joseph's life— which were
those of his greatest suffering—the Holy Virgin never quitted
him, day or night. If she withdrew for a moment, it was only to
serve her Divine Son, who united with His Mother in assisting
our Saint, except when He was unavoidably engaged in other
works. Hence we may say that never was patient so well served.
—*Cité Mystique de Dieu.*

[13] Our august Saint was one of those who enjoyed the privilege of
exemption from the sight of demons at his death.—*Cité Mystique
de Dieu.*

As Pharao said to the Egyptians of old in their
distress, "Go to Joseph," so may we with happy
confidence ask Heaven for favors through the intercession of him to whom the Son of God was subject on earth.

St. Teresa chose him as the chief patron of her
Order. "I choose the glorious St. Joseph for my
patron," she writes, "and I commend myself in
all things to his special intercession. I do not remember ever to have asked of God anything by him
which I did not obtain. I never knew any one
who, by invoking him, did not make great advances
in virtue. He assists all who address themselves to
him in a manner truly wonderful."[14]

> "To all who would holily live,
> To all who would happily die,
> St. Joseph is ready to give
> Sure guidance and help from on high."

[14] In the New World devotion to St. Joseph began at an early
period. Canada chose him as its first patron in 1624. Indian war-
chiefs, converted to the faith, gloried in bearing his name. In 1773
the *first* Catholic church in Philadelphia was erected under the
name of St. Joseph. The cathedrals of Wheeling, Columbus, La
Crosse, and Buffalo are dedicated to God under the patronage of
St. Joseph. Countless churches bear his name and numerous confraternities are found in his honor. Towns and rivers have been called after the head of the Holy Family. The city of St. Joseph in
Missouri is the see of a Catholic bishop. Nearly a dozen colleges
and theological seminaries in our country bear the honored name of
St. Joseph.

SAINT JOHN THE BAPTIST.

THE PRECURSOR OF OUR DIVINE REDEEMER.

DIED A. D. 28.[1]

"Unloose, great Baptist, our sin-fettered lips,
  That with enfranchised voice we may proclaim
The miracles of thy transcendent life,
  Thy deeds of matchless fame."

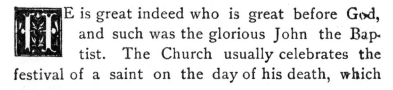HE is great indeed who is great before God, and such was the glorious John the Baptist. The Church usually celebrates the festival of a saint on the day of his death, which

[1] It is to be noted that there is a difference of *four* years between the *exact date* of the birth of Christ and the date given by our common era. The common era was established by the Catholic Church towards the commencement of the sixth century, as a mark of respect to Jesus Christ. Dennis the Little, in computing back from his own time, endeavored to fix the epoch of the birth of our Lord, which, by mistake, he made to correspond to the year 4714 of the Julian period. That was an error of *four* years. St. John the Baptist really died in the thirty-second year of the age of Christ, which, according to our common era, is A. D. 28. Our Lord was thirty-three years of age at His death, yet our common era makes that blessed event A. D. 29. And though this is the year of 1880 of our common era, it is, strictly speaking, 1884 years since the birth of Christ.

[2] John is from the Hebrew, and signifies *the gracious gift of God.*

is his birthday to eternal life. But our noble Saint is excepted from this rule, because he was sanctified in his mother's womb, and came into the world pure and holy.[3]

The birth of this illustrious man, who was sent as a pioneer to prepare the way for Christ, may be ranked with the wonders of history. It is miraculous, and was ushered in with many prodigies.

"There was," says the sacred writer,[4] "in the days of Herod, King of Judea, a certain priest named Zachary, of the course of Abia,[5] and his wife was of the daughters of Aaron, and her name Elizabeth.

"And they were both just before God, walking in all the commandments and justifications of the Lord without blame.

"And they had no son; for that Elizabeth was barren, and they both were well advanced in years.

"And it came to pass, when he executed the priestly function in the order of his course before God, according to the custom of the priestly office, it was his lot to offer incense, going into the Tem-

[3] The Feast of St. John the Baptist is celebrated on the 24th of June—his birthday.

[4] St. Luke.

[5] The family of Abia was one of the twenty-four sacerdotal families into which the children of Aaron were divided, in order that they might all serve in the Temple by turns.

ple of the Lord, and all the multitude of the peo.
ple was praying without at the hour of incense,
and there appeared to him an angel of the Lord,
standing on the right side of the altar of incense.

"And Zachary seeing him was troubled, and
fear fell upon him; but the angel said to him: 'Fear
not, Zachary, for thy prayer is heard; and thy wife
Elizabeth shall bear thee a son, and thou shalt call
his name John.

"'And thou shalt have joy and gladness, and
many shall rejoice in his nativity, for he shall be
great before the Lord; and shall drink no wine nor
strong drink, and he shall be filled with the Holy
Ghost even from his mother's womb.

"'And he shall convert many of the children of
Israel to the Lord their God.

"'And he shall go before Him in the spirit and
power of Elias, that he may turn the hearts of
the fathers unto the children, and the incredulous
to the wisdom of the just, to prepare unto the
Lord a perfect people.'

"Zachary said to the angel: 'Whereby shall I
know this, for I am an old man, and my wife is
advanced in years?'

"An the angel answering, said to him: 'I am Gabriel, who stands before God; and I am sent to
speak to thee, and to bring thee these good tidings.

"'And behold thou shalt be dumb, and shalt

not be able to speak until the day wherein these things shall come to pass; because thou hast not believed my words, which shall be fulfilled in their time.'

"And the people were waiting for Zachary, and they wondered that he tarried so long in the Temple. And when he came out he could not speak to them, and they understood that he had seen a vision in the Temple. And he made signs to them, and remained dumb.

" And it came to pass, after the days of his office were accomplished, he departed to his own house."

Elizabeth, in the sixth month of her pregnancy, was honored by a visit from the Mother of God, in which, at the presence of the Divine Redeemer of mankind, the little Baptist was sanctified.* On this occasion the blessed child, yet unborn, was, by an extraordinary privilege, favored with the use of reason, and was the *first* among men who beheld Christ, and knew Him before his eyes saw the light of this world. His joy was so inexpressible at beholding Him whom the ancient prophets had only foreseen in spirit, that he leaped with delight in his mother's womb.

John was born about six months before the birth of Christ. "The friends and neighbors of

---

* St. Bernard and many other great theologians understand by this gift of sanctifying grace *the remission of original sin.*

Elizabeth," says St. Luke, "heard that the **Lord** had shown His great mercy towards her, and they congratulated with her.'

"A⸱d it came to pass that on the eighth day they came to circumcise the child, and they called him by his father's name, Zachary.   And his mother answering, said: ' Not so—but he shall be called *John.*'

" And they said to her: ' There is none of thy kindred that is called by this name.'   And they made signs to his father, how he would have him called.

"And   demanding   a   writing-table,   he wrote, saying: ' John is his name.'   And they all wondered.   And immediately his mouth was opened and his tongue *loosed*, and he spoke, blessing God.

"And fear came upon all their neighbors; and

¹ There is a Plenary Indulgence on the place where St. John the Baptist was born.   This was the spot where Zachary made the *"Benedictus, Dominus Deus,"* and where he recovered the use of his speech, which he had lost.   At the ruins of the house of St. Zachary there is a Partial Indulgence, and another on the ruins of the Church and Convent of the Visitation.   Here the place is pointed out where St. Elizabeth went to meet the Blessed Virgin, who sang extemporaneously the *Magnificat.*   The desert of St. John the Baptist, and the cave where he lived for a long time, are near this locality.   This is the place where he did penance, where he preached the baptism of penance for the remission of sins, and prepared the ways of the Lord.   Not far off are the tombs of St. Zachary and St. Elizabeth, the parents of St. John the Baptist.—*Vetromile, Travels,* 1869.

all these things were noised abroad over all the hill-country of Judea. And all they that had heard them laid them up in their hearts, saying: 'What a one, think you, shall this child be ?' For the hand of the Lord was with him.''

In order to preserve his innocence spotless, and to improve the wonderful graces which he had received from Heaven, St. John was directed by the Holy Ghost to lead an austere and contemplative life in the wilderness, in the continual exercise of prayer and penance. Thus he lived from infancy[8] till he was thirty years of age.

How much does this precaution of a great Saint, who was strengthened by such uncommon graces and privileges, condemn the rashness of those silly parents who expose the precious souls of their children, in the slippery time of youth, to the contagious air of a hundred dangers, and, above all, to that of worldly, wicked company !

When St. John had reached the age of thirty years,[9] he was perfectly qualified to enter on his

[8] We do not know precisely at what age he retired into the desert. It was *from his tender years*, according to the general impression which appears to have been adopted by the Church. We must not enquire whether he had sufficient discretion to guide himself—he to whom God had granted the use of this faculty in his mother's womb ! The Holy Ghost, who had conducted him into solitude, continued still to be his director and master. —*De Ligny*.

[9] That is the age at which the priests and Levites were permit

sublime mission.   He was the glorious **herald of the Redemption.**   He was to prepare the way **for** Jesus Christ.   Clothed in the garments of penance, he raised his mighty voice ; and the people of a sin-stained land listened to him in awe and admiration.

"In those days," writes the first of the Evangelists, "cometh John the Baptist preaching in the desert of Judea, and saying : 'Do penance, for the kingdom of heaven is at hand.'

"For this is he that was spoken of by Isaias the prophet, saying : *A voice of one crying in the desert, Prepare ye the way of the Lord—make straight His paths.*

"And the same John had his garment of camel's hair, and a leathern girdle about his loins; and his meat was locusts and wild honey.

"Then went out to him Jerusalem and all Judea, and the country about the Jordan ; and they were baptized by him in the Jordan[10] confessing their sins.

---

ted by the Jewish law to begin the exercise of their functions.— *Butler.*

[10] On the shore of the Jordan there is a Plenary Indulgence.   This sacred river is about two hundred miles long, and from fifty to one hundred and fifty feet wide.   It runs from the Sea of Tiberias into the Dead Sea and is called in the East by the Arabs *Banar-el Arden* (River of the Ford), but the Hebrews call it *Jardan* (River of Judgment).   The current is rapid, and the water is brackish.   To cross this river one is nearly certain to be murdered

"And seeing many of the Pharisees and Sadducees" coming to his baptism, he said to them: 'Ye brood of vipers, who hath showed you to flee from the wrath to come? Bring forth, therefore, fruit worthy of penance.

" 'And think not to say within yourselves, We have Abraham for our father. For I tell you that God is able of these stones to raise up children to Abraham.

" 'For now the axe is laid to the root of the trees. Every tree, therefore, that doth not yield good fruit shall be cut down, and cast into the fire.

" 'I indeed baptize you in water unto penance, [11]

---

y the savage descendants of the wild Ismael, unless accompanied by a strong caravan.—*Vetromile.*

St. John the Baptist gave his baptism at a spot on the banks of the Jordan called Bethania. "It was at that place," writes the Abbé Baunard, "that the Hebrews had forded the Jordan under the guidance of Joshua, and it was customary to station thither ferry-boats for the convenience of travelers."

[11] These were two sects among the Jews. The Pharisees were for the most part notorious hypocrites. The Sadducees were a kind of free-thinkers in matters of religion.

[12] The baptism of St. John chiefly represented the manner in which the souls of men must be cleansed from all sin and vicious habits, to be made partakers in the graces of Christianity. It was an emblem of the interior effects of sincere repentance. But it differed entirely from the great Sacrament of Baptism which Christ soon after instituted, and to which it was much inferior in virtue and efficacy. St. John's baptism was a temporary cere

but He that shall come after me is mightier than **I**, whose shoes I am not worthy to bear.[13]   He shall baptize you in the Holy Ghost and fire.

" 'Whose fan is in his hand, and He will thoroughly cleanse His floor, and gather His wheat into the barn, but the chaff He will burn with unquenchable fire.'

" Then cometh Jesus from Galilee to the Jordan unto John to be baptized by him.

"But John stayed Him, saying: 'I ought to be baptized by Thee, and comest Thou to me?'

"And Jesus answering, said to him: 'Suffer it to be so now.   For so it becometh us to fulfil all justice.'   Then he suffered Him."[14]

mony, by which men who were under the Law were admitted to some new spiritual privileges, which they had not before, by him who was the messenger of Christ and of His new covenant. Whence it is called by the Fathers a partition between the Law and the Gospel.   It prepared men to become Christians, but did not make them so.   It was not even conferred in the name of Christ, or in that of the Holy Ghost.—*Butler.*

The baptism of John did not confer the remission of sins; but disposed towards that remission by penance which should follow, and which became the next disposition to the baptism of Christ, in which alone is to be found the remission of sins.—*De Ligny.*

[13] Or as another Evangelist has it—"the latchet of whose shoe I am not worthy to loose."

[14] Our Saint had then been baptized about six months.   He knew Christ by a special revelation.   The Saviour of sinners was pleased to be baptized among sinners, not to be cleansed Himself, but to sanctify the waters, says St. Ambrose—that is, to

"And Jesus being baptized, forthwith came out of the water; and lo! the heavens were opened to him; and he saw the spirit of God descending as a dove and coming upon Him.

"And behold a voice from heaven, saying: 'This is my beloved Son, in whom I am well pleased.' "

The kindness, charity, and angelic life of St. John the Baptist won the hearts of all, and his zeal and manly energy gave him a commanding influence over the minds of his hearers. He toiled on, having only God and His holy will in view. He boldly reproved the vices of all classes of men. With an undaunted authority he raised His voice against the hypocrisy of the Pharisees, the profanity of the Sadducees, the grasping extortion of the publicans, the brutality and injustice of the soldiers, and the grossly scandalous life of King Herod [15] himself.

give them the virtue to cleanse away the sins of men. St. Augustine and St. Thomas Aquinas think that He then instituted the holy Sacrament of Baptism, which He soon after administered by His disciples, whom doubtless He had first baptized Himself.—*Butler.*

[15] This Herod, known in history as Herod Antipas, was the son of that barbarous Herod who ordered the massacre of the innocents, hoping to kill the infant Jesus. The tyrant not only murdered St. John the Baptist, but it was he who sent Christ to Pilate, and had him robed in derision with a white garment. But his hour came. In the year 38, under the Emperor Caligula, he

King Herod, urged on by a criminal passion, had, contrary to all laws human and divine, married Herodias, his sister-in-law, the wife of his brother Philip, who was yet alive.   St. John boldly rep rehended the royal sinner.   "It is not lawful," said the holy Precursor, "for thee to take thy brother's wife."

Knowing him to be a blessed man, Herod feared and reverenced John.   He even did many things by his advice.   But the scandalous con- nection which he kept up with the guilty Hero- dias was a sore spot which he could not bear to have touched; and, of course, he was highly of fended at the liberty which the great preacher took in that direction.   Thus, while he respected him as a Saint, he hated him as a censor; and felt a violent struggle in his own breast between his veneration for the sanctity of the prophet, and the pointed reproaches of his nameless con- duct.

Herodias, however, acted like an enraged fury of hell.   She left no artifice untried to take away the life of him who spoke words of warning and wisdom, and raised his pure, angelic finger to point at her shameless career.   The wretched

---

fell into disgrace, lost his crown, and was banished into Gaul.   Jo- sephus assures us that both Herod and Herodias died in extreme misery

woman clamored for his death, and, to content her, Herod cast the Saint into prison.

"And having a mind to put him to death," says St. Matthew, "he feared the people; because they esteemed him as a prophet.

"But on Herod's birthday the daughter of Herodias danced [16] before them; and pleased Herod.

---

[16] In itself dancing is an indifferent amusement; but it is often the *occasion* of sin. Round dances are condemned by good sense and Christian modesty.

"In order that playing and dancing may be lawful," writes the holy Doctor, St. Francis de Sales, "we must use them as a recreation, without having any affection for them; we may use them for a short time, but we should not continue them till we are wearied or stupefied with them; and we must use them but seldom, lest we should otherwise turn a recreation into an occupation. . . .

"I have the same opinion of dances, Philothea, that physicians have of mushrooms; as the best of them, in their opinion, are good for nothing, so I tell you the best balls are good for nothing. If upon some occasion, which you cannot well avoid, you must go to a ball, see that your dancing be properly conducted. But you will ask me how must it be conducted? I answer, *with modesty, gravity, and a good intention.*"

The eminent Roger de Rabutin, Count of Bussi, lived for many years with dignity and applause at the French Court. In his book, "On the Uses of Adversity," addressed to his children, he cautions them in the strongest terms against a love of dancing. From his own experience he touchingly assures them that this amusement is dangerous to many people. "A ball," he writes, "is generally a post too hot even for a hermit. If it may be done by aged persons without danger, it would be in them ridiculous;

"Whereupon he promised, with an oath, to give her whatsoever she would ask of him.

"But she, being instructed before by her mother, said: 'Give me here in a dish the head of John the Baptist.'

"And the king was struck sad; yet because of his oath,[17] and for them that sat with him at table, he commanded it to be given.

"And he sent, and beheaded John in prison.

"And his head was brought in a dish; and it was given to the damsel, and she brought it to her mother[18].

"And his disciples came and took the body, and buried it,[19] and came and told Jesus."

----

and to persons that are young, let custom say what it will, it is dangerous. In a word, I assert that a mixed ball is no place for a Christian."

[17] It is a sin to take a bad oath, but it is a still greater one to keep it.

[18] St. Jerome tells us that the wicked Herodias made it her inhuman pastime to pierce the sacred tongue of St. John the Baptist with a bodkin.

[19] "The Baptist's head," writes Butler, "was discovered at Emisa in Syria, in the year 453, and was kept with honor in the great church of that city, till, about the year 800, this precious relic was conveyed to Constantinople, that it might not be sacrilegiously insulted by the Saracens. When that city was taken by the French in 1204, Wallo de Sarton, a canon of Amiens, brought a part of this head—that is, all the face except the lower jaw—into France, and bestowed it on his own church, where it is preserved to this day."

Thus died the holy, humble, and illustrious Precursor of the Divine One, about two years and three months after his entrance upon his public ministry, and a year before the death of our Blessed Redeemer. He was a martyr, a virgin, a doctor, a prophet, and more than a prophet. His immortal eulogy comes from the sacred lips of Christ Himself.

"Jesus," writes the Evangelist,[20] "began to say to the multitudes concerning John: 'What went you out into the desert to see? A reed shaken with the wind?

" 'But what went you out to see? A man clothed in soft garments? Behold they that are clothed in soft garments, are in the houses of kings.

" 'But what went you out to see? A prophet? Yea I tell you, and more than a prophet.

" 'For this is he of whom it is written: *Behold I send my angel before Thy face, who shall prepare the way before Thee.*

" 'Amen I say to you, there hath not risen among them that are born of women a greater than John the Baptist.' "[21]

[20] St. Matthew xi.

[21] In the "Litany of the Saints," the Church places St. John the Baptist immediately after the Most Blessed Virgin and the Angels but *before* all other Saints.

The Cathedral of Savannah bears the name of St. John the

Baptist. The same is true of churches in New York, Brooklyn, Boston, Buffalo, Providence, St. Louis, New Orleans, San Francisco, Cincinnati, Ottawa the capital of Canada, and many other towns and cities of North America. The French Canadians are very devout to the great Precursor of Christ, and the name, perhaps, most commonly given to their sons is that of *John Baptist.* Four or five Catholic colleges in this Republic bear the honored name of St. John.

SAINT JAMES THE GREAT,

APOSTLE, MARTYR, AND PATRON OF SPAIN.,

DIED A. D. 43.

T. JAMES was the first of the apostles who had the sublime honor of dying for Jesus Christ and the Catholic faith. He was surnamed the Great to distinguish him from another Apostle of the same name, and was the brother of the "beloved disciple," St. John the Evangelist. Zebedee and Salome were his parents. On his mother's side he was nearly related to our Blessed Lord,[1] before whom he was born about twelve years. He was many years older than his brother John.

St. James was born at Bethsaida, in Galilee, to which place St. Peter also belonged. One day

---

[1] It is generally thought that St. James the Great and St. John the Evangelist were nearly related to our Lord.

73

as Christ was walking by the Sea of Galilee, He saw Peter and Andrew fishing. He invited them to follow Him, and promised to make them fishers of men. Passing on a little farther along the shore, He saw the two brothers James and John in a ship with their father Zebedee. He called them, and, at once, they left their nets and father to follow the Master of Life.

When our Lord formed the College of Apostles St. James and his brother became members of that sacred institution. To these two Christ gave the title of *Boanerges*, or the Sons of Thunder. This, it seems, was to denote their active zeal. When a town of Samaria refused to entertain the Redeemer of mankind, they suggested that He should call down fire from heaven to consume it; but He gave them to understand that meekness and patience were the celestial arms by which they were to conquer the world.

Christ distinguished St. Peter, St. James, and St John among the other apostles by many special favors. They alone were spectators of his glorious transfiguration; and they alone beheld his agony and bloody sweat in the garden.

On one occasion, the mother of St. James made a rather worldly request of Our Divine Redeemer. She wished him to grant that her two sons, James and John, might have the honor of sitting, one on His right and the other on his left in His kingdom.   She imagined that Christ was about to establish a powerful monarchy on earth.

" You know not what you ask, " replied Christ. Then, turning to James and John, He said: "Can you drink the chalice that I shall drink? "

"We can," they answered with confidence.

"My chalice," continued the Son of God, "indeed, you shall drink; but to sit on my right or left hand is not mine to give you, but for them to whom it is prepared by my Father."

Thus they were promised suffering and a place in heaven according to their merits; nor was it long before the promise of Christ was fulfilled to both, though St. James was the first to get his reward.

After the Ascension[2] of our Blessed Redeemer and the descent of the Holy Ghost, St. James left Judea and preached the Faith in various countries.   At length he arrived in Spain.   Here

---

[2] On the very top of the lovely Mount of Olives there is a small octagonal mosque, the remains of a church built there by St. Helena. This is erected on the spot whence Christ ascended into heaven after His Resurrection.   On this rock I saw the print of our Lord's left foot.   It shows that our Saviour had His face towards the west. Here a Plenary Indulgence can be gained.   The Catholics go thither on Ascension Day to celebrate Mass.   The place is in charge of a Santon, who receives some backsheesh (money) to open the door and show the spot.   I asked him for some pieces of the rock; and he broke off a very little piece near the print, but he expected more backsheesh, of course.— *Vetromile, Travels,* 1869.

he was the first to announce the Gospel; and hence he has always been venerated by the Spaniards as their patron saint.

During the Apostle's stay in Spain, it is said he was favored with a remarkable vision. He was living in Saragossa. One night, after a long day's preaching, he went out to refresh himself by praying near the river Ebro, on which the city stands. While at his devotions, he saw the Immaculate Virgin standing before him on a jasper pillar, and all around her were multitudes of angels, of enrapturing beauty, singing the sweetest hymns he had ever heard.

St. James wondered how our Blessed Lady could be there, because he knew that she was still alive, and residing at Jerusalem with his brother, St. John. Seeing, however, that it was really she, he saluted her with deep veneration.

She then addressed him, saying: "Build a church in this place in my name. I know that this part of Spain will be particularly devout to me, and from this moment I take it under my protection."

These words were no sooner uttered than the Virgin Mother and her troop of beautiful angels disappeared.

St. James lost no time in carrying out her gracious command. On the very spot where he beheld the vision, he erected a chapel, which he called *Chapel of our Lady of the Pillar.* A chapel of the same name is there to-day, and is held in great veneration by the whole Spanish people.[8]

Eleven years after our Lord's Ascension, St. James again returned to Jerusalem. The thunder of his eloquence touched many hearts, and conversions were numerous. The Jews, however, soon became enraged at his success, and plotted to kill him. They had barbarously crucified the

---

[8] "Lives of the early Martyrs."

A recent traveler writes : "I started for Saragossa early on the morning of the 18th. . . . About half-past eight in the evening we crossed the Ebro, memorable in the traditions of Spain ; for it was on the banks of this river, a short distance from where we crossed it, that St. James saw the Heavenly Queen and received the sacred Pillar *still to be seen there*, a symbol of the Faith he had planted in Spain, and which still lives strong in the hearts and affections of her people notwithstanding the storms of persecution.

"The Chapel of the Pillar is enclosed in a very large church, of which it occupies the centre. There are three altars in the chapel. The one at the Epistle side is the shrine of our Lady, but no Masses are celebrated on this altar. The Masses are said on the middle altar, or on that at the Gospel side, St. James's.

"Many Masses were celebrated before mine, and at every hour of the day people might be seen prostrated before the altar of our Lady. . . . Tradition says that St. James obtained this statue from the Blessed Virgin herself, when she appeared to him near the river Ebro, and that the statue and pillar still stand on the very spot where they were placed by St. James himself, having never been touched or removed by human hands."— *Rev. J. Adam, Letter of July* 29, 1877, *in the Ave Maria.*

Divine One ; but the disciple is not better than **his** Master.

Having failed on several occasions in their malignant designs on the life of the holy Apostle, his enemies now determined on a plan for his destruction.   It was arranged to raise a sudden disturbance while he was preaching.   Two Roman centurions were hired to have their soldiers in readiness to seize his person at a given signal.

One day while St. James was in the midst of a discourse on the divinity of Jesus Christ, some of the listening multitude exhibited displeasure at his burning words.   The sign was given.   A Scribe, named Josias, rushed on the Saint, and threw a rope around his neck.   The soldiers then seized him and led him prisoner to the king.

This was Agrippa, the grandson of that infamous Herod who beheaded St. John the Baptist.   In his desire to please the Jews, he began to persecute the followers of Christ ; and without making any enquiry as to the truth of the charges brought against St. James, the barbarous king at once ordered him to be executed. [4]

[4] Agrippa was the *first* prince who persecuted the Church. After having put St. James to death, he imprisoned St. Peter, but God delivered him out of the persecutor's hands.   Nor was it long before this king felt the effect of divine vengeance.   After the feast of the Passover, in the year 43, he returned to Cæsarea to exhibit there public games in honor of the Emperor Claudius.

His hour was come. The Apostle, no doubt, recalled Calvary, and, with joy, passed on his way to the block. No longer was he annoyed with ambitious thoughts about whether he would be honored with a place on the right or the left of his Divine Master. His only desire was to prove the depth of his faith and hope and love by giving up his life for the Son of God; his only wish was to glorify Him before heaven and earth.

and was attended thither by a numerous train of nobility. He appeared early on the second morning of the exhibition at the theatre, in a costly robe of silver tissue, artfully wrought, and so bright that the sunbeams which darted upon it were reflected with such an uncommon lustre as to dazzle the eyes of the spectators, who foolishly beheld him with a kind of divine respect. In an elegant speech he addressed the deputies of Tyre and Sidon, who had come to beg his pardon for some offence. Whilst he spoke, the ambassadors and some court sycophants gave a great shout, crying out that it was the voice of a god and not of a man. Agrippa, elated with pride, seemed to forget himself, and to approve instead of checking the impious flattery. But at that instant, an angel of the Lord smote him with a dreadful disease, and he felt himself seized with a violent pain in his bowels. Seeing the distemper to be mortal, he rejected the flattery of his sycophants, telling them that he whom they called immortal was dying. Yet still full of false ideas of human grandeur, though he saw death inevitable, he comforted himself with the remembrance of the splendor in which he had lived. So true it is, that a man dies such as he lives. After lingering five days in dreadful torments, under which no remedy gave him any ease, being eaten up by worms, he expired in all the miseries that can be expressed or imagined. This account is given us by Josephus and by St. Luke.—*Butler.*

As St. James was moving along the street, a poor paralytic saw him, and cried out that he wished to be healed. The Saint granted his request. He was instantly cured. But this miracle led to one still greater.

Josias the Scribe was struck with the matchless peace and courage that marked the conduct of the great Apostle as he went to death ; but the cure of the paralytic worked a wondrous change, and at the sight of the miracle he was suddenly converted. Then and there he repented of what he had done, and cried out that Jesus Christ was the true God.

His sincerity was soon put to the test. He was led with St. James to execution, and begged pardon of the latter for having apprehended him. The Apostle paused a moment, turned to him and embraced him, saying : " Peace be with you. " Having arrived at the block, he kissed him, and they were beheaded together.[5] And thus passed to their heavenly home, in the year 43, the glorious " Son of Thunder " and the lowly, repentant Scribe, each, in his degree, to partake for ever of

[5] On the highest summit of Mount Sion (at Jerusalem) is one of the most elegant and richest churches of the city. It is called the Church of the Apostle St. James. This is where the Apostle of Spain was beheaded by order of King Agrippa. A Partial Indulgence is here obtainable. Stains of the blood of this Apostle can be seen yet on the stone where he received martyrdom.—*Rev. Dr. Vetromile, Travels,* 1869.

that mysterious joy which eye cannot see, nor ear
hear, nor the mind of man comprehend.[6]

[6] The body of St. James was interred at Jerusalem; but, not long
after, it was carried by his disciples into Spain, and deposited at
El Pardon, on the borders of Galicia. In the beginning of the ninth
century the sacred relics were there discovered, and translated to
Compostella. Here they rest in the stately cathedral, and are held
in great veneration.

Many authentic miracles have been wrought through the intercession of St. James ; and during the long struggle between the
Cross and the Crescent in Spain he is said to have appeared several
times, affording visible protection to the Catholic armies of that
nation against the fierce and powerful Moors. Compostella is famous for the number of pilgrims who come to visit the shrine of the
illustrious Apostle of Spain.

Even in the New World the roving and chivalrous Spaniard
brandished his sword and dashed into the fight only after utter-
ing his battle-cry of "San Jago," or St. James. On the first great
battle of Cortes with the Indians the historian Prescott writes:
"It was not long before the ears of the Christians were saluted
with the cheering war-cry of *San Jago and San Pedro!* (St. James
and St. Peter), and they beheld the bright helmets and swords of
the Castilian chivalry flashing back the rays of the morning sun,
as they dashed through the ranks of the enemy, striking to the
right and left, and scattering dismay around them. The eye of
Faith, indeed, could discern the Patron Saint of Spain himself,
mounted on his gray war-horse, heading the rescue, and tramp-
ling over the bodies of the fallen infidels."—*History of the Conquest
of Mexico.*

"Cortes," says Pizarro y Orellana, ''supposed it was his own
tutelar saint, St. Peter; but the common and undeniable opinion is
that it was our glorious Apostle St. James, the bulwark and safeguard
of our nation."

Of this event the brave old soldier-historian, Bernal Diaz, who
was in the battle writes: "I acknowledge that all our exploits

and victories are owing to our Lord Jesus Christ, and that in this battle there was such a number of Indians to every one of us that if each had thrown a handful of earth they might have buried us, if by the great mercy of God we had not been protected. It may be that the person whom Gomara mentions as having appeared on a mottled gray horse was the glorious Apostle St. James or St. Peter, and that I, being a sinner, was unworthy to see him."—*Hist. de la Conquista.*

St. James's Church is the oldest Catholic place of worship in Brooklyn N. Y. All the large cities of the United States have churches dedicated to divine worship under the patronage of this great Apostle.

SAINT PETER,

"THE PRINCE OF THE APOSTLES." [1]

DIED A. D. 65.

S T. PETER, the first Vicar of Christ on
earth, was the son of Jona, a fisherman,
and was originally named Simon. He
was born at Bethsaida, a city of Galilee, situated
on the Sea of Galilee.[2] Some authors have fixed
the date of his birth three years before that of the
Most Blessed Virgin, and seventeen years before the
birth of Christ. St. Andrew, the Apostle, was his
brother.

Peter removed from Bethsaida to Capharnaum, probably on account of his marriage, for

---

[1] Some may, perhaps, think that this title is of modern origin;
but it is at least as old as St. Jerome, who uses these very
words.

[2] The Sea of Galilee, sometimes called the Sea of Tiberias, is
about sixteen miles long by eight wide, and is the largest of two
fresh-water lakes through which the river Jordan passes. It is
said that the river flows through it without mingling its waters
with those of the lake. The latter still abounds in fish as when
the Apostles left their nets to become ' fishers of men"; but the fish-
ery is now of little importance.—*Mitchell, Sacred Geography.*

his wife's mother dwelt in the latter town. Capharnaum ³ was equally well suited for fishing
purposes, as it was built on the shore of the Sea
of Galilee, near the mouth of the river Jordan.
Here Peter and Andrew followed the hardy, la-
borious calling of fishermen.

When about forty years of age, Peter was in
troduced by his brother to our Divine Redeemer,
who, looking upon him, said: " Thou art Simon
the son of Jona; thou shalt be called Cephas,
which is interpreted, *Peter*." ⁴

For some time the future Prince of the Apostles
did not make it a habit to attend our Lord on His
journeys; but he always went to hear Him when
He taught the multitudes. One day as Christ
was walking by the Sea of Galilee, He saw Peter
and Andrew casting their nets into the water.
" Come after Me," said the Great Teacher, "and
I will make you fishers of men." They at once
obeyed the divine call. It was on the same occasion that our Lord invited James and John to
follow Him.

The attachment of St. Peter to his Divine Mas-

³ Our Lord often resided in Capharnaum, which was an important
town. Here He performed many miracles, and in its neighborhood
He delivered the great "Sermon on the Mount," but as its
hardened inhabitants " repented not, " their city, with two others,
was included in a fearful malediction. To-day no vestige of it exists.

⁴ Peter is from the Greek, and signifies a *rock*.

ter was from the first loving, faithful, and **enthu**-siastic.   When certain weak disciples deserted Him—being offended at His doctrine concerning the Holy Eucharist—He asked the twelve: "Will you also go away?"   And Peter nobly answered: "Lord, to whom shall we go?   Thou hast the words of eternal life.   And we have be-lieved and have known that Thou art Christ, the Son of God."

Out of affection he twice cast himself into the sea to meet Jesus Christ.   He had not patience to wait till the boat neared the shore.   On the first of these occasions, the Apostles were crossing the tempest-tossed water at night: and as our Lord approached the vessel, walking upon the waves, **they** were troubled.

In the words of the Holy Book, they exclaimed: "It is an apparition.   And they cried out of fear. And immediately Jesus spoke to them, saying; 'Be of good heart; it is I, fear not.'

"And Peter making answer, said: 'Lord, if it be Thou, bid me come to Thee upon the waters.'

"And He said: 'Come.'   And Peter going down out of the boat, walked upon the water to come to Jesus.

"But seeing the wind strong, he was afraid; and when he began to sink, he cried out, saying: 'Lord, save me!'

"And immediately Jesus stretching forth His hand took hold of him, and said to him: 'O thou of little faith! why didst thou doubt ?' "

By Peter's confidence in God we learn what we can do with the divine assistance; and by his fear we are wisely taught what we are in ourselves.

On a certain occasion, Christ asked His disciples: " ' Whom do men say that the Son of Man is ? '

"But they said: 'Some John the Baptist, and some Elias, and others Jeremias, or one of the prophets.'

"Christ said to them: 'But whom do *you* say that I am ?'

"Simon Peter answered and said : 'Thou art the Son of the living God.'

"And Jesus answering, said to him : 'Blessed art thou, Simon Bar-Jona; because flesh and blood hath not revealed it to thee, but my Father who is in heaven.'

"And I say to thee: *That thou art Peter; and upon this rock I will build my Church, and the gates of hell shall not prevail against it.*

"*And I will give to thee the keys of the kingdom of heaven: and whatsoever thou shalt bind upon earth; it shall also be bound in heaven; and whatsoever thou shalt loose upon earth, it shall also be loosed in heaven.*"

Thus Peter confessed the divinity of our Lord, and, in return for that confession, he was honored with the promise of being made the foundation of the Church and the Vicar of Christ on earth, with wonderful powers and privileges.[5]

Our Blessed Redeemer, who loved His own that were in the world, and loved them to the end, washed the feet of His disciples at the Last Supper. He came first to Peter, who said: "Lord, dost Thou wash my feet?"

"What I do," answered Christ, "thou knowest not now, but thou shalt know hereafter."

Peter said : "Thou shalt never wash my feet."

"If I wash thee not," replied the Divine One, "thou shalt have no part with Me."

Peter was confounded at these words, and exclaimed: "Lord, not only my feet, but also my hands and my head."

This zealous Apostle, however, was permitted to fall, doubtless in punishment of a secret presumption, and that we might learn with him more clearly to discover the weakness of our nature

---

[5] Which powers and privileges descend, of course, to his successors, as the Church is to last till the end of time.

On that singularly misunderstood truth of faith, the *Infallibility of the Popes,* see Archbishop Gibbons's excellent work, ".The Faith of Our Fathers," chap. xi.

For a full explanation of the Pope's place and power in the Church of God, see Archbishop Kenrick's treatise on " The Primacy of the Apostolic See."

and to fear the dangers of human pride. "Lord, whither goest Thou?" said Peter to Christ during His last discourse.

"Whither I go," answered the Great Master, "thou canst not follow me now, but thou shalt follow hereafter."

"Why cannot I follow Thee now?" said Peter; adding with energy: "I will lay down my life for Thee."

But Christ replied : "Thou wilt lay down thy life for Me! Amen, amen I say to thee, the cock shall not crow, till thou deny Me thrice."

Alas! this prophecy was to be fulfilled only too soon. Christ was betrayed by the wretched Judas, and led to the high-priest. Peter followed, and sat without in the court.

"There came to him," writes the Evangelist, " a servant-maid saying: 'Thou also wast with Jesus the Galilean.'

"But he denied before them all, saying: ' I know not what thou sayest.'

" And as he went out of the gate, another maid saw him, and said to them that were there: ' This man also was with Jesus of Nazareth.' And again he denied with an oath, ' That I know not the Man.'

"And after a little while they came that stood by, and said to Peter: ' Surely thou also art one of them ; for even thy speech doth discover thee.' Then he began to curse and swear that he knew not the Man. And immediately the cock crew.

"And Peter remembered the words of Jesus which He had said: 'Before the cock crow, thou wilt deny Me thrice.' And going forth he wept bitterly."

Though St. Peter sinned, and sinned most grievously, he did not lose his faith in Christ. "He had a lie in his mouth," says St. Augustine, "but his heart was faithful." Besides, his repentance was speedy, perfect, and life-long. So abundant were the bitter tears which he shed for denying his Lord that they are said to have formed two furrows in his cheeks, which remained there to the end of his days. From that hour the life which he led was so mortified that he usually ate nothing but herbs and roots.[6]

As the chief of the Apostles fell by presumption, St. Chrysostom tells us that he ever after

[6] St. Peter is the only Apostle whom the Gospel mentions to have been married before his vocation to the apostleship; though we are assured by ancient Fathers and historians that St. Philip and some others were also married men when they were called by Christ. St. Clement of Alexandria, St. Jerome, and St ʹpiphanius expressly affirm, however, that from the time of their call to the ministry, or the commencement of their apostleship, they *all* embraced a state of perpetual continency; and St. Chrysostom proposes St. Peter as an illustrious model of chastity.— *Butler.*

lived in the light of profound humility. By his fall he learned to treat sinners with tenderness and compassion; and by the graces and dignities to which Christ exalted him after his denial, we see the boundless mercy of God, and how sin is perfectly blotted out by that wonderful beautifier of spiritual deformity—true repentance.

After the Resurrection, Christ manifested Himself to His Apostles as they were fishing on the Sea of Galilee. So overjoyed was Peter at seeing his Lord on the shore that he girt his coat about him, plunged into the water, and boldly struck for the land, that he might the sooner pay his respects to the Great Master. The other Apostles followed, dragging a net full of large fishes.

On landing they saw some live coals and a fish broiling upon them, with bread lying near. The kind, adorable Redeemer had just prepared this repast for his toil-worn disciples. When it was over, He asked Peter if he loved Him *more* than the others did.

"Lord," modestly answered Peter, "Thou knowest that I love Thee."

"Feed my lambs," said Christ.

Again our Lord asked Peter if he loved Him.

"Lord, Thou knowest that I love Thee," replied Peter.

"Feed my lambs," said Christ.

Even the third time He asked Peter if he loved Him.

But Peter was grieved on hearing himself asked the question a third time. He was troubled, fearing lest our Divine Saviour had seen some secret defect in his love. "Do you not see," writes St. Chrysostom, "that the better he is grown, the more modest and timorous he has become?"

Peter, however, from the depth of his glowing heart answered: "Lord, Thou knowest all things. Thou knowest that I love Thee."

"Feed my sheep," said Christ.

Thus did Jesus Christ confide to St. Peter the care of the whole flock, both lambs and sheep. He placed him over His Church. He made him His representative on earth, giving him the keys of the kingdom of heaven and the spiritual charge of all mankind. This, in brief, was how the *first* Pope received that wonderful power and supreme jurisdiction which to this day are exercised by his successors in the Eternal City.[1]

[1] "Peter," says the great Bossuet, "appears the *first* in every way —the first in making profession of faith, the first in the obligation of exercising charity, the first of all the Apostles who saw our Saviour risen from the dead, as he was also the first to witness before the people, the first when there was question of filling up the number of the Apostles, the first to confirm the faith by a miracle, the first to convert the Jews, the first to receive the Gen-

After the Ascension of our Lord, Peter first exercised his authority by calling together a council in Jerusalem, at which both the Apostles and disciples were present. The object was to fill the place of the wretched Judas Iscariot in the Apostolic College. Matthias was chosen. Peter presided over that venerable assemblage, and reminded it that the crime of Judas had been foretold by David.

When the Holy Ghost shed His wondrous graces on the disciples, Peter's application of the Scriptures was again most happy.

"And when the days of Pentecost were accomplished," says the Sacred Book, they were together in one place.

"And suddenly there came a sound from heaven, as of a mighty wind coming, and it filled the whole house where they were sitting.

"And there appeared to them parted tongues as it were of fire,[8] and it sat upon every one of them.

---

tiles, the first everywhere. But it is impossible to say all. Every thing concurs in establishing his primacy."—*Sermon sur l' Unité.*

[8] We are not to suppose that this was real fire. Nothing is ever likened to itself; hence, no one thinks of saying : "Water is like water." So it is with the wind, of which it is written that the noise it made was *like* that of a mighty wind ; therefore, it was not really wind, but only a sound like it. So, too, the tongues had but the brightness and agility of flame. They were so many *symbols* whereby the Holy Ghost made known His nature, H s properties, and His effects.—*De Ligny.*

"And they all were filled with the Holy Ghost, and they began to speak with divers tongues according as the Holy Ghost gave them to speak." [9]

The Apostles were so transported by the fervor of zeal that their eloquent language astonished the people of Jerusalem, and even the strangers who listened to their bright and burning words. But some of the Jews jeeringly said: "These men are full of new wine." Then Peter arose, and with such supernatural power did he preach Jesus Christ triumphant over death that three thousand persons were converted and asked to be baptized. This discourse of the Prince of the Apostles was at once wise and noble.

Nor did he confine himself to words. He brought the sanction of miracles to confirm the divinity of his mission. One day St. Peter and

[9] Through the gift of tongues which the Apostles had received, (1) they spoke the respective languages of all those whom they had to address; (2) they understood each of those tongues when spoken to themselves ; (3) when they spoke at the same time to men of different countries and of various tongues, they were understood by all the men at once, as it is proved by the discourse of St. Peter. But how could this be so? God, who operated the miracle, alone knows. We can, however, understand this much — that every word spoken by the Apostles on that occasion, in any language whatsoever, was, by the power of God, so modulated on the air that it struck Grecian ears as the Greek word of the same meaning, while to Roman ears it sounded as a Latin word, and so on with all the others.—*De Ligny.*

St. John were going to the Temple in the after-
noon. "And a certain man," writes St. Luke,
"who was lame from his mother's womb, was
carried—whom they laid every day at the gate
of the Temple which is called Beautiful, that
he might ask alms of them that went into the
Temple.

"He, when he had seen Peter and John about
to go into the Temple, asked to receive an alms.

"But Peter, with John, fastening his eyes upon
him, said: 'Look upon us.'

"But he looked earnestly upon them, hoping that
he should receive something of them.

"But Peter said : ' Silver and gold I have none;
but what I have I give thee. In the name of Jesus
Christ of Nazareth, arise and walk.'

"And taking him by the right hand, he lifted him
up, and forthwith his feet and soles received
strength. And he leaping up stood, and walked,
and went with them into the Temple—walking, and
leaping, and praising God."

The first Christians learned from the lofty example
of their teachers so perfect a spirit of dis-
interestedness, contempt of earthly riches, and
desire after the things of heaven that they lived
in common. The wealthy sold their estates, and
laid the price at the feet of the Apostles. This
was then distributed according to the wants of
all. But even the example of the saints and the

force of miracles cannot always destroy the grovelling spirit of avarice.

"A certain man," relates the Holy Book, "named Ananias, with Saphire his wife, sold a piece of land, and by fraud kept back part of the price of the land, his wife being privy thereunto; and bringing a certain part of it, laid it at the feet of the Apostles.

"But Peter said: 'Ananias, why hath Satan tempted thy heart, that thou shouldst lie to the Holy Ghost, and by fraud keep part of the price of the land?

" 'Whilst it remained did it not remain to thee? And after it was sold, was it not in thy power? Why hast thou conceived this thing in thy heart? Thou hast not lied to men, but to God.'

" And Ananias hearing these words, fell down, and gave up the ghost. And there came a great fear upon all that heard it.

" And the young men rising up, removed him, and carrying him out, buried him.

" And it was about the space of three hours after, when his wife, not knowing what had happened, came in.

"'And Peter said to her: 'Tell me, woman, whether you sold the land for so much.' And she said: 'Yea, for so much.'

" And Peter said unto her: 'Why have you

agreed together to tempt the Spirit of the Lord? Behold the feet of them who have buried thy husband are at the door, and they shall carry thee out.'

"Immediately she fell down before his feet, and gave up the ghost.   And the young men coming in, found her dead, and carried her out, and buried her by her husband.

"And great fear came upon the whole Church, and upon all that heard these things."

So great was the fame and sanctity of the Prince of the Apostles that the people laid their sick friends on beds and couches in the streets, " that when Peter came his shadow might at least pass over any of them, and they might be delivered from their infirmities."

Persecution now came.   The Apostles were scourged, but the faith triumphed.   The holy spirit of Christianity, like a mighty fire, forced its way on all sides.   St. Stephen was crowned with martyrdom.   St. Paul was converted, and after his conversion the persecution ceased at Jerusalem.

St. Peter remained in Judea five years after the Ascension of our Lord.   But when the storm of persecution had blown over, he took his way through the surrounding country to visit the faithful, as a general makes his round to see if all things are everywhere in good order.   Miracles marked his footsteps.   He held his first dispute with Simon the Magician in Samaria.[10]

Thence he proceeded to Cæsarea to baptize Cornelius the centurion, who commanded the garrison in that city.   Cornelius was the *first* Gentile who received baptism.   He afterwards became Bishop of Cæsarea.

From Palestine, Peter passed to Antioch, the capital of Syria.   This was then the most famous city of the East.   It was considered the third city of the Roman Empire, coming immediately after Rome and Alexandria.   He founded the Church of Antioch, and fixed his see there for seven years—that is, from the year 33 to 40.[11]

"This" writes St. John Chrysostom, [12] "is one of the privileges of this our city (Antioch), that it had at first as teacher the chief of the Apostles.

---

[10] Samaria is the first place mentioned in the Acts where Peter went with John, at the request of Philip the Deacon, to impose their hands on those Philip had converted—that is to say, to confirm them in the faith by calling on them the Holy Ghost. Samaria is thus the *first* city where the doctrine of Christ was preached out of Jerusalem.—*Father Thébaud, The Church and the Gentile World*, vol. i.

This Samaria was the capital of a small division of Palestine of the same name.   It is now a mean village.   Some ancient ruins remind the traveler of its former greatness.

[11] St. Peter "really *founded* the Church of Antioch, and was its first bishop."—*Father Thébaud, S. J.*

[12] St. John Chrysostom is one of the great Doctors of the Church. He was Patriarch of Constantinople, and died in 407.

For it was befitting that that city which, before
the rest of the world, was crowned with the
Christian's name,[18] should receive as shepherd the
first of the Apostles ; but after having had him as
our teacher, we did not retain him, but gave him to
regal Rome."

In the partition of nations among the Apostles,
St. Peter chose Rome for the scene of his labors.
This great city was then the headquarters of
idolatry and superstition.   God, who, it seems,
had raised up the Roman Empire that the Gospel
might be more easily spread in many countries, was pleased to fix the fortress of the faith
in its very capital.   Thus the light of truth was
the more readily diffused from the head to the
most distant parts of the known world, which then
acknowledged the imperial sway of the Cæsars.
The spiritual dominion of Peter, however, was
destined to extend far beyond the bounds of this
vast empire.

The Prince of the Apostles arrived at Rome in
the year 40.   "Under the reign of Claudius,"
writes the ancient historian Eusebius, "by the
benign and gracious providence of God, Peter,
that great and powerful Apostle, who by his
courage took the lead of all the rest, was conducted to Rome.   He was a noble general ap-

[18] It was in Antioch that the followers of Christ were *first* called
Christians.

pointed by God and armed with heavenly weapons.
He brought the precious merchandise of intellectual light from the East to the dwellers in the
West, announcing the light itself and the salutary
doctrine of the soul—the proclamation of the kingdom of God." [14]

The holy Pontiff first lived near the site of the
church of St. Cecilia.   In a short time, however,
Pudens, a Roman senator, having heard the
preaching of Peter, declared himself converted, and
the Apostle was conducted to a beautiful palace
which Pudens possessed on Mount Viminal.

St. Peter soon returned for a time to the East.
While visiting the afflicted Church of Jerusalem,
he was arrested, in the year 44, by order of Herod
Agrippa; but Christ did not permit his Vicar to remain long in the clutches of the tyrant.   He was
miraculously delivered by an angel, who led him
from the prison.

Again we find St. Peter in Rome, but only for
a short time, as he was banished by order of the
Emperor Claudius.   In the year 51 he was present
at the first General Council held by the Apostles

[14] As to the testimony of ancient writers with respect to the
long-continued presence of St. Peter at Rome and of his death
by martyrdom, it is so convincing that many learned Protestant
writers have been compelled to admit both.   In fact, all Christian
antiquity is unanimous on the subject . — *Thébaud. The Church
and the Gentile World,* vol. ii.

in the city of Jerusalem. [15]   On this occasion he made a discourse in which he showed that the obligation of the Jewish ceremonies was not to be laid on the Gentile converts.   It immediately became a decree of the council.

One of the last events in the life of this illustrious Apostle was his glorious conflict, at Rome, with that prince of impostors, Simon the Magician. So highly was Simon honored in the imperial city that even during his life a statue was erected to him on an isle of the Tiber, bearing the blasphemous inscription, *Simoni Deo Sancto*—"To the Holy God, Simon."

Simon and the brutal tyrant Nero became fast friends.   The magician even boasted that he would fly in the air, carried by his "angels," in imitation of the Ascension of our Blessed Redeemer.   He was to perform this daring feat for the amusement of the emperor and the corrupt Roman populace.   The day came.   "He went to the Capitoline Hill," says St. Ambrose, "and, throwing himself from the rock, began his ascent.   Then Peter, standing in the midst, said: 'O Lord Jesus, show him that his arts are vain!'   Hardly were these words pronounced

[15] St. Peter, " certainly left Rome once to go to Jerusalem, where he undoubtedly held the *first* rank in the *first* Christian Council there; so that the supremacy of the Bishop of Rome can claim a pretty high antiquity."—*Thébaud.*

when the wings which Simon had made use of became entangled, and he fell." And great was the
fall thereof. He was dashed to the ground with a
bruised body and fractured thigh ; and, in a few
days after, the mighty magician died in rage and
confusion.

The progress of the faith and the miracles of the
Apostles soon drew down the crime-stained hand
of Nero on the Church; and Christians were
persecuted, hunted down, and put to death like wild
beasts of the wilderness. The faithful entreated
St. Peter to conceal himself from the pursuit
of the imperial monster. It was with some
unwillingness that the venerable Apostle yielded
to their earnest desire and made his escape by
night. As he was passing out of the gate of the
city, he met Christ in a vision. "Lord, where
are you going?" asked Peter. "I am going
to Rome, " answered Christ, "to be crucified
again."

To the loving soul the Prince of the Apostles this vision was most suggestive. It seemed
to be a pointed reproof for turning his back upon
death and suffering. He retraced his steps, was
soon arrested, and, with St. Paul, was cast into
the Mamertine Prison.[16] After eight months' imprisonment they were led to execution on the
same day. St. Peter was scourged, and, at his
own desire, crucified with his head downward,

[16] This famous prison may be seen to this day. " Here St. Peter and St. Paul, " writes Rev. Dr. Neligan, "were both imprisoned. We kissed with respect the column to which they were

humbly deeming himself unworthy to suffer in the same position as his Divine Master. And thus died at Rome, on the 29th of June in the year 65, the wonderful fisherman of Galilee, whom Jesus graciously took from his nets, made a fisher of men, placed him over his whole Church, gave him the keys of the kingdom of heaven, and who will be known for time and eternity as the first Pope and Vicar of Christ on earth.[17]

bound, we drank water from the fountain which St. Peter caused to come forth from the floor that he might baptize St. Processus and St. Martinianus, their jailers, with the twenty-seven soldiers, who were all martyred in their turn." See Neligan's *Rome*, p. 79.

[17] As regards the devotion of the Catholics of this Republic to the chief of the Apostles, the following scattered facts may perhaps convey a faint glimpse. The oldest Catholic Church in New York City bears the name of St. Peter. The cathedrals of Cincinnati, Richmond, and Wilmington are dedicated to divine worship under the patronage of St. Peter ; and Baltimore, Washington, Brooklyn, Boston, Milwaukee, San Francisco, Buffalo, Newark, Chicago, and many other places have churches bearing the name of the Prince of the Apostles. There is one Catholic College called after him—St. Peter's, Jersey City. It possesses the powers of a university.

See the New Testament for the two canonical Epistles of St. Peter.

In the church of St. John of Lateran, at Rome, is the wooden altar used by St. Peter, and now reserved for the exclusive use of his successors; also the heads of St. Peter and St. Paul, and the sacred table used at the Last Supper.

"The body of St. Peter," says Artaud, "was at first interred in the Catacombs, and then transferred to the Vatican. His head, as well as that of St. Paul, is over the high altar of the basilica of St. John of Lateran, where they were placed by Pope Urban V., A. D. 1370."—*Lives of the Popes.*

SAINT PAUL,

DIED A. D. 65.

ST. PAUL[2] is a towering figure in the **early** history of the Catholic Church. Every thing about him was remarkable—his miraculous conversion, his boundless zeal, his shining virtues, his manly character, and his heroic death. Though not one of the twelve, he is justly entitled to hold a place among the great Apostles.

He was born of a Jewish family at Tarsus,[3] in

[1] Both Scripture and patristic tradition agree in securing to St. Paul his high attribution of Apostle of the Gentiles—that is, mainly of the Greeks, since the civilized gentile world had been universally invaded by Greek language, customs, and religion—*Fr Thébaud, S. J.*

[2] Paul is from the Latin, and signifies *little*. It is generally thought that on his conversion he changed his name from Saul to Paul.

[3] Tarsus was the capital of Cilicia, and a seat of learning so famous as almost to rival Athens and Alexandria. The Cydnus river, which flows past the city, was noted for the coldness of its waters, and was nearly fatal to Alexander the Great on his bathing in it, when in a state of perspiration. —*Mitchell Ancient Geography.*

Asia Minor, but was educated in the schools of Jerusalem. Mention is first made of him in the New Testament at the stoning of St. Stephen. The murderers of the proto-martyr, we are told, " laid down their garments at the feet of a young man whose name was Saul." This was the future Apostle of the Gentiles. He was then, however, such an active, bitter persecutor of the Christians that he ardently wished to see them destroyed with something like the force and rapidity of lightning.

"And Saul," says the Holy Book, " as yet breathing out threatenings and slaughter against the disciples of the Lord, went to the high-priest, and asked of him letters to Damascus, to the synagogues, that if he found any men or women of this way he might bring them bound to Jerusalem.

"And as he went on his journey, it came to pass that he drew nigh to Damascus; and suddenly a light from heaven shone round about him. And falling on the ground, he heard a voice saying to him: 'Saul, Saul, why persecutest thou me?'

"Who said: 'Who art Thou, Lord?' And He: ' I am Jesus whom thou persecutest. It is hard for thee to kick against the goad.'

"And trembling and astonished, he said: 'Lord, what wilt Thou have me to do?'

"And the Lord said to him: 'Arise and go in. to the city, and there it shall be told thee what thou must do.' Now the men who went in company with him stood amazed, hearing indeed a voice but seeing no man.

"And Saul arose from the ground, and when his eyes were opened, he saw nothing. But they leading him by the hands, brought him to Damascus. And he was there three days without sight, and he did neither eat nor drink."

The Lord appeared to a good Catholic of Damascus, the disciple Ananias, and told him to go and see the converted persecutor, naming the street and house where he would find Saul. Ananias expressed some fear on hearing the terrible name of Saul mentioned; but he was soon reassured.

"Go thy way," said Christ, " for this man is to Me a vessel of election, to carry my Name before the Gentiles and kings, and the children of Israel. For I will show him how great things he must suffer for my Name's sake."

"Ananias went to the house," continues the sacred narrative, " and laying his hands upon him, said: 'Brother Saul, the Lord Jesus hath sent me— He that appeared to thee in the way as thou camest — that thou mayest receive thy sight and be filled with the Holy Ghost.' And immediately there fell from his eyes scales as it were, and he received his sight; and rising up he was baptized." [4]

Such was the extraordinary conversion of St. Paul, an event which the Church celebrates on the 25th of January.

He immediately preached Christ and His holy faith to the synagogues.[5] "And all that heard him, " writes St. Luke, " were astonished, and

---

[4] Mount Hermon, which has been seen towering from many places of the Holy Land, is now close at hand, and nigh to this locality, on the right, the spot is pointed out where the miraculous conversion of St. Paul took place, to which is attached a Partial Indulgence. Damascus, the oldest city in the world, founded by Ur, the grandson of Noe, contains about 160,000 inhabitants, the majority of whom are Mohammedans; still the number of Christians is large. . . . The streets are narrow, crooked, and dirty. . . . On the site of the house of Ananias, where the conversion of St. Paul was completed by his baptism, and where by the hands of the same saint he recovered his sight, there is the Catholic chapel, to which is attached a Partial Indulgence. There is also a Partial Indulgence on the window from which St. Paul was let down.   It is an old tower of Roman architecture.   Near it they point out the grave of St. George, the name of the soldier who is believed to have been instrumental in the Apostle's escape; he became a convert, and was crowned with martyrdom on the spot.— *Vetromile.*

Damascus is situated in a fertile and delightful region. The Turks and Arabs believe it to have been the original Garden of Paradise, and that it has not its equal on earth.   It is one hundred and thirty-six miles north of Jerusalem, and about forty-five miles east of the Mediterranean.

[5] St. Paul began his apostleship *eight* or *ten* years, probably, after the day of Pentecost.   This date depends on the exact epoch

said : ' Is not this he who persecuted in Jerusalem those that call upon this Name; and came here for that intent, that he might carry them bound to the chief priests? ' "

But Paul daily increased in grace and power, and confounded the Jews who dwelt at Damascus. Those people finally became so enraged that they determined to kill him, and even placed watches, day and night, at the gates of the city, in order to render his escape impossible. "But the disciples," says St. Luke, " taking him in the night, conveyed him away by the wall, letting him down in a basket."

St. Paul now went to Jerusalem, where he stayed fifteen days, during which time he enjoyed the conversation of the Prince of the Apostles.[6] He was very active in disputing with the Jews; but such was their hateful obstinacy that they shut their ears to the glowing truths of salvation.

His words fell like flashes of light. The wonderful force and clearness of his discourses, which the Jews tried in vain to answer, aroused their wrath and malignity, and again his life was in danger. Some Catholic friends, however, took

---

of his conversion, which is not perfectly well ascertained. Thus, when he commenced to preach, Palestine and a great part of Syria had already received the Gospel.—*Father Thébaud, S. J.*

[6] This was on the part of St. Paul a visit of respect which he believed it his duty to pay to him whom Jesus had established as Head of His Church —*De Ligny.*

nim to Cæsarea, and thence sent him by sea to Tarsus, his native city.   There he remained for over three years, and preached the faith with great success in Cicilia and Syria.

St. Paul next proceeded to Antioch[7] to assist St. Barnabas in the work of evangelizing that historic city.   After a year thus spent, he went to Jerusalem, bearing alms to the faithful of that distressed and famine-stricken portion of the Church. He returned to Antioch, however, on fulfilling his mission.

It seems to have been about this time that St. Paul was favored with that sublime ecstasy in which he was carried up to the third heaven, and saw and heard divine mysteries which man could not utter, and to which, many years after, he referred in one of his public discourses.

By the command of the Holy Ghost, St. Paul and St. Barnabas were especially set apart for the office of preaching, and were now sent forth with full authority to spread the Faith over all nations.

---

[7]Antioch, at one time, was considered the third city in the world, and was called the Queen of the East.   It is now a place of no importance.   It was here, according to St. Luke (Acts xi. 26), that "the disciples were *first* named CHRISTIANS."   This was about the year 44.   "Julian the Apostate," writes Father De Ligny, S. J., "published an edict suppressing the name of Christians, which he changed into that of *Galileans*.   He feared that name, says one of the Fathers, even as the demons fear it."—*History of the Acts of the Apostles.*

Though the other Apostles lived by the **Gospel,** St. Paul chose not to make use of that liberty. He earned his bread by making tents. But if he was not ignorant of what it was to have plenty, he also possessed that lofty Christian spirit which knew how to live in want and hunger.

To follow the steps of this illustrious preacher and founder of churches in his many missions and long and countless journeys would, indeed, be impossible in our short sketch. We can merely glance at his glorious labors.

Taking with him St. Barnabas, in the year 44, he left Antioch, and after a short sea voyage arrived in the famous island of Cyprus,[8] which he traversed, spreading the truths of the Gospel on all sides, and making many converts. Among these was Sergius Paulus, the Roman proconsul.

Paulus was a wise and prudent man ; but he had been led astray by the magical arts of a Jewish impostor named Barjesus, the Sorcerer. The proconsul desired to hear St. Paul speak. Barjesus opposed the preaching of the Apostle. But the Saint smote the wretch with blindness ; and the sight of the miracle so impressed Sergius

[8] Cyprus is the largest island in the Mediterranean Sea, except Sicily and Sardinia. It was famous for the variety and abundance of its products, and its delightful climate. The range of Mount Olympus extends through the whole length of the island. —*Mitchell.*

Paulus that he was converted and received the Sacrament of Baptism.

The next scene of the Saint's zeal was Asia Minor.[9] He cured a man who was lame from his birth, in the city of Lystra; and, on witnessing this wonder, the dull heathen multitude hurried to offer him and Barnabas sacrifices, as if they were divine beings. The Apostles, of course expressed their abhorrence at such a thoughtless action. But the same giddy mob soon after stoned St. Paul, and he was dragged out of the city as dead. Friendly hands however, cared for him, and he soon recovered. The two returned to Antioch after an absence of three years; and during the four years that followed, St. Paul preached the faith over Syria and Judea.

In the year 51 we find him again at Antioch whence he went to Jerusalem, and assisted at the first General Council held by the Apostles in that city. The twelve were present. It was

---

[9] Asia Minor is a large peninsula which forms the most western division of Asia. It is bounded on the north by the Black Sea, and on the south by the Mediterranean. Its inhabitants formed many different nations, as Cilicia in the south, Pontus in the north, Galatia and Cappadocia in the interior, and many others. "St. Paul," says Father Thébaud, S. J., "evidently attached an immense importance to the conversion of Asia Minor —that celebrated country which is now expiring in the pangs of poverty, war, and hunger under the barbarous sway of the Turks."

on this solemn occasion that St. Paul recounted
to the assembled Fathers the progress which the
Gospel had made by his preaching among the Gentiles.[10]

He soon gave another mission in Asia Minor,
sowing the good seed from city to city as he
passed along.   One night, while at Troas, he had a
vision in which a Macedonian seemed to stand before him earnestly beseeching the holy Apostle
to visit his country and enlighten its people in the
truths of the Catholic religion.   St. Paul regarded
this as a pressing invitation, and, accompanied by
St. Luke[11] and others, he boarded a vessel and passed into Europe.

[10] The brevity of our narrative, no doubt, makes St. Paul hasten
on rather rapidly in the eyes of the reader.   But in reality it was
not so.   He remained long enough in each place to give the
faith a solid foundation; and he everywhere established *bishops*,
who continued the good work when he departed.   See Father
Thébaud's learned work, *The Church and the Gentile World, vol*, ii.
chap. x.

[11] St. Luke, the Holy Evangelist and favorite companion of St.
Paul, was a native of Antioch, a physician by profession, and a man
of great learning.   St. Jerome assures us that he was very eminent
in his profession, and St. Paul, by calling him his most dear physician, seems to indicate that he had not laid it aside.   He was a
convert to the Catholic faith.   He remained with St. Paul to the
last, and after the death of the Apostle of the Gentiles, St. Luke
preached the Gospel in various nations, and was finally crucified
on an olive-tree in Greece.   This accomplished Saint was one of
the four inspired historians of our Lord, and the author of the
only inspired history of the infant Church—the "Acts of the

The first place blessed with his labors was Phi-
lippi, a famous city and Roman colony.   Here he
confirmed his teachings with miracles, and founded
a church eminent in the early annals of Christianity.   He next visited Thessalonica, the capital of Macedon.   The divine seed of the Gospel
fell on good ground, and many Thessalonians be,
came model Catholics, especially dear to their great
spiritual father.

We glance again at the ever-active Apostle of
the Gentiles, and we see him traversing the streets
of a city equally renowned in history and literature.   Athens[12] had not so far degenerated in the

Apostles."   "He was a man," says Rev.   Dr.   O'Reilly, whose
"heart was as pure and beautiful as his mind was cultivated.'
What a model for the Catholic physician of our day!   The Church
has always esteemed and honored the great profession of medicine.   Tertullian called medicine "the sister of philosophy."
Saints Cosmas and Damian, who are daily commemorated by the
Church in the Canon of the Mass—a most extraordinary distinction—were brothers and famous physicians, who suffered martyrdom about the year 303.   The true Christian physician has a
great mission.   He can do much to save the soul as well as to
heal the body—something he should never forget.   "Acknowledge and appreciate your dignity," said the immortal Pius IX.,
in reply to an address of the Catholic doctors of Italy.   "The first
doctor is God.   You are called upon to cure the diseases of the
body, but *these often depend upon the diseases of the soul.*"

[13] Athens, anciently the capital of Attica, was the most important and splendid city in Greece.   It was called by the ancients
the Eye of Greece, and also of the civilized world.   It was the great
seat of learning and the arts, and was the birth-place of the

arts and sciences but that it still counted among
its people many wise and learned men. The
Athenians, however, were very superstitious ; and
so careful that no deity should want due honor
from them that they had an altar inscribed, "*To
the unknown God.*"

St. Paul refers to this in the discourse which he
made in the great court of the Areopagus. "Men
of Athens," he said, "I perceive that in all things
you are too superstitious. For passing by and
seeing your idols, I found an altar also on which
was written: *To the unknown God.* What, therefore, you worship without knowing it, that I preach
to you."

Among those whom the Saint converted was
Dionysius, one of the judges of the Areopagus.[17]
"Thus was formed," says the venerable Father
Thébaud, S.J., " the first Christian congregation at
Athens."

St. Paul now proceeded to Corinth, where he
lodged in the house of a tent-maker named Aquilia.
It was from this city that he wrote his two "Epis-

most eminent orators, philosophers, and artists of antiquity.—*Mitchell.*

[13] The renowned tribunal of the Areopagus flourished long after
St. Paul—as late as the close of the fourth century, when Christianity put an end to it as well as to all other national, provincial,
or local traditions and customs. Strange, indeed, but so it was.
Whatever had seen so many ages of duration vanished at once like
the fabric of a dream.—*Fr. Thébaud S.J.*

tles" to the Thessalonians in the year 52. These
are his first writings.[14]

After a stay of eighteen months at Corinth, the
Apostle set out for Jerusalem, where he kept the
festival of the Passover. He then passed on to Antioch and traveled again through Asia Minor,
everywhere encouraging the faithful and watering
his young plants.

He remained nearly three years in the city of
Ephesus, preaching both in public places and private houses, and performing great miracles, even
by handkerchiefs and other articles that had touched
his person. For some months he addressed himself chiefly to the Jews; but it was in vain that he
thundered in their obstinate ears. Seven
sons of Sceva, a Jewish high-priest, foolishly attempted to cast out devils in the holy name
of "Jesus, whom Paul preaches," though they were
not Christians. "But the wicked spirit," writes St.
Luke, "answering said to them: ' Jesus I know,
and St. Paul I know; but who are you ?' And
the man in whom the wicked spirit was, leaping upon them and mastering them, prevailed against
them so that they fled out of that house naked and
wounded."

After another journey to Macedon, we find St.
Paul again in Jerusalem in the year 58. This was

[14] St. Paul also wrote "Epistles" to the Romans, Galatians, Ephe-
sians, etc See the New Testament.

the fifth visit which he paid to the church of that city.   He was in Jerusalem, however, but seven days when certain Jews who had opposed him in some distant mission came into the city to cele‹ brate a religious festival: and seeing the great Christian preacher in the Temple, they stirred up the anger of the people, and even laid violent hands upon him, crying out:

"Men of Israel, help !   This is the man that teaches all men everywhere against the people, and the Law, and this place; and, moreover, he has brought in Gentiles into the Temple, and has violated this holy place."

This wild, lying harangue had the desired ef‹ fect.   The wrath of the Jews was aroused.   In a moment the whole city was in an uproar.   The fanatical people ran together, and taking St. Paul, they threw him out of the Temple, and were about to kill him when Claudius Lysias, the commander of the Roman garrison, inter‹ fered.

The Apostle now obtained permission to speak, and, addressing the angry multitudes, he told the story of his miraculous conversion to the Faith. But no sooner had he finished than the Jews yell‹ ed out: "Away with such a one from the earth! It is not fit that he should live."

Claudius Lysias was no doubt irritated, and, wishing to learn from him the true state of the matter, he ordered that St. Paul should be tied to a pillar and scourged.   But while the executioner was binding his hands, the Apostle asked the centurion that stood by: "Is it lawful for you to scourge a man that is a Roman and uncondemned?"   On hearing that St. Paul was a Roman citizen, the commander was afraid and had him at once unloosed.   He was then lead to the castle of Antonia."[16]

As the Roman commander was anxious to know the real nature of the charges brought against the Apostle of the Gentiles, he next day called the Jewish priests together in council; "and bringing forth St. Paul he set him before them."

"I have conversed," said the Saint, looking at his bitter enemies, "with all good conscience before God, until this present hour."   On hearing this, the high-priest, Ananias, with brutal malignity, commanded those that stood near him to strike the illustrious speaker on the mouth.

"God," answered Paul, with the spirit and noble boldness of a man defending the sacred cause of truth—"God shall strike thee, thou whited wall. For sittest thou to judge me according to the law, and

---

[16] The castle of Antonia, with its four elegant turrets of polished marble, kept jealous and unceasing watch over the precincts of the Temple.—*Orsini.*

contrary to the law commandest me to be struck?"[16]

This meeting ended in nothing but disputes among the Jewish priests themselves: and fearing that the Apostle would be torn in pieces during the war of words, the Roman commander prudently sent a party of soldiers, who led him from the council-hall into the castle. Jesus Christ to show that He is nearest His servants when they are in affliction, graciously appeared to St. Paul the second night after this adventure, and encouraged him with the assurance that the Apostle would have the honor of giving testimony to Him in imperial Rome itself.

Hearing that certain Jews had banded together for the purpose of murdering St. Paul, the Roman commander of Jerusalem sent him under a strong guard to Felix, the governor of the province, who resided at Cæsarea.[17] His wrathful accusers followed the Apostle: but he defended himself before Felix. This wicked governor, however, kept him for two years in prison.

Festus soon succeeded Felix in the government of Judea; and again St. Paul was impeached by

[16] This was a prophecy, if it be true, as people think, that this Ananias is the same who was massacred, together with his brother, by a rival faction of the Jews.— *De Ligny.*

[17] Cæsarea, in the time of the Romans, was the chief city of Samaria. Under Herod it became one of the renowned seaports of the Mediterranean.

his fiendish enemies.   The Apostle made a manly and Christian defence.   "Neither against the law of the Jews," he answered his accusers, "nor against the Temple, nor against Cæsar, have I offended in anything."

But Festus, wishing to favor the Jews, said : "Will you go up to Jerusalem, and there be judged of these things before me ?"

"I stand at Cæsar's judgment-seat," replied St. Paul, "where I ought to be judged.   To the Jews I have done no injury, as you very well know.   If I have injured them or have done anything worthy of death, I refuse not to die.   But if there be none of these things whereof they accuse me, no man may deliver me to them.   I appeal to Cæsar."

This was final.   His appeal was recognized by the governor, as it was a right granted by the laws to Roman citizens.   Some days after King Agrippa came to visit Festus, who told him of St. Paul.   The King was very desirous to see such a famous personage.   The hall of audience accordingly was prepared, and the Apostle brought forth.   He preached before the king, and at the end of his touching discourse said : "Believest thou the prophets, O King Agrippa?   I know that thou believest."

"In a little," answered Agrippa, "thou persuadest me to become a Christian."   He was *almost* converted.   How many, unhappily, in our own day are like Agrippa!

As St. Paul had appealed to Cæsar, Festus sent him on board of a vessel bound for Italy.   He was accompanied by his dear companion, St. Luke, and several others.   This memorable voyage was marked by storms and adventures.   The ship was wrecked on the island of Malta, but all, numbering two hundred and seventy-six persons, reached the shore in safety.   "See what it is," exclaims St. John Chrysostom, " to live in the company of a saint—though a prisoner—and to have him for a protector in all dangers!"

The inhabitants of Malta treated the shipwrecked strangers with courteous hospitality, and kindled large fires to enable them to dry their water-soaked clothes, and to warm their chilled bodies.   While St. Paul, however, was actively engaged in throwing a bundle of sticks on the fire, a viper, maddened by the heat, slipped out of the wood, and fastened its deadly fangs in his hand.

"Undoubtedly this man is a murderer," whispered the people of Malta to one another, "who, though he has escaped the sea, yet vengeance does not suffer him to live."

But the Saint shook the reptile into the flames, and received no injury.   They imagined, however, that after the poison would begin to operate.

he would swell up and suddenly die. "But expecting long," says St. Luke, "and seeing that no harm came to him, they said that he was a god."

The Apostles arrived at Rome in the year 61. No accusers appeared against him, and after two years he was set at liberty. He then left the imperial city, returning to the East. There he undertook new voyages, again preached the faith over many nations, and suffered chains, prisons, conflicts, torments, and continual dangers of death.

About the year 64 he returned to Rome. He soon fell under the anger of the barbarous Nero, and was cast into the Mamertine prison. Here, in company with the Prince of the Apostles, he was closely confined from October to the following June; and when both passed out of its gloomy walls together, they were on the road to execution and to everlasting glory and happiness. St. Paul was beheaded on the spot where stands the beautiful church now dedicated to him, on the 29th of June in the year 65.

"In this church," writes Dr. Neligan, "are three springs of water which miraculously gushed forth from the earth where the head of the Apostle touched it. In an angle is the column to which the Apostle was bound when he was beheaded. Near it is the altar of the Saint, ornamented with columns of black porphyry. As the Apostle was led to the place where he was martyred he converted three of the soldiers of the escort, who were martyred three days afterwards. As his head was cut off, instead of his blood flowing from the body a stream of milk issued from it, which covered the ground and the lictor. The head made three bounds, and three fountains sprang up where it touched the earth, each still preserving a different temperature." [18]

[18] The cathedrals of Pittsburg, and St. Paul, Minnesota, are dedicated to God under the patronage of the Apostle of the Gentiles. There are also churches in New York, Brooklyn, Cincinnati, Philadelphia, and many other places in this Republic bearing the name of St. Paul. The capital of Minnesota, which is the see of a bishop, is called after him. He is the patron of the Congregation of the Missionary Priests of St. Paul the Apostle, commonly called Paulist Fathers. This congregation was founded at New York by Father Hecker, C. S.P., in 1858.

SAINT JOHN,

THE APOSTLE AND EVANGELIST.

DIED A. D. 100.

JOHN,[1] "the disciple whom Jesus loved" and the greatest of the Evangelists, was born in Bethsaida, a town of ancient Galilee. It stood upon a slight elevation overlooking the Sea of Galilee, a few miles beyond Nazareth. To-day its site is only marked by some desolate ruins. But one lofty column, lone and magnificent, still points its shaft towards the skies, and kindly marks the historic birthplace[2] of St. John and his brother, St. James the Great.

John's father and mother were Zebedee and Salome. Salome seems to have been a generous-

------

[1] John is from the Hebrew, and signifies *divine grace and beauty, or the gracious gift of God.*

[2] The spot containing these noble ruins is desolate and uninhabited. The lake splashes its waters sadly against the stones heaped together or scattered along the shore. Its very name of Bethsaida is lost to it. The Turks know the place only under the name of Tell-Houm or Tell-Hum. The duplicate column alone is left standing, as if to mark by a sign the cradle of the two brothers inseparably united in the faith and in the apostolate of Jesus. —*Baunard.*

hearted woman whom love made ambitious to see her sons great, as we learn from an anecdote in the Gospel.[8] Zebedee was a hardy, honest fisherman—a trade held in high estimation among the Jews. He owned a bark on the Sea of Galilee, and with the aid of his two sons and others enjoyed the luxury of daily toil and a modest competence. It appears there was a great intimacy between the family of Zebedee and that of Jona, the father of Peter and Andrew.

Our first sight of John, the future Apostle, is in the society of the greatest of prophets, John the Baptist. Besides the multitudes who flocked to receive baptism from the Holy Precursor of Christ, he had his disciples, whom he instructed in the secrets of a higher doctrine, preparing them in solitude and recollection for the approaching revelations of the kingdom of heaven. John was one of that faithful band.

He had listened for about a year to the preaching of John the Baptist and his praises of the Son of God. He now longed for the arrival of the great One, and the day of His appearance was at hand.

"The next day again," writes our Evangelist himself, "John[4] stood and two of his disciples.

"And seeing Jesus walking, he said; '*Ecce Agnus Dei* '—Behold the Lamb of God!

[8] St. Matthew xx. 20   [4] John the Baptist.

"And the two disciples heard him speak, and they followed Jesus.

"And Jesus, turning and seeing them following Him, said to them: 'What seek you?'   Who said to Him: 'Rabbi, where dwellest Thou ?'

"He said to them: 'Come and see.'   They came and saw where He abode, and they stayed with Him that day.   Now it was about the tenth hour.[5]

"And Andrew, the brother of Simon Peter, was one of the two who had heard of John, and followed him."[6]

There is no doubt that the other was St. John. One he never names in his beautiful Gospel, and that one is himself.

Soon after Christ began his public life.   He was one day walking on the shores of the Sea of Galilee.   Peter and Andrew were just casting their net into the water, as the great Master of Life called them to be "fishers of men," and they followed Him.   Passing along some distance farther, He came to the ship of Zebedee.   John and James were there with ·their father mending nets.   Christ called the brothers, and leaving " their nets and father they followed Him." Such, in brief, is the simple story of how St. John made the acquaintance of our Blessed Re-

[5] About four or five o'clock in the evening.
[6] St. John, chap. i. 35-40.

deemer, and finally became His disciple, "the beloved disciple."

St. John is said to have been the youngest of
all the Apostles. He was probably about twenty-
five years of age when he was called by Christ,
for he lived seventy years after the suffering of
his Divine Master. Piety, wisdom, prudence, and
simplicity made him in his youth equal to those
who with gray hairs had been long exercised in the
practice of virtue.

For him our Blessed Redeemer had an affection
wholly particular. He was "the disciple whom
Jesus loved." Nor was this without good reason.
Love is gained by love. St. John loved his Divine
Master with a boundless love. He was the very
soul of meekness, and his virginal purity and
beautiful innocence made him dear to Christ.

"The singular privilege of his chastity," says
St. Augustine, "rendered him worthy of the more
particular love of Christ, because being chosen by
Him a virgin, he always remained such."

It is remarkable that our Lord was pleased to
choose a virgin for His Mother, a virgin for His
Precursor, and a virgin for His beloved disciple.
And the Catholic Church, guided by her Divine
Founder, only permits those who live perfectly
chaste to minister at the altars of the Holy One.
Purity, then, is a great virtue. It is a celestial
virtue. In the words of St. Francis de Sales, it

is " the beautiful and white virtue of the soul."
"Blessed are the pure of heart," said Jesus Christ,
"for they shall see God."

St. John received new lessons in the school of
the great Teacher. He grew in grace and virtue, for he followed Him who was "the way, the
truth, and the life." He saw the miracles, the
holy life, and the heavenly charity of the Son of
God. He was one of those who had the rare
privilege of being present at the Transfiguration
of Christ[7] and at His agony in the Garden.[8]

---

[7] Mount Thabor rises, glorious and majestic, from the luxuriant
plains of Esdrælon. It has the appearance of a truncated cone,
and, at a distance, looks like a loaf of sugar cut from the top.
Its sides are rich with vegetation, and the centre place is stocked
with an immensity of game of every variety. But its glory is for
having been the mountain on whose top Christ, in company with a
few Apostles, transfigured Himself, and in the presence of Moses
and Elias appeared clothed with white garments shining like the
sun.—*Vetromile.*

[8] The Garden of Gethsemani is now enclosed with a high and
massive wall. Outside, near the gate, there is a small pillar
marking the spot where our Saviour was betrayed by Judas with
a kiss. There is a Plenary Indulgence attached. The Garden is
cultivated by a Franciscan brother, and is laid out in beds of
flowers. To this spot our Lord used to retire; here he prayed
entire nights; here He ate, drank, and conversed with His disciples;
here He gave commencement to his bitter Passion. In this
place and on this spot He said to the eight Apostles to sit till He
went yonder to pray; and here He commanded the three Apostles to
stop and pray, removing from them a stone's throw. What a precious locality!—*Vetromile.*

Even at the Last Supper he was the favorite.

The awful hour of the crucifixion was not far distant. "Amen, amen," exclaimed our Lord to the twelve, "I say to you, *one* of you shall betray me."

"The disciples therefore looked one upon another," writes our Evangelist, "doubting of whom He spoke.

"Now there was leaning on Jesus' bosom one[9] of his disciples, whom Jesus loved.

"Simon Peter therefore beckoned to him, and said to him: 'Who is it of whom He speaketh?'

" He therefore, leaning on the breast of Jesus, said to Him : 'Lord, who is it?'

"Jesus answered: 'He it is to whom I shall reach bread dipped.' And when He had dipped the bread, He gave it to Judas Iscariot."

In reading the Holy Book we discover a particular friendship between St. John and St. Peter. They were old companions. But their affection for each other doubtless had its foundation in the mutual love and zeal which they cherished for their Divine Master. If St. Peter was the head of the infant Church, St. John was its heart.

To the last he was faithful. St. Chrysostom says that when our Lord was apprehended, and the other Apostles fled, St. John never forsook Him. He seems to have accompanied Christ through all his sufferings. He attended Him

[9] St. John himself.

during His crucifixion. He stood under the cross. He confessed his Divine Master in the midst of arms and guards, and in the press of angry multitudes of His most fiendish enemies.

And the dear, dying, and adorable Redeemer, who "loved His own who were in the world, and loved them to the end," did not forget His "beloved disciple." He confided to him the care of His holy Mother.

"Behold thy Mother" was uttered from the cross. "And from that hour the disciple took her to his own," and all mankind had a mother in the Most Blessed Virgin.[10] It was the consummation of fidelity on the part of St. John. Truly, it is good to stand at the foot of the cross and to suffer with Jesus Christ!

When Mary Magdalen brought word to St. Peter and St. John that she had not found Christ's body in the sepulchre, they both hastily directed their steps to the sacred spot. John, being the younger and more active, outran Peter and arrived

[10] The divine legacy did not stop at the disciple. It was addressed to the world, and, under the name of St. John embracing the entire Church, it appointed a mother to the family of souls whose Father is in heaven. . . . Devotion to the Blessed Virgin is not the worship of weak minds and of dreamy souls, since it was implanted by Jesus Christ Himself in the great heart of St. John: that it has its root beside the cross, and that, born among thorns, that lily was watered by the tears of the Mother of God and by the Blood of her Son.—*Baunard.*

first. On examination they found nothing **but** "linen cloths." The "beloved disciple," to use **his** own words, " saw and believed." The glorious Redeemer of mankind had indeed triumphed over sin and death !

Later Christ appeared to the Apostles as they were fishing on the Sea of Galilee.[11] He stood on the shore and spoke to them ; yet, according to the Sacred Book, "the disciples knew not that it was Jesus." They had toiled all night and caught nothing. He requested them, however, to cast their net "on the right side of the ship." It was done, and great was the multitude of fishes taken.[12] This instantly opened the eyes of St. John. His spiritual nature was touched, and he recognized the presence of something more than mortal. Turning to St. Peter, he said : "It is the Lord !"

After the Ascension of Christ, St. John seems to have remained for a long time at Jerusalem, though he sometimes preached in other cities. A sweet and sacred duty attached him to Judea, where he was detained near the Most Holy Virgin.[13] But when the glorious Mother of God

[11]This was the third time that Christ had manifested Himself to his disciple after His Resurrection.—*St. John xxi.* 14.

[12] "Simon Peter went up, and drew the net to land, full of great fishes, *one hundred and fifty-three.* And although there were so many, the net was not broken."—*St. John xxi.* 11.

[13] The good Boanerges never was a traveling missionary. He

passed to her heavenly home, St. John went to re
side at Ephesus,[14] a famous city of Asia Minor.
We have already learned of the missionary labors of
St. Paul in this region.

St. John took care of all the churches of Asia,[16]
founded new sees, and placed bishops in them.
Even in his extreme old age his zeal led him to
make long journeys in the interest of religion.

had a special charge of the Blessed Virgin given him by Jesus on
the cross.   This was enough honor and profit to the whole Church,
in good conscience although Protestants, and other men perhaps, do
not appear to think so.—*Fr. Thébaud, S. J.*

[14] Ephesus contained the celebrated pagan temple of Diana,
which occupied two hundred years in building.   It was situated
on the shores of the Ægean Sea, an arm of the Mediterranean.   In
the days of St. John, Ephesus was the capital and chief city of Asia
Minor.

But time has laid a heavy hand on this once flourishing centre
of human activity.   Ephesus is a dead city.   A blackish stream
called the Kara-sou waters a miserable village styled Ayasabouk,
inhabited by about fifty ragged Turkish families.   Below, near
the sea-shore, a large mass of ruins, bricks, broken columns, and
crumbling walls, indicates the site of some ancient edifice.   They
are said to be the remains of the temple of the Great Diana.   In
the centre of the village, upon a hill stands an antique building
of which the Mussulmans have made a mosque.   That was formerly the church of the Apostle St. John, and that is the sole
remembrance left by the Angel of Ephesus to **mark** his passage.—
Baunard.

[15] The term Asia, as *now* understood, was not used by the inspir-
ed writers.   The Asia, mentioned in the New Testament was the
Roman proconsulship of Asia, of which Ephesus was the capital.—
Mitchell.

During the second general persecution of the Christians, in the year 95, he was seized by the proconsul of Asia. It is asserted by some that the following letter, the original of which is in the British Museum, was sent by that pagan official to the Emperor Domitian in relation to the great Apostle :

"To the most pious Cæsar Domitian ever Augustus, the proconsul of Ephesus, greeting :

"We make known to your glory that a man named John, of the race of the Jews, has come into Asia, where he preaches the crucified Jesus, affirming the later to be God and the Son of God. Through him the worship of our invincible gods is forsaken, and the venerable temples built by your predecessors are menaced with approaching ruin. That man succeeds by his preaching, and by his illusive magic is converting the people of Ephesus to the worship of a dead Man who was nailed to a cross. We ourselves, full of zeal for our immortal gods, have summoned that impious wretch before our tribunal, engaging him by caresses and threats to abjure his Christ and offer agreeable libations to the all-powerful gods of the empire. Unable to succeed in persuading him to do so, we have addressed these letters to your power, in order that it may please you to make known to us that which will be most pleasing to your Majesty." [16]

St. John was summoned to Rome. His trial took place at the Latin Gate. He was commanded to sacrifice to the gods, and, on his refusal, was condemned to be executed. Preparations were made. The death of such a man was a public spectacle of importance. The day came. The cruel, pompous emperor was present, and the corrupt Roman nobility gathered in crowds.

The ceremony began by the emperor's cutting off the hair from the venerable head of the Apostle. He was then brutally beaten with rods, and finally plunged into a caldron of boiling oil. But it was like a bath for refreshment. He did not find death therein. "The fiery, seething mass," in the words of Bossuet, "suddenly changed into a gentle dew." The glorious old Saint came forth from the appalling ordeal with renewed strength and courage, untouched and unharmed. This wonderful event took place in the month of May, about the year 96.

Thus St. John was condemned to live, but he did not remain at Rome. The tyrant Domitian banished him to the isle of Patmos. [17]

[16] See Baunard, "Life of the Apostle St. John," p. 344.

[17] Patmos is a small island situated off the western coast of Asia Minor. It has now a population of only about four thousand. "It would be difficult," writes the Abbé Baunard, "to

In this retirement, the Apostle was favored with those heavenly visions, which he has recounted in the " Apocalypse," or Book of Revelations. They were manifested to him on a Sunday in the year 96. The first three chapters are evidently a prophetic instruction given to seven neighboring churches [18] of Asia Minor, and to the bishops by whom they were governed. The last three chapters celebrate the triumph of Christ, and the judgment and eternal reward of the saints. The intermediate chapters are variously expounded.

"Notwithstanding the depths of that divine book," writes the great Bossuet of the " Apocalypse," " we feel in reading it so sweet, yet at the same time so magnificent, an impression of the majesty of God, such high ideas of the mystery of Jesus Christ, so lively gratitude for the nation redeemed by His Blood—we find such noble

find in the Archipelago a more desolate spot than the island whither St. John was banished. . . . The isle which the Italians designate by the name of Palmo has but one solitary palm-tree, which grows in a valley styled the *Garden of the Saint,* in like manner as, in his history, it has but one name, which overrules all others."—*Life of the Apostle St. John.*

[18] The cities in which these " seven churches" were founded were *Ephesus, Smyrna, Pergamos, Thyatira, Sardis, Philadelphia.* and *Laodicea.* These cities are all now, with the exception of Smyrna and Philadelphia, either greatly decayed or in ruins, and the churches—once so distinguished—have hardly an existence. A few Christians, mostly of the Greek faith, are still to be found in Smyrna and some of the other towns.—*Mitchell, Sacred Geography.*

images of His victories and of His reign, with such wonderful songs to celebrate His greatness —that it is calculated to ravish heaven and earth.

"All the beauty of the Scriptures is condensed in that book. Whatever is most touching, most vivid, and most majestic in the law and in the prophets receives therein new splendor, and re-passes before our eyes to fill us with consolation and graces for ever.

"All the men inspired by God seem to have brought thither whatever they possess that is richest and grandest to compose the most beautiful picture imaginable of the glory of Jesus Christ; and one would say that to write this admirable book John had received the spirit of all the prophets."

St. John made his brief stay in Patmos remarkable. Even to-day his memory remains vivid, and the inhabitants point out spots which he blessed by labors and miracles.

The following anecdote is from the Venerable Bede. A magistrate of Patmos, named Aristodemus, seeing the miracles of John, grew enraged instead of being converted. He wished to put an end to them, and one day said to the Apostle: "Do you wish me to believe in your God? If you do, accept this trial. Here is a powerful poison. Take it, and if you do not die from its effects I will become one of your disciples.

"But that you may be clearly aware of its nature, I shall cause a solution of it to be swallowed by two condemned criminals. They will die immediately, and after them you shall drink it."

The barbarous wretch thought to get rid of John by such a cruel artifice; but the Saint cheerfully accepted the proposition. The two criminals drank the poison, and expired in agonies. Then the holy bishop took the fatal cup in his turn, armed himself with the Sign of the Cross, and slowly drank the contents. Smilingly he handed it to the magistrate, after which he hastened to raise to life the two unhappy victims of the deadly beverage. When Aristodemus saw this, his eyes were opened, and grace touched his heart. He believed in Jesus Christ, and became a Christian.

The death of the tyrant Domitian, and the revocation of all his edicts by the Roman Senate, left St. John once more in freedom. He bade adieu to the isle of Patmos, and, after two years' absence was enabled to visit Ephesus in the year 97.

The aged Apostle now recommenced his missionary courses through Asia Minor. Antiquity has preserved to us the remembrance of his closing and beautiful career. One after another he visited the churches, combating heresies, correcting errors, consoling the sorrowful, and everywhere bearing with him that truth and gentle kindness which he learned on the sacred bosom of his Divine Master.

The ancient Fathers inform us that   was chiefly to confute the blasphemies of Ebion and other heretics who denied the divinity of Jesus Christ, and even his pre-existence before his temporal birth, that the glorious St. John composed his Gospel.   There was still another reason.   It was to supply certain omissions of the other three Gospels, which he had read and approved.

The original was written in Greek, and by the Greeks he is styled THE THEOLOGIAN.   St. Jerome relates that when he was earnestly requested by the bishops of Asia to write the Gospel, he answered that he would do it if, by ordering a common fast, they would all put up their prayers together to the Almighty God.   When it was ended, the great Apostle, enlightened from above, began his inspired and beautiful composition: "In the beginning was the Word, and the Word was with God, and the Word was God."

A legend tells us that when St. John began his Gospel, and proclaimed the eternal generation of our Blessed Redeemer by the sublime sentence, "In the beginning was the Word," a clap of thunder resounded, and lightning suddenly flashed in the serene sky.   That fact is an allusion to the name which Christ had bestowed upon him when He Himself styled him "the Son of Thunder," and is the united emblem of the power and splendor of that heaven descended eloquence.

Such a book is not formed of merely human ideas. It requires the thought and dictation of God. It demands prayer and sacrifice. The Divine Spirit of Truth animated the writer with the most wonderful words ever heard on earth.

"The Gospel of St. John," says Origen, "is, so to speak, the flower of the Gospels. He alone could penetrate to that depth whose head had rested upon the bosom of Jesus, and to whom Jesus gave Mary as a mother. That confidential friend of Jesus and of Mary, that disciple treated as a second self by the Master, was alone capable of the thoughts and sentiments condensed in that book."

The Gospel of the "beloved Apostle" is the most noble and sublime writing which the earth has ever possessed, or ever will possess. There is nothing strange in this assertion. The more a word resembles a thought, a thought a soul, and a soul God, the more beautiful is the whole. Hence what equalled beauty and grandeur must emanate from a book whose words are the image of the thought and of the soul of God! [19]

"The hand of an angel," exclaims Herder, "has written it."

Many interesting episodes marked the visitation

[19]Baunard.

of the churches of Asia Minor by the great Apostle. These reveal to us the state of souls, the singular customs of that time, and the almost boundless influence of St. John. We give one as related by Clement of Alexandria.

In a city near Ephesus the Apostle, after having made a discourse, remarked a young man in the multitude that gathered near. He was handsome, of noble stature, pleasing countenance, and his soul was far more beautiful than his body.

Taking the youth with him, St. John presented him to the bishop of that place, saying: "I confide this young man to your care, in the presence of Christ and before this congregation. Christ will be my witness in regard to the sacred deposit which I place in your hands. It is the treasure of my heart."

The bishop promised to take care of him, but the venerable old Saint again repeated his injunction. He then departed for Ephesus.

The youth was received into the bishop's own house. The prelate educated him, loved him, cherished him as his own soul, and at length conferred upon him the celestial grace of Baptism.

When, however, the bishop had signed the young man with the divine seal of salvation, he began to relax somewhat of his former vigilance; and his charge, finding himself thus too

early set at liberty, soon saw himself surrounded
by young men of his own age, idle, daring, and corrupt.

At first they taught him the way to idleness,
merrymaking, intemperance; after a time he became a criminal, and finally a robber. Like a
spirited horse whose mettle carries him over the
precipice, the young wanderer fell into the utmost
excesses. He even tried to outdo his wild companions, thinking that for himself at least all was
lost.

In vain the bishop tried to check him. It was
now too late.

At length the misguided young fellow assembled
the herd of wretches among whom he moved, formed them into a troop of desperadoes, and became
their bold and hardy leader. He was soon the terror of the country.

After a certain time, however, the aged Apostle was summoned to the same city.

Having ended his mission and settled various affairs, he solemnly addressed the bishop, saying:
"Restore to me the deposit which Christ and myself confided to you in the presence of this church
of which you are pastor."

The bishop was sorely puzzled. He thought
that perhaps it was a question of some deposit
of money. But St. John said: "I reclaim from you
the soul of our youthful brother." At these

words the prelate lowered his eyes, wept, and answered: "He is dead!"

"How and by what manner of death?" enquired the Apostle. "Dead," replied the other, "to God; for now he is but a wicked, lost wretch —in short, a robber. He has quitted the Church, and he dwells on the mountain, which he has seized with an armed troop of men like himself."

On hearing this, St. John, overcome with sorrow, wept bitterly, and exclaimed: "Is this the sort of guardian that I have set to watch over a brother's soul!" He then asked for a horse and guide, and hastily took his way towards the mountains.

He reached the spot and was soon in the hands of the advance guard of the robbers. He coolly allowed them to take possession of all his, merely saying: "Lead me to your chief; it is for him that I have come."

The armed chief awaited the captive. He saw him as the party approached, and, recognizing the holy and venerable Apostle. he was seized with shame and ran away.

St. John, however, urged on his steed, and, forgetting his great age, called out loudly: "My son, why do you flee from me—an unarmed old man? Have pity on me, my child. Do not fear. There is still hope for you. I will be your guarantee to Christ. If necessary I will cheerfully give my life for you, even as the Lord has given His life for us all. I will give my soul to purchase yours. Stop, my son. Believe me, it is Christ who sends me after you."

These kind, earnest words had the desired effect. The hardened robber—the leader in many a wild and desperate deed — stopped and cast his eyes towards the ground. He then threw away his arms, and trembled as the big, round tears rolled down his still handsome, manly countenance.

St. John approached, and the robber 'chief humbly embraced his feet. The poor penitent was bathed in his tears as in a second baptism, but he still kept his right hand, which had shed so much blood, concealed under his garments.

The Apostle encouraged him and pledged himself that he would obtain his pardon from the great God, whose mercy is above all His works. The holy old man even fell upon his knees, seized that crime-stained hand—for evermore purified — and tenderly kissed it.

"The young man," says the ancient writer, " was brought back into the assembly of the saints. John prayed with him. He fasted with him. Together they did penance. He healed his soul by his words as if by a sovereign charm, and he no more quitted him till he had raised him to the life of grace and restored him to the Church." [20]

[20] Baunard.

Cassian tells another pleasing anecdote of St. John in his old age.   One day while the Saint was playfully caressing a pet partridge, a hunter who observed him thus amusing himself expressed surprise.

"And you,' asked the Apostle, "do you always carry that bow bent which I see in your hands?"

"Not always," replied the hunter: "I unbend it and rest it, that it may preserve its spring and elasticity."

"Then, young man," resumed St. John, "why do you wonder that I likewise unbend and repose my soul, that it may afterwards mount more freely towards heaven?"

St. Jerome relates that when age and weakness grew upon the Apostle at Ephesus, so that he was no longer able to preach, he had himself carried to the church, and on such occasions he simply said to his flock: "My dear children, love one another." After a time the people were wearied at constantly hearing the same words, and they asked him why he repeated this advice so often. "Because," replied the beloved disciple, "it is the precept of the Lord, and if you put it into practice you do enough."

One after another the Apostles had bidden adieu to earth and passed to their heavenly home of their Divine Master, and for many a year St. John alone remained, the last of the glorious

twelve.   But one day the warning from above came.
He was told that the hour of reward was not far
distant.   According to a beautiful belief, it was the
Immaculate Virgin herself who whispered the welcome news.   "O my son!" said the sweet Lady,
"you welcomed me to your dwelling when I was upon
earth.   Come with me now to the mansion of the
great God."

The moment came.   He said farewell to the
weeping faces that crowded around, raised his
eyes to heaven, and, with a prayer on his pure
lips, gently expired.   And thus passed away, at
the age of ninety-four, in the year 100, the good
Son of Thunder and the dear Apostle that Jesus
loved.[21]

What a shining and beautiful life!   It was so
full of faith, hope, love, zeal, purity, gentleness, simplicity, and heroism!   Its splendor dazzles the eye of
faith.   But it was a life of action and suffering.   St.
John was no sleepy Christian, nor did he seek an
easy way to heaven.   He had learned the divine
philosophy of love and labor and suffering on the
bosom of Christ.[22]

[21] At ancient Ephesus with its historic ruins there is still shown
"the tomb of St. John the Evangelist and of St. Timothy, the cave
of the Seven Sleepers, and the Portico of the   Agora where Justin
Martyr disputed with Tryphon the Jew.   This city has long claimed
to have given birth to Homer."— *Vetromile.*

[22] A good many churches in the United States bear the name of
St John the Evangelist.

SAINT CECILIA,

VIRGIN, MARTYR, AND PATRONESS OF SACRED MUSIC.

DIED A.D. 230.

———————

"At last divine Cecilia came,
　　Inventress of the vocal frame ;
The sweet enthusiast, from her sacred store,
　　Enlarged the former narrow bounds
　　And added length to solemn sounds,
With nature's mother-wit and arts unknown before.
　　Let old Timotheus yield the prize,
　　　Or both divide the crown ;
　　He raised a mortal to the skies,
　　　She drew an angel down." [1]

IN the early part of the third century there lived at Rome[2] a beautiful girl who belonged to a family illustrious for bravery and genius. She was a native of the imperial

[1]Dryden.

[2]The city of Rome is on the east side of the river Tiber, fifteen miles from the sea. It is often called the Eternal City. For over two thousand years it has been more or less connected with everything great and memorable enacted in the civilized world. Once the capital of the great Roman Empire, it finally became the patrimony of the successors of St. Peter, and as such—despite political knaves and royal robbers—it will likely remain to the end of time

city. Her pure countenance reflected the divine beauty of her soul; and grace, modesty, and the continual thought of God's holy presence surrounded her, so to speak, with a mysterious charm. This was St. Cecilia,[3] who, in days of girlhood, had consecrated by a vow her virginity to Heaven.

She was now eighteen. The Roman poor knew her charity. Often had they seen her alone in the caves of the martyrs,[4] or perhaps only accompanied by a faithful servant. Her father was a pagan, but he respected the religion of his good and lovely daughter.

It was the earnest wish of her parents[5] that Cecilia should marry, and they chose for her a distinguished husband. He seemed not unworthy of the honor. Valerian, though still a pagan, possessed at least those natural gifts which prepare the soul for faith, hope and charity.

[3] Cecilia is the feminine of Cecil.

[4] Now called the *Catacombs.*

[5] They were both pagans, but Cecilia from childhood had been brought up a Christian—perhaps through the influence of some of her relatives. "History," says Gueranger, "throws no light upon the means used by the Holy Spirit to win her to this celestial doctrine : but we know that from her earliest infancy she was initiated in the mysteries of Christianity. Probably an aged relative or faithful nurse, previously illuminated by the true light, instructed the young girl in the principles of that faith, the profession of which in those days almost necessarily involved the sacrifice of earthly happiness." —*Life of St. Cecilia.*

But who can express the anxious fears of Cecilia? She had offered her heart to God, and He had accepted the precious offering. Could a pagan, however, understand this mystery, and would not this union of the soul with its Creator seem a strange folly to a young man like Valerian, still living in the world of the senses?

More than one Christian soul has felt these chaste doubts. It is honorable to hesitate before making for a mere mortal a sacrifice for which a young girl sometimes can never console herself. Cecilia trembled, and prayed, and hoped almost against hope that she would not be forced to lose the palm of virginity.

It must be said that she was very unhappy, but she threw herself on the protection of the good God. She prayed and fasted, and the nearer the wedding-day approached the more she increased her devotions and her penances. But the Almighty is always near those who call on Him. He could not leave His loving child alone and comfortless. In an hour when her sorrow was deepest He revealed to her that He had accepted her generous vow, in token of which He would send an angel to guard her chastity.

At length, however, the wedding-day arrived, and Cecilia, dressed in shining robes of silk and gold, became a bride against the dearest wishes of her heart. When the wedding-party broke up she found herself alone with him who was to be her life-long companion. It was now that she confided to him, as far as she could, the secret of her pure, anxious breast in a conversation the charm of which has come down to us.

"Valerian," she began, fixing her sweetly brilliant eyes on the attractive young nobleman, "there is a secret that I wish to confide to you. I have a lover, an angel of God, who watches over me with jealous care. If you preserve inviolate my virginity, he will love you as he loves me, and will overpower you with his favors."

Valerian was much astonished, and wished to know this angel.

"You shall see him," said Cecilia, "when you are purified."

"How shall I become so?" asked Valerian.

"Go to Urban," [6] whispered the beautiful Saint. "When the poor hear my name, they will take you to his sanctuary. He will explain to you our mysteries."

Led by an unknown power, the young man consented to go. We know the happy result of this step—his interview with Pope Urban in the catacombs, his conversion, and his baptism. Still dressed in his white robe, he returned to Cecilia.

Valerian could now understand the love of the angels and its perfect beauty. In future he

[6] Pope Urban I.

loved Cecilia with a love that was more than
love ; but it was as his sister in God, to whom
belong the heart, and soul, and intellect.   He understood the value of the soul.   Nor is it mere conjecture to say that others loved in those Christian
ages more as the spiritual and pure-minded Valerian
did.

Valerian's brother, Tiburtius, soon sought the
residence that was blessed by the presence of our
Saint.   They did not labor in vain to show him
that his gods were only idols.   Subdued by the mysterious charm of the Christian virgin, conquered
by the eagerness of his brother, Tiburtius also wished to see the angel who watched over Cecilia.
If for this it was necessary to be purified, purified
he would be; and thus he became the first conquest
of Valerian, who had ardently besought Heaven for
such a result.

Souls such as these were too beautiful for pagan
Rome.   The governor, in the absence of the emper-
or summoned Valerian and Tiburtius before his
tribunal.

"Valerian," said the governor, "your brother's
head is evidently crazed; you, I hope, will be able to
give me a sensible reply."

"There is only one physician," answered Valerian, "who has deigned to take charge of my brother's
head and of mine.   He is Christ, the Son of the
living God!"

"Come," said the governor, "speak with wisdom."

"Your ear is false," replied Valerian; "you cannot understand our language."

The two young nobles, like brave men, proclaimed their faith in Jesus Christ. Valerian died a hero and martyr. He went to wait for his pure and beautiful Cecilia in heaven. Nor was he forsaken by Tiburtius.

Cecilia piously took charge of their bodies, and prepared to follow them on the path to eternity. Soon she was called to answer for her conduct, but she disconcerted the judge. Before such loveliness, purity, heroism, and innocence threats and entreaties utterly failed, and corrupt paganism felt abashed.

The noble young lady, however, received her sentence. She was convicted of loving the poor and of adoring a crucified God, and was instantly confined in the bath-room of her own house. She was to be suffocated in a hot vapor-bath. But in the midst of this fiery atmosphere the holy Cecilia remained uninjured.

The stupefied jailers related that they had discovered her singing the praises of God. On hearing this the wrath of the pagan governor knew no bounds. The executioner was summoned. With a trembling hand he inflicted three wounds on the neck of the virgin-martyr, but

failed to sever the head.   Terrified himself, he then
ran away.

Cecilia, however, lived three days, bathed in
her blood and stretched on the flags. The
Christians gathered around her.   She was able
to bid farewell to the poor, to whom she had given
all her property.   Then, feeling her strength fail,
and while Pope Urban was in the act of giving her
his blessing, she drew her robe around her, and joyfully gave back to God her bright and beautiful
spirit.   This memorable event happened about the
year 230.

According to her last desire, the Pope transformed the house that had witnessed her martyrdom
into a church.   The bath-room became a chapel,
and by its arrangement bears witness to-day to the
truth of the Saint's life.   One can still see the
mouth of the pipes which let in the vapor, covered
with a grating; and on the same flags where the
Roman virgin expired, the kneeling Christian can
ponder down deep in his heart the example of lofty
heroism which the gentle and pure-souled Cecilia
gave to the world. [1]

The Christians of the Eternal City erected a
church in honor of St. Cecilia.   This edifice
however, having fallen into decay, Pope Pascal I.
began to rebuild it · but he felt troubled as to

---

[1] *Revue Générale*, as translated in the *Catholic World*, vol xiii.

how he should find the body of the Saint. It was thought that, perhaps, the Lombards had taken it away, as they had many others from the cemeteries of Rome, when they besieged that city in 755.

One Sunday, as this Pope was assisting at Matins in St. Peter's, he fell into a slumber in which he was told by St. Cecilia herself that the Lombards had in vain sought her remains, and that he should find them. Accordingly, he had a search made, and discovered those sacred relics in the cemetery called by her name. The body was clothed in a robe of gold tissue, with linen cloths at her feet, dipped in her blood. With her body was also found that of her husband, Valerian. The Pope caused them to be translated to the Church of St. Cecilia in 821.[8]

Is it wonderful that such a touching and beautiful story should be repeated, age after age, by poets, painters, and sacred orators? St. Cecilia has been praised by the pen of the venerable Bede

---

[8] In 1599, Cardinal Sfondrate—who grandly rebuilt the church of Cecilia—ordered the tomb to be opened with solemnity. To the great delight and admiration of all, the body of the Roman virgin, respected by long ages, appeared in a state of miraculous preservation. The chaste folds of her dress were restrained by a girdle. At her feet were found the blood-stained cloths which had bound her wounds. Three fingers of her right hand were open, as if even in dying she wished to avow her belief in the sublime mystery of the Holy Trinity.

and other illustrious saints.   The great St. Thomas Aquinas preached sermons in her honor.   Raphael, Rubens, Guido, and Fra Angelico have employed their exquisite genius to picture the divine patroness of music, whose rare soul like a celestial lyre had responded to the faintest inspirations of heaven.   For over fifteen centuries her name has been mentioned in the Canon of the Mass—an honor truly extraordinary.[9]

What food for wholesome reflection there is in the short but sublime life of this virgin-martyr ! It warns us to lift up our hearts.   It points to the skies.   We are made for heaven.   The soul daily whispers this, for it is naturally Christian. Let us, then, know how to turn from the hurry of life and the tinkling sound of human words, and think occasionally of the great God.   It will bring peace to the troubled spirit.   Oh! look at the example of this bright and blessed girl.   Pray to her. Ask her protection.   She has known how to find

---

[9] It was on St. Cecilia's day that the Catholic founders of Maryland sailed from England.   "On the 22d of the month of November, in the year 1633, being St. Cecilia's day," writes Father White, S. J., "we set sail from Cowes, in the isle of Wight, with a gentle east wind blowing ."—*Relatio Itineris in Marylandiam.*

There are churches in New York, Brooklyn, Philadelphia, Louisville, and various other places, dedicated to God under the name of St. Cecilia; and nearly all Catholic societies of sacred music bear her beautiful name.

that love, and peace, and happiness which the world
cannot give.

"Music the fiercest grief can charm,
And Fate's severest rage disarm ;
Music can soften pain to ease
And make despair and madness please:
Our joys it can improve,
And antedate the bliss above.
This the divine Cecilia found,
And to her Maker's praise confined the sound.
When the full organ joins the tuneful choir,
The immortal powers incline their ear :
Borne on the swelling notes our souls aspire,
While solemn airs improve the sacred fire;
And angels lean from heaven to hear.
Of Orpheus now no more let poets tell;
To bright Cecilia greater power is given—
His numbers raised a shade from hell,
Hers lift the soul to heaven."

St. Christophorus

THE MARTYR

THE PATRON SAINT OF TRAVELLERS

DIED A.D. 254.

AN ANCIENT tradition concerning St. Christophorus relates: He was born in the land of Canaan, and was named Reprobus, that is Reprobate, for he was a barbarous heathen. In stature and strength he was a giant. Thinking no one his like in bodily vigor, he resolved to go forth in search of the mightiest master and serve him. In his wanderings, he met with a king who was praised as the most valorous man on earth. To him he offered his services and was accepted. The king was proud of his giant and kept him near his person. One day a minstrel visited the king's castle, and among the ballads he sung before the court was one on the power of Satan. At the mention of this name the king blessed himself, making the sign of the cross. Reprobus, wondering, asked him why he did that. The king replied: "When I make this sign, Satan has no power over me." Reprobus rejoined: "So thou fearest the power of Satan? Then he is mightier than thou, and I shall seek and serve him."

Setting forth to seek Satan, he came into a wilderness. One dark night he met a band of wild fellows riding through the forest. It was Satan and his escort. Reprobus bravely accosted him, saying he wished to serve him. He was accepted. But soon he was convinced that his new master was not the mightiest on earth. For one day, whilst approaching a crucifix by the wayside, Satan quickly took to flight, and Reprobus asked him for the reason. Satan replied: "That is the image of my greatest enemy, who conquered me on the cross. From him I always flee." When Reprobus heard this, he left the devil, and went in search of Christ.

In his wanderings, he one day came to a hut hidden in the forest. At its door sat a venerable old man. Reprobus addressed him, and in the course of the conversation that ensued the old man told him that he was a hermit, and had left the world to serve Christ, the Lord of heaven and earth. "Thou art my man," cried Reprobus; "Christ is He whom I seek, for He is the strongest and the mightiest. Tell me where I **can find** Him."

The hermit then began instructing the **giant** about God and the Redeemer, and concluded **by** saying: "He who would serve Christ must offer himself entirely to Him, and do and suffer everything for His sake. His reward for this will be immense and will last forever." Reprobus now asked the hermit to allow him to remain, and to continue to instruct him. The hermit consented. When Reprobus was fully instructed, he baptized him. After his baptism, a great change came over the giant. No longer proud of his great size and strength, he became meek and humble, and asked the hermit to assign to him some task by which he might serve God, his master. "For," said he, "I can not pray and fast; therefore I must serve God in some other way." The hermit led him to a broad and swift river nearby, and said: "Here build thyself a hut, and when wanderers wish to cross the river, carry them over for the love of Christ." For there was no bridge across the river.

Henceforth, day and night, whenever he was called, Reprobus faithfully performed the task assigned to him. One night he heard a child calling to be carried across the river. Quickly he rose, placed the child on his stout shoulder, took his staff and walked into the mighty current.

Arrived in midstream, the water rose higher and higher, and the child became heavier and heavier. "O child," he cried, "how heavy thou art! It seems I bear the weight of the world on my shoulder." And the child replied, "Right thou art. Thou bearest not only the world, but the Creator of heaven and earth. I am Jesus Christ, thy King and Lord, and henceforth thou shalt be called Christophorus, that is, Christ-bearer. Arrived on yonder shore, plant thy staff in the ground, and in token of my power and might to-morrow it shall bear leaves and blossoms."

And the child disappeared. On reaching the other shore, Christophorus stuck his staff into the ground, and behold, it budded forth leaves and blossoms. Then, kneeling, he promised the Lord to serve Him ever faithfully. He kept his promise, and thenceforth became a zealous preacher of the Gospel, converting many to the Faith. On his missionary peregrinations he came also to Lycia, where, after his first sermon, eighteen thousand heathens requested baptism. When Emperor Decius heard of this, he sent a company of four hundred soldiers to capture Christophorus. To these he preached so convincingly, that they all asked for baptism. Decius became enraged thereat and had him cast into prison. There he first treated him with great kindness, and surrounded him with every luxury to tempt him to sin, but in vain. Then he ordered him to be tortured in the most cruel manner, until he should deny the Faith. He was scourged, placed on plates of hot iron, boiling oil was poured over and fire was lighted under him. When all these torments did not accomplish their purpose, the soldiers were ordered to shoot him with arrows. This, too, having no effect, he was beheaded, on July 25, 254.

Two great saints refer to the wonderful achievements of St. Christophorus. St. Ambrose mentions that this saint converted forty-eight thousand souls to Christ. St. Vincent Ferrer declares, that when the plague devastated Valencia, its destructive course was stayed through the intercession of St. Christophorus.

SAINT LAWRENCE,

THE ILLUSTRIOUS MARTYR.

DIED A.D. 258.

AMONG the most illustrious of the martyrs is the glorious St. Lawrence. He is honored by the whole Church. His name sanctifies one of the great rivers of America, a river whose majestic grandeur is the wonder of travelers and the inspiration of poets—

. . . "the river whose mighty current gave
Its freshness for a hundred leagues to ocean's briny wave." [1]

[1] The conferring of this name, as nearly every one knows, originated with the famous Catholic navigator and discoverer of Canada, James Cartier, whose second voyage is thus described by Parkman: "On the 16th of May, 1535, officers and sailors assembled in the Cathedral of St. Malo, where, after confession and hearing Mass, they received the parting blessing of the bishop. Three days later they set sail. The dingy walls of the rude old seaport, and the white rocks that line the neighboring shores of Brittany, faded from their sight, and soon they were tossed in a furious tempest. But the scattered ships escaped the danger, and, reuniting at the Straits of Belle Isle, steered westward along the coast of Labrador till they reached a small bay opposite the island of Anticosti. Cartier called it the Bay of St. Lawrence, a

We know little as to the birth and education of
St. Lawrence,[2] but the Spaniards call him their
countryman.   While still a youth his remarkable
virtue attracted the notice of St. Sixtus, then
Archdeacon of Rome, who took him under his protection and became his instructor.

When St. Sixtus[3] became Pope, in 257, he ordained Lawrence deacon; and, though he was
yet young, the Pontiff appointed him first among
the seven deacons, who served in the Church of the
Eternal City.   He thus became the Pope's archdeacon.   This was a charge of great importance, to
which was annexed the care of the treasury of the
Church and the distribution of its revenues among
the poor.

In the year 257 the Emperor Valerian published his bloody edicts against the Catholic Church.
He foolishly flattered himself that its destruction
was merely a question of time and rigorous persecution, not knowing it to be the work of the
Almighty.   His plan was as simple as it was
stupid and blindly brutal.   He would cut off the

name afterwards extended to the entire gulf and to the great river
above."—*Pioneers of France in the New World.*

Cartier's pious reason for giving it the name of our Saint was this:
he reached the bay on the 10th of August, the day on which the
Church celebrates the feast of St. Lawrence.

[2] Lawrence is from the Latin, and signifies *crowned with laurel*
The name is also written Laurence.

[3] He was the second Pontiff of that name.

shepherds and disperse the flocks; and hence he
began his barbarously elaborate scheme by ordering all bishops, priests, and deacons to be put to
death.

Pope St. Sixtus II. was seized in about a year
from this date, and led to execution. While on the
way St. Lawrence followed him with tears in his
eyes ; and thinking himself ill-treated because he
was not to die with the holy Pontiff, said :

"Father, where are you going without your son ?
Why do you not take your deacon with you as usual ? Shall you go alone to offer yourself a sacrifice
to God ? What have I done to displease you
that you thus cast me off ?"

"My son, " replied the brave Vicar of Christ, "it
is not I who leave you. Our Lord reserves you
for a sharper battle. I am old and feeble, and I
must die after a slight skirmish ; but you, who are
young and strong, shall have more glory in your
triumph. Dry your tears. In three days you shall
follow me."

The Holy Father then gave Lawrence some directions about immediately distributing all the
treasures of the Church among the poor, lest they
should be robbed of their patrimony by its falling
into the hands of the pagan persecutors. Having
said this, he waved a last adieu to his faithful deacon.

Lawrence was full of joy, for he had just heard

that he should soon be called to God.   But a pressing duty was to be performed.   He set out immediately to seek the poor widows and orphans, and
gave them all the money which he had in his keeping.   He even sold the sacred vessels to increase the
sum.   This was also given to the poor.

In those early days the church at Rome was possessed of considerable riches.   Besides providing
for its ministers, it maintained many widows and
virgins and fifteen hundred poor people.   The Holy
Father or his archdeacon kept a list containing the
names of these persons.

Some of the officers who led the Pope to execution heard him speak of money and treasures, and
took care to repeat his words to the Prefect of
Rome.   This grasping official at once imagined that
the Christians had hidden vast treasures.   He became deeply interested in the matter ; for he was
no less a devout worshipper of gold and silver than
of Mars and Jupiter.

He sent for St. Lawrence.   "You Christians
complain," began the wily hypocrite, "that we
treat you with cruelty ; but now there is no question of tortures.   I simply ask what you can easily
give.   I am told that your priests offer up sacrifices in golden chalices, that the sacred blood is
received in silver cups, and that in your meetings
after night you have wax tapers fixed in golden
candlesticks.

"Bring these concealed treasures to light. The emperor has need of them for the support of his army. It is said that according to your doctrine you must render to Cæsar the things that belong to him. I do not think that your God ever caused money to be coined. He brought none into the world with Him. He brought nothing but good words. Then give us the money, and be rich in words."

"The Church," calmly replied St. Lawrence, "is, in truth, rich; nor has the emperor any treasure equal to its possessions. I will take pleasure in showing you a valuable part; but allow me a little time to set everything in order and to make an inventory."

The prefect was fairly delighted. He did not understand the *kind* of treasure to which Lawrence referred, and fancying that he was already possessed of hidden wealth, he gladly gave the Saint a respite of three days.

During this time Lawrence went all over the city, seeking out from street to street the poor who were supported by the charity of the Church. He knew where to go, and well the poor knew him. On the third day he had his *treasures* gathered together. He placed them in rows before the church, and they consisted of hundreds of the aged, the decrepit, the blind, the lame, the maimed, the lepers, widows, virgins, and young orphans.

He then proceeded to the residence of the prefect, and invited him to come and see the treasures of the Church.   The haughty official was astonished to behold such a number of poor wretches. To him it was a sickening sight that aroused naught but anger, fury, and disappointment. He turned about, and looked at the holy deacon with an air of fierce scorn.

"What are you displeased at?" exclaimed the dauntless Lawrence.   "Behold the treasures I promised you ! I have even added to them the gems and precious stones—those widows and consecrated virgins who form the Church's crown.   It has no other riches.   Take these and use them for the advantage of Rome, the emperor, and yourself."

The enraged prefect, no longer able to control himself, cried out: "Do you thus mock me ?   Are the ensigns of Roman power to be thus insulted? I know that you wish to die.   This is your foolish vanity.   But you will not take leave of life so soon as you imagine.   I will see to that.   I will protract your tortures.   Your death shall be slow and bitter. You shall die by inches."

Lawrence was neither annoyed nor terrified. He feared God alone. "Wicked wretch," he replied with energy, "do you expect to frighten me with these tortures ? To you they may be tortures, but to me they are none.   I have long wished for such dainties."

On hearing this the prefect was in a hurry for nothing but revenge. The Saint was stripped, and his naked body torn with a kind of whips called scorpions. After this severe scourging, plates of red-hot iron were applied to his bleeding sides. Lawrence, in spite of such appaling treatment, presented a joyful countenance, while the prefect raged with the fury of a wild beast. He could not comprehend how any human being could cheerfully endure such punishment. He even accused the martyr of being a magician, and threatened that unless he at once sacrificed to the gods he would add to his torments.

"Your torments," answered St. Lawrence, " will have an end, and I do not fear them. Do what you will to me. I am prepared for the worst."

The p.efect at once oraerea nim to be beaten with leaden plummets, and soon his whole body was a bruised and torn mass. The Saint prayed to God to receive his soul; but a voice from heaven, which was heard by all who stood around, told him that he had yet much to suffer.

"Romans," shouted the brutal prefect, "do you see how the devils help and encourage this fellow, who derides both the gods and the emperor, and has no respect for their sovereign power, no any fear of torments ?"

Lawrence was next placed on a rack, and his suf

fering body stretched so that every limb was dislocated. His flesh was torn with hooks, but he did not flinch. Calm and cheerful, he prayed and suffered. An angel was seen to wipe his face and bleeding shoulders, and the sight of the blessed spirit converted one of the soldiers, who went up to the Saint and asked to be baptized.

The frantic prefect now ordered a large gridiron to be procured. It was soon in readiness, and live coals, partly extinguished, were thrown under it that the martyr might be slowly burned. He was placed naked upon this iron bed, and bound with chains over a slow fire. His flesh was soon broiled, and little by little the cruel heat was forcing its way into his very heart and bowels. A light beautiful to behold shone from his face, and his burning body exhaled a most sweet odor. The martyr, says St. Augustine, felt not the torments of the persecutor, so strong and vivid was his desire of possessing Christ. Thus in the midst of appalling torments he enjoyed that peace which the world cannot give—the peace of God.

Turning to the prefect, St. Lawrence said to him, with a cheerful smile: "Let my body now be turned; one side is broiled enough."

The cruel prefect ordered him to be turned. It was done, and the Saint said, "Eat now, for it is well done." The prefect again insulted him;

but the martyr continued in earnest prayer, with sighs and tears imploring the divine mercy with his last breath for the conversion of the city of Rome. Having finished his prayer, a ray of immortality seemed to light up his manly countenance; he lifted his eyes towards heaven, and his pure, holy, and heroic spirit went to receive the shining reward promised to those who suffer persecution for the sake of justice and religion.

"The admirers of pagan fortitude," says Dr. MacHale, "may dwell with rapture on the many trophies which were won by the primitive patriots of Rome. They may quote the devotion of a Curtius leaping into the lake, the courage of a Scævola flinging his hand into the fire, or the exorable fidelity of a Regulus returning to Carthage with the certainty of the exquisite tortures he was fated to endure. Yet these and similar instances of extraordinary fortitude with which Roman history abounds cannot bear a comparison with the calm and tranquil patience with which this holy servant of God bore the slow tortures of the gridiron."

An ancient writer ascribes the entire conversion of the city of Rome to the prayers of St. Lawrence. God even began to grant his request at the moment it was made. Several senators who were present at his death were so moved by his piety and heroic fortitude that they became Christians on the spot.   The death-blow was given to idolatry.   From that day it declined, and soon pagan Rome lived only in the pages of history.[2]

How sublime is that ancient faith which can produce such a man as the glorious St. Lawrence! We have the same holy and beautiful faith. We are Catholics. But in the practice of virtue how little heroism we commonly display! Yet virtue demands sacrifice. Pain is the path to holiness. We are in the world only to please God. We must learn the nobility of suffering. It is the true test of love. Christ suffered, the Blessed Virgin suffered, the Saints suffered; and no soul has ever become truly great and good and virtuous that

---

[2] On the very eastern confines of the ancient city (Rome) stands the venerable church of St. Lawrence, the celebrated deacon whose heroic sufferings and death form one of the most interesting episodes in ecclesiastical story. No traveler or pilgrim could visit the "Eternal City" without likewise visiting a spot which is consecrated by the memory of one of the most illustrious in the entire catalogue of its numerous martyrs........ .... This church is ranked among the seven to the visit of which the popes have annexed a Plenary Indulgence. Under the canopy of the great altar the bodies of the Saint and of St. Stephen, the first martyr, repose, united in sepulchre as they were in the office of deacon and in the glory of martyrdom.—*Archbishop MacHale, Letter L V.*

There are churches in New York, Baltimore, Cincinnati, and various other places in this republic bearing the name of St. Lawrence. Montreal, Canada, has its college of St. Lawrence.

has not been disciplined in the school of affliction.
In short, without some suffering there can be no
real greatness, no heroism, no carrying of that blessed and mysterious burden—the cross!

SAINT AGNES,

THE YOUNG ROMAN VIRGIN AND MARTYR.

DIED A.D. 304.

A T the beginning of the fourth century there lived in Rome a rich, noble and beautiful girl who was happily named Agnes.[1] In accordance with her high birth, her parents had her carefully educated; but her chief glory was a stainless purity of soul, for she had consecrated her young heart to Heaven by a vow of virginity. [2]

[1] Agnes signifies *pure* or *chaste*.

[2] "What is a vow ?" it may be asked.   A vow," writes Perry, "is a free and deliberate promise made to God of doing something good, with an intention of binding one's self to do it.   A vow, in the making of it, is a free act; but when made is binding under the strictest obligation. . . . It is more meritorious to perform good works by a vow than without a vow, because by a vow we sacrifice our liberty to God—we give Him not only *the fruit* but the *tree itself.*"—*Instructions.*

A vow to God, however, is something so good and holy that it should never be made lightly or without careful consideration. This is especially true as regards the vow of chastity.   "No one," says the learned Dr. Weninger, S.J., "must take such a vow without long previous reflection and the advice of a prudent

Beauty is the reflection of heaven in the human countenance.   The soul as it grows lovely transforms in its turn the body which it animates, and thus the living mirror of the face reflects strength and gentleness, peace and purity.[3]

As Agnes was one day returning from school,

---

confessor ; still, should any one have bound himself to its observance, let him carefully attend to his promise." — *Lives of the Saints,* vol. i.

"It is much better not to vow," declares the Holy Book, "than after a vow not to perform the things promised."—*Eccles.* v. 4.

[3] The last sentence expresses a *physiological truth.* " No act we perform," says Steele, " ends with itself. It leaves behind it in the nervous centres a tendency to do the same thing again. Our physical being thus conspires to fix upon us the habits of a good or an evil life.   Our very thoughts are written in our muscles, so that the expression of our faces and even our features grow into harmony with the lives we live."—*Human Physiology.*

"The muscles of the features." writes Holden, "are generally described as arising from the bony fabric of the face, and are inserted into the nose, corners of the mouth, and the lips.   But this gives a very inadequate idea of their true insertion.   They drop fibres into the skin all along their course, so that there is hardly a point of the face which has not its little fibre to move it. The habitual recurrence of good or evil thoughts, the indulgence in particular modes of life, call into play corresponding sets of muscles which, by producing folds and wrinkles, give a permanent cast to the features, and speak a language which all can understand, and which rarely misleads.   Schiller puts this well when he says that *it is an admirable proof of infinite wisdom that what is noble and benevolent beautifies the human countenance ; what is base and hateful imprints upon it a revolting expression."* — *Medical and Surgical Landmarks.*

her modesty and fascinating beauty attracted the idle glance of Eutropius, son of the governor of Rome.   In a moment he was desperately in love, for never before had he seen such a sweet angelic countenance.   Day and night that vision of loveliness haunted his excited mind.   At length he visited the parents of Agnes and asked her hand in marriage.   But as their daughter was only twelve years of age, they did not encourage the young man's proposal.

Not so easily, however, was Eutropius to be put off.   He determined to speak to Agnes herself, hoping that she would listen better than her father and mother.   He watched for her daily in the street.   One day as she passed he ran up, told his love, and begged her to accept some costly and brilliant jewels which he held in his hand.

Agnes declined the gifts, and with great dignity and earnestness said : "Leave me !   There is Another who possesses my whole heart.   I love Him more than my own life and soul.   He is so great, noble, and beautiful that I will ever remain true to Him."

It is not likely that the young Roman heathen grasped the full meaning of the Saint's words.   But he went away sad at heart.   He became distracted with grief and disappointment, and in a short time fell sick.

When the governor of Rome learned the cause
of his son's illness, he sent a third person to the
home of St. Agnes to ask her to accede to the wishes of Eutropius. It was in vain. She gave a final
refusal.

As may be readily conceived, this affair was
talked over again and again in the governor's residence. On one occasion an officer present remarked in a tone of sarcasm: "It is useless to waste
time in the matter. Agnes, being a Christian,
is a witch, and imagines Christ to be her bride-
groom."

This was a new and delightful item of information. The governor immediately ordered her to
be arrested. Under the pretext of proceeding
against her as a Christian, he hoped to be able to
gain another point by forcing her to marry his in-
fatuated son.

The holy and beautiful Agnes soon stood an accused prisoner before his tribunal. In the sweetest
words possible the governor urged his request a
second time. He promised honors and estates, but
soon saw he was wasting his breath to no purpose.
Then he began to threaten with all the cunning of an
experienced knave.

"Either renounce your Christ," said he sternly,
"and consent to the marriage, or, if you desire
to remain a virgin, offer sacrifice to the goddess Vesta, and enroll yourself among the Ves-

tals.⁴ Make your choice. If you refuse both offers, however, I will have you sent to an infamous abode, where the vilest wretches may treat you just as they please."

Agnes quailed not before the dangers that now threatened her on every side. "It is in vain you hope for my consent," replied the holy heroine. "I will neither renounce Christ nor offer sacrifice to Vesta. The one true God only do I adore. You threaten me with disgrace, but I have an angel of the Lord for protector. He will guard my frail body. You shall soon learn that my God is a God of purity. He will bring your wicked purpose to naught."

Such a bold and noble answer enraged the pagan governor. With all the malignity of a base nature, this monster ordered the pure, lovely girl to be stripped of her clothing and led in a state of complete nudity to a den of iniquity. But the great God was near, and took this occasion to work a grand and never-repeated miracle in order to prove His love for holy chastity. In a moment the rich hair of her head grew in such a profusion of length and thickness that it en-

⁴ Vesta was the goddess of fire among the pagan Romans, and the Vestals were virgins consecrated to Vesta and the service of watching the sacred fire, which was kept perpetually burning upon her altar. They were six in number, and their term of service lasted thirty years— *Webster.*

circled her entire person like a close-woven garment.

When the abode of infamy was reached, St.
Agnes saw an angel of God who was sent there for
her special protection. He handed her an exqui
site dress whiter than snow. She put it on. A
dazzling brilliancy now surrounded her divine-
ly-protected person: and many whose brutal instincts brought them near turned away with feelings of awe and mysterious respect on beholding
the shining grandeur of that spotless young
maiden.

Eutropious alone had the wicked audacity to
approach the dear Saint and offer violence; but
in the twinkling of an eye he was struck blind by
the angel, and fell trembling to the floor. He
was dead. It was the swift punishment of an impure scoundrel.

Soon it became known that the governor's son
was killed, and a great outcry was raised through
the whole city. Agnes was a wretched Christian
and a witch, they exclaimed, and Eutropius had
perished by her vile enchantments. The unhappy father rushed to the place and like a madman
tore his hair in grief and anguish.

"O you sorceress and infernal monster!"
shouted the furious governor, " born for my misery,
why have you killed my son?"

"I have not killed your son," answered the

young Saint. "He perished by his own wicked
rashness. Unlike others who came here, he did
not heed the brightness of this room, or respect the great God and the angel who guards
my virginity; and Heaven instantly chastised his
blind and brutal obstinacy."

The anger of the governor gave way to calmness,
and he said: "Then I beg of you to restore
my son again to life. If you do the world will
know that he did not die of your magic."

"Your hardened unbelief," replied Agnes,
"merits not that Almighty God should raise
your son from the dead; but I will beg this
favor of Him, that Rome may know His glory
and greatness." The sweet Saint prayed, and lo!
the dead Eutropius arose and said in a loud voice:
"The idols are devils. The God of the Christians is the only true God, and He alone is to
be adored!"

The news of this strange event passed rapidly
over the city. The pagan priests began to fear that
the worship of their idols was in danger, and
stirred up the fury of the low and ignorant
masses by proclaiming that Agnes was a sorceress,
who plotted the downfall of the sacred gods.
This sealed the fate of the Christian
maiden.

A mob gathered, crying out: "Death to the
sorceress! Death to the infamous and sacrile-

gious witch who blinds the minds of men by her enchantments !"

The governor did not desire the death of St. Agnes,
but the wild attitude of the mob frightened him ;
and though he refused to meddle in the case, he
quietly placed it in the hands of his deputy, Aspasius. He was a mean dodger of duty. He belonged
to that list of cringing cowards which history hands
down to us headed by the infamous name of Pontius
Pilate.

Agnes was brought before Aspasius, and condemned to be burned alive. It is said that she was transported with joy on hearing the cruel sentence.
She went to death "more cheerfully," says St Ambrose, "than others go to their wedding.'

She was placed on the funeral pile, the fire shot
up on every side, and soon the heroic virgin was en-
circled by flames. But God worked another wonder.
Agnes, thus surrounded, sat untouched and sang the
praises of her Almighty Master.

The heathen priests, full of anger and malignity asserted that this striking wonder was the result of
magic. They demanded that the Saint should be
put to death in another way ; and Aspasius ordered
the executioner to thrust his sword through her
neck.

The spectators wept to see that tender and
beautiful girl subjected to such revolting punish-
ments ; but, with more than the fearless intrepidity

of a veteran warrior, Agnes turned to the pale, hesitating executioner, and said: "Do not hesitate. Perish this body, which is pleasing in the eyes of those whom I desire not to please."

As she raised her eyes to heaven, breathing a last prayer for the eternal safety of her stainless soul, the cruel sword of the executioner did its work, and the glorious battle was ended. Peerless purity was crowned by martyrdom. It was the famous victory of a child of thirteen, in 304, over the tender weakness of her years, the power of pagan Rome, and the malice of men and demons.

St. Agnes was buried with all honor by her parents. Fondly they cherished the memory of their dear and beautiful daughter, often praying on her tomb. On the eighth night, however, after her martyrdom she appeared to them, shining with a radiance truly celestial, and said: " My dearest father and mother, mourn not as if I were dead, but rejoice with me that I am now in heaven, crowned with fadeless glory." [5]

> Saint Agnes, bright gem in the grand court of heaven,
>   Whose jewelled gates glisten with jasper and gold,
> What words to the children of earth have been given,
>   To speak of thy worth, of thy glory untold !

[5] There are churches dedicated to divine worship under the name of St. Agnes in New York, Brooklyn, Baltimore, Pittsburgh, Cincinnati, and many other places in the United States.

What pearl could compare with thy pure soul so holy ?
> What ruby's rich depths with thy heart's fervent love ?
What amethyst's glow with thy meek life so lowly ?
> What diamond with thy dazzling beauty above ?

"Saint Agnes, sweet patroness, teach us to follow
> The footsteps of Him whom thy young heart loved best,
That after life's night-time of tears and of sorrow
> May dawn a glad morning of peace and of rest.
With scorn thou didst look upon earthly ambition
> And long from its fettering links to be free;
It seemed in thy sight but a vain apparition—
> The real, the true One was waiting for thee!" [6]

[6] **E. M. V.** Bulger in the *Ave Maria.*

SAINT BASIL THE GREAT,

ARCHBISHOP OF CÆSAREA AND DOCTOR OF THE CHURCH.[1]

DIED A.D. 379.

S T. BASIL,[2] whose name shines with such resplendent lustre after fifteen centuries have passed away, was born in 329 at Cæsarea, the capital of the kingdom of Cappadocia. [3]   His noble and saintly parents were St. Basil the Elder and St. Emmelia, who left behind them a family so illustrious in learning and virtue that one of them is considered the light of his age and is numbered among the great Doctors of the Church, and four have an honored place on the golden list of canonized saints.

Basil's first teacher in virtue was his grandmother, St. Macrina the Elder, under whose ten-

----

[1] Of all the holy, learned, and illustrious men produced by the Catholic Church, but *nineteen* are honored with the title of *"Doctor of the Church."* "There are many Doctors *in* the Church," writes Pope Benedict XIV., " but few Doctors *of* the Church."

[2] Basil is from the Greek and signifies *royal* or *kingly*.

[3] Cappadocia was the largest division of Asia Minor, and was at one time an important kingdom.

der care he passed the early years of childhood at a country-house in Pontus.[4] He assures us that during his whole life he never forgot the impressions of piety which this venerable lady's lofty example made upon his infant mind. His father, who was a man of much learning and eloquence, gave the bright boy his first lessons in literature.

The Saint's early studies were made in the schools of Cæsarea, where his progress in piety and learning was the astonishment of his preceptors. He was deemed equal in oratory to the best masters in his native country, when he removed to Constantinople, where Libanus, a pagan, but the most famous rhetorician of his time, gave public lectures. This professor was charmed with his gifted pupil. In his letters he says that he was in raptures as often as he heard Basil speak in public, and ever after he kept up an epistolary correspondence with the future Doctor of the Church.

The love of useful knowledge next carried Basil to Athens. Here he was delighted to meet his young friend and fellow-countryman, Gregory Nazianzen.[5] Gregory, who had arrived there a little be-

[4] Pontus was a kingdom lying north of Cappadocia. Its shores were washed by the Black Sea.

[5] St. Gregory Nazianzen (from Nazianzus, his birthplace) afterwards became Patriarch of Constantinople. Like his friend St. Basil, he is honored with the extraordinary title of Doctor of the Church. He died in 389.

fore, had influence enough to procure his friend a welcome reception, and the reputation and dignified manners of Basil happily protected him from the rough treatment which new-comers generally received at the hands of the students.

Harmony of inclinations, an equal enthusiasm for virtue and learning, and a mutual esteem for each other's worth formed between Basil and Gregory a friendship as lasting as it was beautiful. To these pure young minds this holy affection was a shield from bad company and a great consolation. Everything was in common. They had the same lodging and the same table. Together they cheerfully toiled up the hill of knowledge, and seemed to have but one heart and one soul.

"We knew but two streets," writes Gregory, "and chiefly the first of these, which led us to the church, and to the saintly teachers and doctors who there attended the service of the altar and with the food of life nourished the flock of Christ. The other street with which we were acquainted—but which we held in much less esteem—was the road to the schools and to our masters in the sciences. To others we left the streets that led to the theatre, spectacles, feastings, and diversions. It was our only great affair, our only aim, and all our glory to be called and to live Christians."

St. Basil became a master in the liberal arts and sciences. He excelled in philosophy and literature. It is said that his knowledge of nature was more accurate and comprehensive than that of Aristotle himself. St. Gregory tells us that his power of reasoning was most remarkable. But he wisely seasoned all his vast acquirements by meditation on the Holy Scriptures, and by carefully reading the precious works of the Fathers. Thus he stored his capacious mind with the riches of knowledge *ad majorem Dei gloriam*—"to the greater glory of God."

In the year 355, Basil returned to his native city and opened a school of oratory. He was also induced to plead at the bar. The most brilliant success smiled on his undertakings; and soon the young nobleman found himself on the foremost wave of fame and popularity. On all sides he was greeted with applause. It was, however, a time of danger. Nor is it wonderful to learn that Basil's heart was assailed by temptations to vainglory and a secret satisfaction in the empty praises of men.

He felt there was some peril, and the timely words of his sister, St. Macrina, and his friend, Gregory Nazianzen, added to his thoughtfulness. Basil's was a brave, manly, cultivated nature, ever open to the influence of the good and the beautiful. Besides, he was faithful to the inspirations of grace.   The light of celestial wisdom flashed its brightness on his soul, and he triumphed over the obstacles that seemed to crowd that narrow path which leads to the skies, and with heroic greatness he bade adieu to the fleeting joys and glories of a worldly career.   He gave nearly all his estate to the poor, and became a monk.

Convinced, however, that the name of a monk would only be his condemnation if he did not strictly fulfil the obligations of the religious state, he traveled over Syria, Mesopotamia, and Egypt in 357, visiting the most renowned hermits and monasteries in those countries, and thus carefully instructing himself in the duties and exercises of a monastic life.

During the following year he returned to the house of his grandmother on the banks of the river Iris.   Here his mother, St. Emmelia, and his sister, St. Macrina, had founded a nunnery, which at that time was governed by the latter lady.   On the opposite side of the river Basil established a monastery for men, which he ruled five years, resigning the position of abbot in 362 to his brother, St. Peter of Sebaste. [a]

He founded several other religious houses in different parts of Pontus, which he continued to superintend even after he became archbishop.

[a] Another of St. Basil's brothers was the celebrated Father of the Church, St. Gregory of Nyssa.

It was for their direction he drew up his "Longer and Shorter Rules." [1]

As to Basil himself, his retired life was a model of virtue and rigorous mortification. He never had more than one coat. He lay on the ground, and sometimes passed whole nights in watching. At night he wore a long hair-shirt, but not in the day-time, that it might be unseen by men. He inured himself to the sharp cold of the mountains of Pontus, and never allowed himself to enjoy any other heat than that of the sun. His one meal a day consisted of bread and cold water. But he chiefly studied to practise the interior virtues of purity, meekness, and humility.

Libanus, the pagan philosopher, admired nothing in the Saint so much as his unvarying sweetness towards all : but he tempered this rare and beautiful virtue with an amiable gravity. He was a great lover of chastity, and built several convents for young virgins, to whom he gave a written rule.

During a wide-spread famine in 359 he sold the remainder of his estate for the benefit of the poor, and his friend, St. Gregory Nazianzen, tells us

[1] The Rule of St. Basil is universally followed to this day by all the Oriental monks, even by those who call themselves the Order of St. Anthony.—*Butler.*

that **ever after** he lived in the greatest poverty possible.

When Julian the Apostate ascended the imperial throne in 361, he wrote to St. Basil—whom he had known at Athens—and invited him to his court. The man of God answered that the state of life upon which he had entered rendered it impossible to comply with the emperor's request. This aroused the anger of Julian, and, some time after, he wrote to the Saint, ordering him to pay five thousand dollars in gold into his exchequer. In case of refusal he even threatened to level the city of Cæsarea with the ground.

St. Basil calmly replied that far from being able to raise so large a sum of money, he had scarcely enough to purchase subsistence for one day. He boldly added in his letter that he was surprised to see Julian neglect the exalted duties of his position, and provoke the just anger of the Almighty by openly opposing His worship. The emperor was enraged at this pointed rebuke, and he marked out Basil as a victim for severe punishment as soon as he should return from his Persian expedition. But the hand of God was already raised against the profane tryranny. He perished in the summer of 363.

It was with great reluctance that some time after this St. Basil permitted himself to be ordained priest by Eusebius, Archbishop of Cæsa-

rea; and when that prelate died, in 370, our Saint
was chosen and consecrated archbishop. Placed
in that high dignity he seemed to surpass himself
as much as he had before surpassed others. Even
on working days he preached to the people both
morning and evening; and such was the touching
beauty of his discourses that multitudes eagerly
thronged to hear his burning words. He established many pious practices. We learn from his letters
that the good people of Cæsarea received Holy
Communion every Sunday, Wednesday, Friday, and
Saturday.

He was the guardian of the poor and the unfortunate. Besides other countless charities, he
founded a vast hospital, which Gregory Nazianzen
calls a new city, and one of "the wonders of the
world." It continued long after his time, and was
called from him *Basiliades*. The illustrious Saint
often passed through its wards, comforting the
patients, instructing them, and ministering to their
spiritual miseries.

St. Basil was a fortress of the faith, and such was
his fame, the power of his learning, and the holiness
of his life, that his name awed even the imperial
heretics of his time. Of this we have a glorious
proof in the remarkable triumph which he gained
over the Arian emperor, Valens.

With his hands reeking in the martyr blood of
Catholics, Valens passed rapidly through the prov-

inces of Asia Minor. On his arrival in Cappa. docia he stood ready to dart the thunder of his power on the great Archbishop of Cæsarea. He took the precaution, however, of sending before him the prefect, Modestus, with orders to induce Basil, either by threats or promises, to communicate with the Arians.

Modestus summoned the archbishop to appear before him. The Saint came. The prefect, seated on his tribunal, gave him a courteous reception. He tried smooth words and great promises, but all to no purpose. Seeing, however, the failure of this method, the hypocritical Modestus assumed an insolent air.

"Basil, he exclaimed in an angry tone, "what do you mean by opposing a great emperor that all obey? Fear you not the effects of the power with which we are armed?"

"To what does this power extend?" said the Saint.

"To the confiscation of goods, banishment, tortures, and even death," returned the prefect.

"Perhaps you can threaten me with some greater punishment," observed Basil. "None of all these things give me the least uneasiness."

"How so?" demanded Modestus.

"He that has nothing to lose," said the noble archbishop, "is secure against confiscation. I am master of nothing but a few books and the rags I wear—for neither of which, I presume, you have any pressing necessity. As to banishment, I do not see what you could do. Heaven alone is my country. I as little fear your torments. The first stroke would despatch my frail body, and thus put an end both to my life and pain. Death I dread not ; I regard it as a favor. It would bring me sooner to that Almighty Father for whom alone I live."

"Never did any man," exclaimed the astonished prefect, "talk at this rate of freedom to Modestus."

"Perhaps," said Basil, "this is the first time you have had to do with a bishop."

"I give you till to-morrow," shouted the annoyed Modestus, "to deliberate upon the matter."

"I shall be the same man to-morrow," quietly observed the Saint, "that I am to-day."

Valens was enraged at the prefect's want of success, and cited the archbishop to appear before himself. But he the better understood his own littleness after coming in contact with Basil's majestic virtue and dauntless character. The prefect ventured upon a third attack ; but it only added to the Saint's greater glory. "We are overcome," said Modestus to the emperor. "This man is above our threats."

Valens, however, daily importuned by the Ari-

ans, resolved to banish the intrepid archbishop.
The order was drawn up and only remained to be
signed.   He seized one of those reeds which the
ancients used as a pen, and was about to put his
signature to the document, when lo ! the reed broke.
The second and third reed broke in the like manner ; and as he was taking up a fourth, he found his
hand tremble and the tendons of his arm began
to slacken.   In a fright he tore up the paper and
Basil remained unmolested.

The Saint had, indeed, fought the good fight ; but
not many years rolled away when he fell sick.   He
knew the happy end had come.   For him death had
no terrors.   "Into Thy hands, O Lord ! I commend
my spirit," were the last words whispered by the
eloquent lips of this illustrious Doctor of the Church.
He died at the age of fifty-one years, on the 1st of
January, A. D. 379.

The writings of St. Basil are of the very highest order.[8] "When I read his treatise 'On the
Creation,' "says the great Doctor, St. Gregory Nazianzen, "I seem to behold my Creator striking
all things out of nothing.   When I run over his
writings against the heretics, the fire of Sodom

[8] St. Basil wrote in Greek.   His genius brightened everything
touched by his pen.   Many good critics have not hesitated to call
him the most accomplished orator that ever lived, and his style the
best model of genuine eloquence.   He was, indeed, a great master
of eloquence.

sparkles in my view, flashing upon the enemies of the faith and consuming their criminal tongues to ashes. When I consider his work 'On the Holy Ghost,' I feel God working within me, and I am no longer afraid of publishing the truth aloud. When I look into the 'Explanations of the Holy Scripture,' I dive into the most profound abyss of mysteries. His panegyrics on the martyrs make me despise my body, and I seem to be animated with the same noble ardor of battle. His moral discourses assist me to purify my body and soul, that I may become a worthy temple of God, and an instrument of his praises to make known His glory and His power.'"

[9] There is a Church at Toronto, Canada, bearing the name of St. Basil. The Fathers of St. Basil conduct St. Michael's College, Toronto. and Assumption College, Sandwich, Canada.

SAINT MONICA,

MOTHER OF THE GREAT SAINT AUGUSTINE.

DIED A.D. 387

————

MONICA, whose name is one of the glories of the Church in the fourth century was born in Numidia,[1] in the year 332. She belonged to a good Catholic family. From her early life we may learn the power of habit, and the golden value of prudence and temperance. The promising girl by degrees contracted a liking for wine, as she took a sip now and then when sent to the cellar by her mother to draw some for the use of the family.

Though this sipping became habitual, it never grew excessive. It is not hard to see, however, where it might have terminated had not God mercifully checked Monica. A servant-maid was His instrument. One day a curious glance into the cellar revealed her young mistress in the act

---

[1] A country in the north of Africa bordering on the shores of the Mediterranean. It embraced what is now the eastern portion of Algeria.

of drinking. It was not forgotten; and some time after, on words arising between them, the servant taunted Monica by calling her a "wine-bibber." This pointed rebuke acted like the lancet in a happy surgical operation. The future Saint reflected, prayed, and was cured for ever.

Not long after this moral change Monica received baptism,[2] and henceforth her life was that of a true Christian. On reaching the age of womanhood her parents gave her in marriage to a citizen of Tagasté named Patricius, a man of honor, but, unhappily, a heathen. Here was a new field of labor. Monica served her husband with matchless amiability, and toiled to gain him to God. But it was, in truth, a tedious and most difficult undertaking.

As a pagan, Patricius was the slave of vices both nameless and countless. Monica's chief argument to reclaim him was the sanctity of her own conduct, backed by those kind, affectionate manners which could not fail to inspire his love, respect, and esteem. She bore all his sallies of passion with angelic patience. He was a man of hasty and violent temper, but his prudent wife

---

[2] The custom of deferring Baptism was common, it seems, in the early ages of the Church. It was done lest the grace of that holy sacrament should afterwards be stained. See note under the life of St. Augustine.

never annoyed him by the least word or action while she saw him in anger. When, however, the fit was over and Patricius was calm and sensible, she gave him her reasons in a way that was both gentle and impressive.

When Monica saw other women bearing only too visible marks of the anger of their husbands, and heard them bitterly blaming their rough tempers and vicious lives, she would simply reply: "Rather lay the blame on yourselves and your tongues." It was a truth well said, and her own example was a convincing proof. In spite of the unhappy fact that Patricius was a man who often foolishly flew into a towering passion, yet he never forgot the sacred respect due to his wife's person. The storm lasted but a moment And thus Monica, by silence and kindly tact, always had her home lighted up with the blessed sunshine of peace.

This illustrious lady had also the happy gift of making peace among quarrelling neighbors—often a very thankless task. On such occasions she spoke with a force, prudence, and tender charity that was truly wonderful.

It was her great delight to serve the poor. She assisted daily at Mass, and studied to imitate the actions of the Saints. But she never allowed any exercise of piety to stand in the way of the most careful attention in watching over the education of her children,[8] in which, however, Almighty God gave her numberless occasions of merit and suffering—particularly in Augustine—that He might in the end more amply crown her holy toil.

Augustine was born in 354. As he grew up Monica was unceasing in her cares to plant the seed of virtue in his young soul. Still, she was, perhaps, immoderately fond to see him excel in learning, but she flattered herself that he might one day make a good use of it in promoting the honor and glory of God. Her husband desired the same thing, but merely that his son might one day raise himself in the world.

One of the happy fruits of Monica's patience and prayers was the conversion of Patricius. Henceforth he became pure in his life and faithful to the duties of a good Christian. He died in 371 — a year after his baptism.

Augustine, who was then seventeen years of age, was pursuing his studies at Carthage, where, unhappily, he was led astray by the Manichees and joined those vain heretics. His mother was informed of the misfortune, and her grief was inexpressible. Augustine had lost the precious treasure of faith, and to Monica the news was more heartrending than if he were laid in the silent tomb. So deep was her indignation that she would neither

[8] Two sons and one daughter.

suffer him to eat at her table, nor even to live under the same roof with her.

"Thou hast heard her vows," exclaims St. Augustine in after-years, addressing himself to God, "and Thou hast not despised her tears; for she shed torrents in Thy presence—in all places where she offered her prayers to Thee."

Nor were the prayers of the saintly woman unheard. An angel appeared to her in a dream and told her to wipe away her tears, adding: "Your son is with you." She was comforted. She told this dream to Augustine, but he ventured to infer that she would come over to his sentiments in matters of religion. "No," she said with energy, "it was not told me that I was with you, but that *you were with me.*" Such a pointed answer made a great impression on Augustine, as he afterwards acknowledged. This happened in the year 377, and Monica again permitted her son to eat and live in her own dwelling.

Almost nine years, however, passed away before Augustine's conversion; and during all this time Monica appealed to Heaven with sighs and tears and prayers. Once she engaged a learned prelate to speak to him. "The heart of the youth," said he, "is yet too indocile; but God's time will come." On another occasion she urged him with renewed earnestness. "Go," answered the good old bishop, "continue to do as you do.

It is impossible that a child of such tears should perish." Monica went home, bearing these words in her mind as a message from heaven.

When Augustine was twenty-nine years of age, he resolved on going to Rome to teach rhetoric. His mother opposed such a design, fearing it might delay his conversion. She even followed him to the sea-side, determined either to bring him back or to accompany him to Italy. He pretended, however, that he had no intention of going; but one night, while his mother was praying in a chapel, he secretly boarded a vessel bound for Europe.

" I deceived her with a lie," writes St. Augustine, " while she was weeping and praying for me ; and what did she ask of Thee, my God, but that Thou wouldst not suffer me to sail away ! But Thou graciously heard her main desire—that I might be engaged in Thy service—and refused to grant what she asked then, in order to give what she always asked !"

Next morning, on finding that her son had sailed, Monica's grief was boundless. "God," says Butler, " by this extreme affliction would punish her too human tenderness ; and His wisdom suffered her son to be carried by his passions to a place where He had decreed to heal them.

This devoted mother followed her gifted but erring son, and found him at Milan, the city of the great St. Ambrose, where she learned from his own lips that he was no longer a heretic. She now redoubled her tears and prayers for Augustine's thorough conversion, which she had the joy to witness in the summer of 386. He was baptized at the following Easter, with several of his friends.

"My son," said the illustrious Monica, "there is now nothing in this life that affords me any delight. What have I to do here any longer, or why I am here, I know not. All my hopes in this world are at an end. The only thing for which I desired to live was that I might see you a Catholic and a child of Heaven. God has done much more. I see you now despising all earthly felicity and entirely devoting yourself to His service. Then what further business have I here?"

Soon after the Saint and her converted son set out for Africa; but on the road the great woman was seized with a fever. A friend asked her if she was not afraid of being buried so far away from her own country. "Nothing is far from God," she replied. " Nor need I fear that he will not find my body to raise it with the rest."

On reaching the port of Ostia,[4] where they were to embark, she said to her two sons : "You will bury your mother here." Augustine was silent;

---

[4] Ostia, at the mouth of the Tiber, was the port of Rome.

but Navigus expressed a wish that she might not die in a foreign land.

"Lay this body anywhere," she said. "Be not concerned about that. The only thing I ask of you both is—remember me at the altar of God wheresoever you are."

She grew weaker, and soon the beautiful spirit winged its flight to that happy abode where tears and sorrow and suffering are unknown. St. Augustine, who was then thirty-three years of age, closed her eyes — those loving eyes which were so often raised to heaven, so often drowned in the floods of bitter tears that gushed forth for his conversion. And thus died the dear St. Monica, model of all good mothers, at the age of fifty-six, in the year 387.[5]

[5] There is a church bearing the name of St. Monica in New York City, and one at Jamaica, Long Island.

SAINT JEROME,

PRIEST AND DOCTOR OF THE CHURCH.

DIED A. D. 420.

———

ST. JEROME, one of the very greatest lights in the history of learning and Christian literature, was born in the year 329, at Stridonium,[1] in Pannonia.[2] His good Catholic parents gave him an excellent education — that gift more precious than gold or lands.

"Next to the blessing of Redemption," says the celebrated Dr. Doyle,[3] "and the graces consequent upon it, there is no gift bestowed by God equal in value to a good education. Other advantages are enjoyed by the body: this belongs entirely to the spirit. Whatever is great or good

[1] Now Sdrigni, a small town.

[2] Pannonia comprised that part of Hungary which lies west of the Danube, with portions of the provinces of Lower Austria, Styria, Croatia, and Sclavonia. — *Mitchell, Classical Geography.*

The birthplace of St. Jerome was, it seems, near the northeastern borders of Italy.

[3] Bishop of Kildare and Leighlin, Ireland.

or glorious in the works of men is the fruit of educated minds. Religion herself loses half her beauty and influence when not attended or assisted by education ; and her power, splendor, and majesty are never so exalted as when cultivated genius and refined taste become her heralds or her handmaids."

Jerome studied under the first professors at Rome, and became master of the Latin and Greek languages. It was the delight of his soul to collect a good library, and to spend his days and nights with the best authors. He was so carried away by the love of his book-friends that sometimes he even forgot to eat or drink. Cicero and Plautus were his favorites. He not only purchased many works, but copied several with his own hand, and had others transcribed by his friends.[4]

Unhappily, however, there was one drawback. Under pagan teachers and the heathen influences of Rome, Jerome nearly forgot the piety of his boyhood, and became full of refined vanity and worldly sentiments. He had acquired knowledge at the expense of virtue.

On arriving at manhood the ardent student resolved to travel with the view of improving his education. One of his points of attraction was

---

[4] It is to be remembered that this was centuries before the art of printing was invented, and that books were then rare, extremely valuable, and very difficult to multiply.

Treves,[*] then famous for its schools. It was there that his early piety was revived and his heart entirely converted to God. Henceforward he resolved to devote himself wholly to the service of heaven and to a life of chastity. He also began the study of the sacred sciences, and carefully collected everything that might add to his literary treasures. After visiting various other cities, and contracting friendships with many pious and learned men, he returned to Rome, resolved to give himself with his whole soul to study and retirement

But complete solitude could only be found in some distant country; and our Saint set out for the East, accompanied by a priest of Antioch, who acted as guide. The travelers passed through Asia Minor, visiting the hermits and other persons famous for sanctity. Jerome pushed on to Antioch, stayed awhile in that city, and then retired to a hideous desert between Syria and Arabia. He received a warm welcome, however, in that wild, lonely region from the holy Abbot Theodosius.

It was in such an abode of desolation that Jerome, wasted by sickness, was fiercely assailed by nameless temptations. Truly, this was a hard battle, carried on as it was in " the company of scorpions and wild beasts."

[*] Treves, or Trier, is on the Moselle, in Germany.

"I loved solitude," he exclaims, " that in the bitterness of my soul I might more freely bewail my
miseries and call upon my Saviour. My hideous,
emaciated limbs were covered with sackcloth. My
skin was parched, dry, and black, and my flesh was almost wasted away.

"The days passed in tears and groans, and
when, against my will, sleep overpowered me, I
cast my weary bones—which barely hung together
—upon the hard ground, not so much to give them
rest as to torture myself. Of eating and drinking
I say nothing. The monks in that desert,
even when they are sick, know no other drink
than cold water, and look upon it as sensuality ever
to taste anything touched by fire."

Yet, in this dreary den of penitential solitude,
Jerome had to battle long and manfully with temptations against the virtue of purity.

"Finding myself," continues the Saint, "abandoned, as it were, to the power of this enemy, I
threw myself in spirit at the feet of Jesus, watering them with my tears, and I tamed my flesh by
fasting whole weeks. I am not ashamed to dis-
close my temptations; but I grieve that I am not
now what I then was.

"I often joined whole nights to the days—weeping, sighing, and beating my breast till the desired calm returned. I feared the very cell in which
I lived, because it was a witness to the foul sug-

gestions of my enemy; and being angry and armed with severity against myself, I went alone into
the most secret parts of the wilderness, and if I
discovered a deep valley or a craggy rock anywhere, that was the place of my prayer — there I
threw this miserable sack of my body.   The same
Lord is my witness that after so many sobs and
tears, after having in much sorrow long looked
up to heaven, I felt most delightful and interior
sweetness."

It was during this period of severe trial that
he began the study of Hebrew. [6] "That I might
subdue my flesh," writes the great Doctor, "I
became a scholar to a monk who had been a Jew,
to learn of him the Hebrew alphabet; and after
I had most diligently studied the judicious rules of
Quintilian, the flowing eloquence of Cicero, the
grave style of Fronto, and the smoothness of Pliny,
I inured myself to hissing and broken-winded words.

"What labor it cost me, what difficulties I went
through, how often I despaired and left off, and
how I began again to learn, both I myself who
felt the burden can witness, and they also who

[6] Hebrew was carefully cultivated in the Jewish academy or
great school of Tiberias (in Palestine), out of which St. Jerome
had a master.   It has long since become very imperfect, reduced
to a small number of radical words, and only to be learned from
the Hebrew Bible—the only ancient book in the world extant in
the language.—*Butler.*

lived with me. But I thank our Lord that I now gather sweet fruit from the bitter seed of those studies."

Jerome, however, had still a passion for the Latin classics, especially the writings of Cicero. He relates that on one occasion, while prostrated by a burning fever, he fell into a trance or dream, in which he seemed to be summoned before the awful tribunal of Christ. He was asked his profession. "I am a Christian," answered Jerome.

"It is a lie," said the Judge. "You are a Ciceronian. The works of that author possess your heart." And the Saint was condemned to be scourged by angels. The remembrance of that dream—for dream it was—made a vivid impression on his imagination. He looked upon it as a divine admonition. "From that time," he says, "I gave myself to the reading of divine things with greater diligence and attention than I had ever read other authors."

As an unhappy schism divided the church of Antioch, St. Jerome wrote to Pope Damasus, about the year 376, asking for advice in relation to the delicate state of affairs. "I am joined in communion with your Holiness," he writes, " that is, with the Chair of Peter. I know the Church is built upon that rock. Whoever eats the lamb out of that house is a profane person. Whoever is not in the ark shall perish in the flood. . . . Whoever gath-

ers not with you, scatters.   He who is not Christ's
belongs to Antichrist.''

The Pope's reply is not extant.

In 377 St. Jerome, at the age of forty-eight, was
raised to the sacred dignity of the priesthood by
Paulinus, Patriarch of Antioch.   He consented to
this promotion, however, only on the express condition that he would not be obliged to serve any
church in the office of his ministry.

Soon after this he passed into Palestine, perfect-
ed himself in the Hebrew language, and visited and
carefully examined all the places made sacred by the
presence of Jesus Christ.

We find our admirable Saint, always a student,
at Constantinople, about the year 380, making a
profound study of Holy Scripture under St. Gregory Nazianzen.   He considered it a great honor
and happiness to have this celebrated doctor for
his master.

On visiting Rome in 381, Jerome was detained
by Pope Damasus as his secretary.   But the
light of his life could not be hidden.   He was
soon loved and esteemed by all.   Priests, monks,
and nobles sought his instruction and asked his
guidance in the way of Christian virtue.   He had
likewise the charge of many devout ladies whose
names have since adorned the calendar of the
saints.'

---

¹ The most illustrious of the Roman ladies whom St. Jerome

St. Jerome wrote his work "On the Perpetual Virginity of the Blessed Virgin Mary" in the year 383. It was composed in answer to the blasphemies of a malignant heretic named Helvidius, a man of coarse and brutal instincts. The holy Doctor placed his iron grip on this vile assailant of the Immaculate Mother, in order, as he says, "to

instructed was St. Paula, who persuaded him to accept a lodging in her hospitable home during his stay at Rome, that she and her family might the more easily have recourse to him as their spiritual guide. This St. Paula was a lady of culture and extensive learning—one who did not forget that lofty sentiments and noble aspirations are incompatible with mental poverty. She was a model for the earnest women of our age and country.

"Amongst other lessons," says the great Bishop Dupanloup, "to be derived from the biography of St. Paula, we may learn the immense advantage accruing to spiritual life from mental culture, and the need in which women stand, both on account of their exalted mission and of the immense influence it is given them to exercise on human character, of vigorous training and well-grounded instruction, if they are to be equal to their important duties and to escape that frivolity by which so many lives are wasted. To be for man the helpmate and stay which God has meant her to be; to form the mind, heart, conscience, and character of her children; to be the guiding, regulating spirit, the active centre of a Christian home, is a task far beyond the capacity of an ignorant, narrow, frivolous, and superficial mind—a task requiring habits of vigorous, self-denying virtue. But it were vain to look for such unless the soul be prepared by a serious training and real instruction. This is the only solid groundwork of a serious life, without which there is no promise of stability, and all we may look for is to behold the choicest endowments of mind and character stunted by a wretched mediocrity of aims and of practice."
—*Studious Women.*

teach one who had never learned to speak the art and wisdom of silence."

We need not say how well the task was accomplished. St. Jerome never did anything by halves, and his pen was like a mighty battle-axe that clove the toughest and most obstinate skulls. "Having thus worsted you in argument," he says in taking leave of the foul Helvidius, "I know full well that you will seek to decry my life and to soil my character; but I glory therein beforehand, since such abuse will proceed from lips that have blasphemed Mary, and I, a servant of the Lord, will, even as His Mother, be the butt of your brawling insolence."

After the death of Pope Damasus our illustrious Doctor retired to Palestine and journeyed through Egypt to improve himself still more in the sacred sciences. On returning to the Holy Land he made his abode at Bethlehem. Here the noble lady, St. Paula, followed him from Rome, built him a monastery, and placed under his wise direction a convent of nuns which she founded and governed.

It was at this period that St. Jerome, living on the spot where Christ came into our sin-dimmed world, and where the angels sang "*Gloria in Excelsis Deo*," began those vast critical labors on the Holy Scriptures which have rendered his name so celebrated.

"For this," says Butler, "the Church acknowledges him to have been raised by God through a special providence and particularly assisted from above; and she styles him the *greatest* of all her doctors in expounding the Divine Oracles. Pope Clement VIII. scruples not to call him a man, in translating the Holy Scriptures, divinely assisted and inspired.'"

[8] Latin was the language of the Roman Empire, and a Latin translation of the Bible was made in the time of the Apostles, and approved, it seems, by St. Peter himself. But in the fourth century great variations had crept into many copies of the Sacred Book. To remedy this evil, and to correct the faults of bold or careless copiers, Pope Damasus commissioned St. Jerome to revise and correct the Latin version of the Gospels by the original Greek. He did his work to the great satisfaction of the whole Church, and some time later he translated the remainder of the New Testament. "His new translation," says Butler, "of the books of the Old Testament, written in Hebrew, made from the original text, was a more noble and more difficult undertaking." This version of St. Jerome was approved by Pope St. Gregory the Great, and since the seventh century it has been used by the Catholic Church under the name of the *Vulgate*—from the Latin *vulgatus*—that is, for general or common use. In 1546 the General Council of Trent placed its seal of unerring approval on the *Latin Vulgate*. Our Douay Version was made directly from the Vulgate. The late General Council of the Vatican, presided over by the immortal Pius IX., passed the following important decrees:

"If any one shall not receive as sacred and canonical the Books of Sacred Scripture, entire with all their parts, as the Holy Council of Trent has enumerated them, or shall deny that they have been divinely inspired, let him be anathema."—*Canon IV., on Revelation.*

"These Books of the Old and New Testament are to be re-

He defended the faith against the vain Pela‑
gius with his usual vigor and success. "I nevei
spared heretics," he writes, "and have done my
utmost endeavors that the enemies of the Church
should be my enemies." Nor did the Pelagians
ever forgive St. Jerome. Their blind and head‑
strong leader became so infuriated that he excited
his followers to a high pitch against the holy Doc‑
tor. A troop of these ruffians plundered and burn‑
ed his monastery; and the Saint only escaped their
fury by a timely flight.

After this storm blew over the great old Doctor
—veteran soldier of Jesus Christ—still continued
his precious labors. He toiled on to the last,
a lover of God and truth and books. Some re‑
markable sayings are attributed to him. "Wheth‑
er I eat or drink," he observed, "or whatever
else I do, the dreadful trnmpet of the last day seems
always sounding in my ears: *Arise, ye dead and come
to judgment !*"

ceived as sacred and canonical, in their integrity, with all their
parts, as they are enumerated in the decree of the said council
(Trent), and are contained in the ancient Latin edition of the Vul‑
gate. These the Church holds to be sacred and canonical, not
because, having been carefully composed by mere human indus‑
try, they were afterwards approved by her authority, nor merely
because they contain revelation with no admixture of error, but
because, having been written by the inspiration of the Holy Ghost,
they have God for their Author, and have been delivered
as such to the Church herself."—*Decrees and Canons of the Vatican
Council.*

His boldness and manly vigor in defending the sacred cause of truth did not fail to make many bitter enemies. "You are deceived," he would say, "if you think that a Christian can live without persecution. He suffers the greatest who lives under none. Nothing is more to be feared than too long a peace. A storm puts a man upon his guard, and obliges him to exert his utmost efforts to escape shipwreck."

On his deathbed he said to his dear disciples, who had mournfully gathered around : "My children, I am at the point of death ; and I declare to you that it is my firm, unwavering conviction—a conviction strengthened by a long experience of over fifty years—that out of a hundred thousand persons who continue in sin till the hour of death scarcely one is saved."

Having manfully subdued himself, and triumphed over vice, heresy, and ignorance, the illustrious St. Jerome, who had used all his splendid genius in promoting the glory of God, passed from toil to reward at the ripe age of ninety-one, on the 30th of September, 420.[9]

[9] There are Catholic churches in the diocese of Springfield and several other places in this republic called after St. Jerome ; and a college at Berlin, Ontario, Canada, bears the name of the renowned Doctor.

ST. AUGUSTINE,

BISHOP OF HIPPO AND DOCTOR OF THE CHURCH.

DIED A. D 430.

S T. AUGUSTINE,[1] the model of penitents, the Doctor of Doctors, and the most illustrious champion of the faith, was born at Tagasté,[2] a small town of Numidia,[3] Africa, on the 13th of November, 354. His parents, Patricius and Monica, were in good circumstances. His father was a pagan, but his mother was a Saint; and, as we shall soon see, it is a precious blessing to have a saintly mother.[4]

[1]Augustine is from the Latin, and signifies *belonging to Augustus.* It is sometimes contracted into *Austin.*

[2]Tagasté was in the interior, at some distance from the sea, "which," says Butler, "the Saint had never seen till he was grown up."— *Lives of the Saints,* vol. viii.

[3] Numidia was a nation in the north of Africa, its shores being washed by the Mediterranean Sea. Under the Carthaginians and Romans it was a fertile land, distinguished for wealth, prosperity, and population. St. Augustine is, doubtless, its most illustrious son. Numidia occupied what is now the eastern portion of Algeria.

[4] See the life of St. Monica.

Monica was unceasing in her cares to plant the golden seed of virtue in the tender soul of her boy She taught him to pray. She pointed out to him the glory and beauty of the Catholic religion. He was made a catechumen. [5] Once while Augustine was going to school in his native town he fell dangerously ill, and asked to be baptized, and his mother got everything ready for the ceremony; but he suddenly grew better, and it was deferred. This was done lest he should afterwards stain the grace of that holy sacrament. [6]

The worldly Patricius was not slow in perceiving the budding genius of Augustine, and he spared nothing to make him a scholar. Monica eagerly backed the good work, and every effort was made to press him forward on the road of knowledge. When a little one he greatly dreaded correction, as he tells us in his "Confessions," and often did he pray to Heaven with childish earnestness that he might escape punishment

[5] A catechumen was made by being marked with the sign of the cross and by blessed salt being put in his mouth.—*Butler.*

[6] This custom of deferring Baptism, for fear of sinning under the weight and obligations of that sacrament, St. Augustine most justly condemns; but then the want of a sense of the sanctity of that sacrament, and the frequent perfidiousness and sacrileges of Christians in defiling it by relapsing into sin, is an abuse which, in these latter ages, calls for our tears and for all our zeal. The Church has long since forbidden the Baptism of infants ever to be deferred.—*Butler.*

at school, deeming it the most gigantic of evils.
The Saint complains, and justly too, of those
hard, austere teachers who cloud the bright days
of boyhood by multiplying that labor and sorrow
through which all the children of Adam are obliged
to pass.[7]

Augustine was a most gifted student. He read
the Latin poets with delight, and was noted for
his lively wit. But in after-years he deplored
that pernicious spirit in the schools which made
scholars more afraid of an offence against the rules
of grammar than a violation of the commandments
of God.

But the fatal rock on which he struck was bad
company. It was his first step down the slippery
path of sin—that highway to perdition.

> "He that once sins, like him that slides on ice,
> Goes swiftly down the slippery ways of vice;
> Though conscience checks him, yet, those rubs gone o'er,
> He slides as smoothly and looks back no more."[8]

It is a curse to have wicked companions, for

---

[7] It is a great abuse of the young intellect to overtax the memory
of children. Such a course often blights both mind and
body. Many teachers and parents display a sad lack of knowledge
on this important point. Nothing but vanity or criminal
ignorance will ever allow children to injure either health or eyesight
in the pursuit of knowledge. All study that is to redound to the
glory of God and the good of the student must be guided by religion,
prudence, and good sense.

[8] Dryden.

example is powerful. It seduces the young, the thoughtless, the weak-willed. "Let us go," "Let us do it," exclaims youthful scoundrelism, and every one is ashamed not to be shameless.

Augustine went down step by step, until at last he fell into the cesspool of impurity. He was led into this mire of iniquity as much by the dangerous example of others as by idleness and the reading of immodest plays in Terence. He did not pray, he did not avoid the occasions of sin; and let nobody wonder that this bright, promising young man soon found himself swimming in the putrid waters of vice.

Patricius, as a pagan, was ignorant of the very meaning of that Christian word, *virtue;* and, in relation to the reprehensible conduct of his son, he used no fatherly restraint. He merely winked at his vices and follies, provided Augustine toil-ed hard to be a scholar. But how the tender, motherly heart of Monica bled! She prayed and admonished.

It "seemed to me," says the Saint himself, "but the admonitions of a woman, which I was ashamed to obey; but, O God! they were Thy admonitions, and I knew it not. By her Thou didst speak to me, and in her I despised Thee. Yet I knew it not, and with such blindness did I rush on that among my equals I was ashamed of being less guilty than others when I heard them bragging of their atrocious actions. I had a mind to do the same."

In his seventeenth year Augustine was sent to Carthage,[9] where he easily held the first place in the school of rhetoric. He flung himself into study with all the ardor and energy of genius, but his motives, as he avows, were neither lofty nor Christian. He labored merely through vanity and ambition. Nor did progress in knowledge improve his life; for he was still the base slave of his passions. A year passed, and his father Patricius died in the Catholic faith—a happy result brought about by the example, tears, and prayers of the kind, devoted St. Monica.

Augustine continued to pursue his studies at Carthage. He carefully read Cicero, Aristotle, and other heathen philosophers. At length, however, he grew weary of their company and turned to the Holy Scripture; but he was too proud and unspiritual to profit by the perusal of that sacred volume. He disliked its simplicity of style. Nor

[9] Carthage was one of the great cities of ancient times. At one period it was twenty-three miles in circumference and had 700,000 inhabitants. It was for more than seven hundred years the capital of the republic of Carthage, which became a great commercial and maritime power, and planted colonies all along the coasts of Northern Africa, and also in Spain, Sicily, Corsica, and Sardinia. —*Mitchell.*

was it long till unfortunately he fell into heresy by joining a vain sect called the Manichees. [10]

For nearly nine years he continued wandering in error—from the age of nineteen to that of twenty-eight. Thus corruption of heart degraded and blinded the intellect, and created an intense loathing of all things spiritual. Thus the mind was predisposed to error, and poor misguided reason fell into heresy. "I sought with pride," says the Saint in his 'Confessions,' "what only humility could make me find."

Unhappily, Augustine's vanity was flattered by the wily Manichees. They pretended to try everything by the test of reason alone. [11] They scoffed at the authority of the Catholic Church. They made a foolish parade of science. But these hardened, short-sighted heretics were too blind to comprehend that there has ever been and ever must be complete harmony between sound reason and true science and the divine authority of the Church of God. [12] "All heretics," declares

[10] Originated by Manes, an apostate priest.

[11] The sublime mysteries of religion are *above* reason—but not *contrary* to it—hence it is not the sphere of reason to sit in judgment on those heavenly truths. Reason cannot logically constitute itself judge of the supernatural.

"If any one shall say," declares the Council of the Vatican "that human reason is so independent that faith cannot be enjoined upon it by God, let him be anathema."—*Decrees and Canons.*

[12] Faith and reason can never be opposed to one another

the great Doctor himself, "generally deceived **by**
a parade of science, and blame the simplicity of
believers."

But in spite of Augustine's errors of mind and
heart, his progress in learning was truly extraordinary. At twenty years of age he had mastered
most of the liberal sciences. "What did this
profit me," he exclaims, "when it did me harm?"
Alas! he knew everything but himself and the true
knowledge of God.

The grief of St. Monica at the fall of her gifted son into heresy was inexpressible. She prayed, and wept, and admonished. She regarded him
as worse than a heathen, because he would not
hear the Church; and when he returned to his
native town she forbade him to eat at her table,
or even to enter her door. The noble mother
used this severity and pointed indignation in
order to make Augustine enter into himself. He
was mentally intoxicated. He was bloated with
conceit.

St. Monica besought a learned bishop to speak
to her son; but the prelate excused himself, say-

" Although faith is above reason," say the Fathers of the Vatican
Council, " there can never be any real discrepancy between faith
and reason, since the same God who reveals mysteries and infuses
faith has bestowed the light of reason on the human mind; and
God cannot deny Himself, nor can truth ever contradict truth."
—*Decrees ana Canons*.

ing that the misguided young man was not yet fit for profitable instruction. " Only pray to our Lord for your son," he said, "and he will at length discover his error and impiety."

Soon the devoted lady came again with the same earnest request ; but the good old bishop dismissed her, saying : "Go, and God will bless your son. It cannot be that the child of such tears should perish.'' She was comforted, and received those words as if they had been whispered by an angel from heaven.

After having opened for a time a school of rhetoric at Carthage, Augustine determined to go to Rome, which seemed to offer a wider field for his ambition. He went against the wishes of his mother. On reaching the imperial city, however, he fell sick, and was soon at the point of death "Where would I have gone," he writes, "if I had then died, but into those flames and torments which I deserved?"

On regaining health he opened a school of rhetoric in the great city, and students flocked to fill the benches. He soon became very popular. His kind ways and sweetness of temper were as much admired as the sparkle of his wit and the brilliancy of his learning. But in a short time he was called to Milan, where the Emperor Valentinian the Younger kept his court.

The reception of Augustine at Milan was very

flattering.   Even the great St. Ambrose,[13] then
archbishop of that city, showed him particular
marks of respect.   The young professor often attended his sermons, and no doubt many a grain of
good seed fell on the hard ground of his soul.
Though full of pride and prejudice, his eyes were,
by degrees, opened to the beauty of virtue and the
sublimity of the Catholic Church.

At length, he addressed himself in his difficulties
to Simplician, an aged and learned priest of Milan.
This was a wise step on the way to truth; but
Augustine was still held captive by the tyranny of
his passions.   "I sighed and longed to be delivered,"
he exclaims mournfully, "but was kept fast bound,
not with chains or irons, but with my own iron will.
The enemy held my will and made a chain of it that
fettered me fast."

Truly, in the words of the old hymn, two men were
striving within him :

> "Mon Dieu ! quelle guerre cruelle—
> Je trouve deux homme en moi."[14]

It was the vice of impurity especially that par-
alyzed the effort of this gifted man to rise at once
from the mire of sin and walk in the bright way

[13] "St. Ambrose is one of the nineteen immortal Doctors of the
Church. He died in 397.

> [14] "My God ! what war I wage—
> Two men within me strive."

of virtue.   The divine dignity of chastity, it is
true, forced itself upon his keen, cultured mind;
but, on the other hand, the power of evil habits
was terrible.   He was chained down; but he wept
and cried to Heaven.   At length the grace of
God came, and Augustine triumphed over himself.   His conversion happened at the age of
thirty-two, in the year 386.   In company with his
now overjoyed mother—who had devotedly followed him to Italy — he retired to a country-house
near Milan.

While thus in solitude, employed in prayer and
penance, he tells us that God, "by his grace
brought down the pride of his spirit, and laid low
the mountains of his vain thoughts by daily bringing him to a greater sense of that misery and bond-
age from which he had just escaped."

He wept over the wounds and spiritual miseries
of his tempest-tossed soul.   He thought of the
precious time he had lost in pursuing toys of vanity and phantoms of shame, and, looking up to
heaven, he exclaimed from the bottom of his now
burning and repentant heart: "O Beauty, ever
ancient and ever new, too late have I known Thee,
too late have I loved Thee !"

Augustine was baptized by St. Ambrose on
Easter Eve, in the year 387.   No sooner had he
received the sacrament of regeneration than happily he found himself freed from all anxiety in re-

lation to his past life.   Thus he began to taste the
sweets of virtue; he began to know the peace and
beauty of a good life. "Keep a good conscience,"
says à Kempis, " and thou shalt always have
joy."

The illustrious convert resolved to return to
Africa, but had only reached the port of Ostia
when he lost that model of good, tender, and heroic mothers—St. Monica.   It was only after she
was piously interred that he gave vent to tears,
and then they flowed in streams down his manly
face. "If any one think it a fault," he exclaims,
"that I thus wept for my mother some small part
of an hour—and a mother who during many years
had wept for me that I might live in Thy eyes, O
Lord! — let him not scoff at me for it, but, if his
charity is great, rather let him weep also for my
sins before Thee."

He landed at Carthage in 388.   Retiring at
once to his country-house, he lived for nearly
three years entirely disengaged from all temporal
concerns, meditating day and night on the law of
God, fasting, praying, and instructing others by
his books and discourses.   A few pious friends
gathered around him.   He settled his paternal
estate on the church of Tagasté, only on condition that the bishop should furnish him with a
yearly sum sufficient for his support among his
religious companions.   In their house everything

was in common.   It is from this period that the Order of St. Augustine dates its origin.

Augustine was ordained priest, much against his own wishes, in 390.[15]   "O my father Valerius !" he said to the Bishop of Hippo, "do you command me to perish?   Where is your charity? Do you love me?   Do you love your church?   I am sure you love both me and your church.   But many things are wanting to me for the discharge of this employment, which are not to be attained but as our Lord directs us, by asking, seeking, and knocking—that is, by praying, reading, and weeping."

Feeling in the depth of his great soul that the instruction of the flock is the chief duty of the pastor, death alone interrupted the course of the Saint's eloquent sermons.   He preached every day, and sometimes twice a day.   Often he was so weak that he could scarcely speak, but he ceased not to instruct.[16]   Such was his ardor for the salvation of souls that he forgot the pains of sickness.

As Valerius, Bishop of Hippo, was bending under the weight of years, he had Augustine

[15] The disorders of his youth would have been a perpetual disqualification or irregularity, had they happened *after* his baptism ; but from that time he was become a new man, and was then more conspicuous for piety than for his great learning.—*Butler.*

[16] St. Augustine always preached in Latin.

nominated his coadjutor; but the Saint **vigor-**ously opposed the project. He was compelled, however, to submit to the will of Heaven, and was consecrated in December, 395. Valerius died the year following.

We have not space to speak at length of St. Augustine in his new dignity as Bishop of Hippo."
He was a bishop of bishops.

> " He tried each art, reproved each dull delay,
>   Allured to brighter worlds, and led the way."

The Saint's clothes and furniture were modest and in good taste, but rigidly simple. With the exception of spoons, no silver was used in his house. His dishes were of earth, wood, or marble. He exercised a kind hospitality. During meals he loved reading or the discussion of literary topics rather than ordinary conversation. He abhorred detraction, and in order to warn his guests to shun it, the following lines were written on his table

> " This board allows no vile detractor place,
>   Whose tongue shall charge the absent with disgrace."

Should any one forget himself on that point, the great Bishop at once arose and retired to his room. His love for the poor was intense ; nor was he afraid

---

" Hippo (often called Hippo-Regius) was a city on the seacoast of Numidia. Its chief glory is that St. Augustine was its bishop.

to contract considerable debts that he might supply
their wants. He scarcely ever made any other
visits than to orphans, widows, the sick, and the distressed. But his zeal for the salvation of his whole
flock seemed boundless.

"I desire not to be saved without you," said he
to his people. "What shall I desire? What shall I
say? Why am I a bishop? Why am I in the world
only to live in Jesus Christ? It is but to live in
Him with you. This is my passion, my honor, my
glory, my joy, and my riches."

The charitable zeal of St. Augustine in combating the heretics of his time is beyond all praise.
In public and private he made war on religious error; and his kindness and vast learning carried all before them. Nor was his golden pen ever idle. He
was the light of his day and country as well as of
after-ages.

When his last illness came, this great Doctor
ordered the *Seven Penitential Psalms* to be written
out and hung in tablets on the wall near his bed.
Thus, lying on the couch of death, he read and
re-read the contrite words of David with tears
streaming down his venerable cheeks. He made
no will, for he possessed nothing. To the end his
luminous intellect shone out clear and vigorous,
and his last days were an almost ceaseless prayer.
He died, with the blissful calmness of one who
knows that he is going to receive the reward of

the faithful servant, at the ripe age of seventy-six years—over forty of which he had spent in the service of Heaven—on the 28th of August, A. D. 430.

St. Augustine is the prince of the Fathers and Doctors. Popes, councils, and the whole Church have honored his holy memory and his immortal writings.[18] But the greatness and sanctity of this illustrious man were built up on the broad and deep foundations of humility. He was little in his own eyes. "Attempt not," he writes, " to reach true wisdom by any other road than that which God has appointed. In the first, second, and third place, this is *humility;* and as often as you ask me I must give the same answer. There are

[18]His "Confessions" and "The City of God'" are, perhaps, the best known of all his works. In his "Confessions" the great Saint lays open the errors of his conduct with the most sincere humility and compunction. The "City of God" is a profoundly learned defence of the Christian religion. It is one of the greatest monuments of human genius. Others among the Fathers and Doctors of the Church may have been more learned or masters of a purer style, but none more powerfully touched the heart and kindled within it the fire of religion.

His famous remark on the name Catholic is even more sugges-tive in our day than it was when penned over fourteen centuries ago. "I am retained in the Church," he says, "by her very name of CATHOLIC; for it was not without a cause that she alone, amid so many heresies, obtained that name. All the heretics de-sire to be called Catholics ; but if a stranger asks them which is the Church of the Catholics, none of them venture to point out their Church."

indeed, other precepts, but unless humility go before, accompany, and follow, all the merit of our good actions is snatched away by pride."[19]

[19] The Order of St. Augustine was introduced into the United States in 1790. St. Augustine's Church, in Philadelphia, was committed to the flames by a mob of fanatics in 1844. (See our "Popular History of the Catholic Church in the United States," p. 240.) It was afterwards rebuilt. The Augustinian Fathers now direct over twenty churches in various states. They also conduct Villanova College, Pa. The *first* American Indian who was raised to the dignity of priesthood was educated by the Augustinians and became a member of their order. He belonged to the Iroquois, or Five Nations, and was captured by the Spaniards in the early part of the seventeenth century. The *oldest* city in the United States is named after this great Doctor. It was founded by Melendez, a Spanish admiral, in the year 1565.

SAINT PATRICK,

THE APOSTLE OF IRELAND.

DIED A.D. 465.

"All praise to St. Patrick, who brought to our mountains
 The gift of God's faith, the sweet light of His love;
All praise to the shepherd who showed us the fountains
 That rise in the heart of the Saviour above !

"There is not a Saint in the bright courts of heaven
 More faithful than he to the land of his choice;
Oh ! well may the nation to whom he was given
 In the feast of their sire and Apostle rejoice.
    In glory above,
    True to his love,
He keeps the false faith from his children away—
    The dark, false faith
    Far worse than death."
       —Faber.

T. PATRICK, whose noble name [1] is re-
vered in many lands, was born in the
year 387, at Boulogne, in the north of
France. [2] His father, Calphurnius, and his moth-

----

[1] Patrick is from the Latin, and signifies *noble*.

[2] There is a curious want of unanimity amongst ecclesiastical historians as to the birthplace of St. Patrick. Baronius and

er, Conchessa, a niece of St. Martin, Archbishop of Tours, were persons of rank and virtue. Conchessa, it is said, was noted for elegance of manners and beauty of person.

The Saint's childhood was marked by many miraculous incidents. We can give but one. While running about in a field one of his sisters slipped and fell, striking her forehead against a sharp stone. The girl was so stunned and severely wounded that she seemed to be lifeless. Friends anxiously gathered around, and her little brother was soon on the scene. Patrick's surgery was wonderful. He made the sign of the cross on her blood-stained countenance, and instantly the wound was healed. But the scar remained as a sign to mark the spot where faith and holiness had gained a victory.

The boy grew up in the bright way of virtue. His merits far surpassed his years. In the words of the venerable monk Jocelin, he went "forward in the slippery paths of youth and held his feet from falling. The garment that nature had woven for him—unknown to stain—he preserved whole, living

others say he was born in Ireland ; Usher and his followers make him a native of Scotland ; and others give him a still different origin. But this disputed point seems to have been finally settled by the learned Dr. Lanigan in his ''Ecclesiastical History of Ireland." He proves that the Saint was born at Boulogne, in France. See Lanigan's ''Ecclesiastical History of Ireland" and Sister Cusack's "Life of St. Patrick."

a virgin in mind and body.   On the arrival of the
fit time he was sent from his parents to be instructed in sacred learning.

"He applied his mind to the study of letters,
but chiefly to psalms and hymns and spiritual
songs, retaining them in his memory and continually singing them to the Lord ; so that even from
the flower of his first youth he was daily wont to
sing devoutly unto God the whole psalter, and
from his most pure heart to pour forth many
prayers."[3]

But the day of trial was at hand.   The future
Apostle of Erin was to be tested as gold in a furnace.   When he had reached the age of sixteen,
the famous King Niall of the Nine Hostages,
monarch of Ireland,[4] swept along the coast of
France on a marauding expedition, and captured
the good youth with many of his countrymen.
Patrick was carried to the shores of Ireland, and

---

[3] "The Life and Acts of St. Patrick."

[4] Niall the Great, or, as he is usally called, Niall of the Nine
Hostages, was the one hundred and twenty-sixth monarch of Ireland.

Ireland is a fertile and beautiful island 306 miles in length and
180 in breadth.   It has been known at various periods of history as
Erin, Hibernia, and *Scotia.* It was called Hibernia by Cæsar, Pliny
Tacitus, and other Roman writers.   The name of Scotia was ex-
clusively applied to Ireland until the eleventh century, when it was
transferred to Scotland, called Alba, and sometimes Scotia Minor,
before that period.   Ireland has been so named by the English during the last seven or eight centuries

sold as a slave to Milcho, a chief ruling over a portion of the county of Antrim

The young captive was chiefly employed in tending herds of sheep and swine on the mountains. It was a period of sore adversity. But his soul rose above such lowly occupations and held unbroken communion with Heaven. Thus, in the heat of summer and the biting blasts of winter, on the steep sides of Slieb-mish[5] or on the lone hill-tops of Antrim, he recalled the sacred presence of God; and made it a practice to say "a hundred prayers by day and nearly as many more by night."[6]

---

[5] *Slieb-mish* (the dish-shaped mountain) is one of the most beautiful elevations in Ireland. It rises in the form of a truncated cone to the height of eighteen hundred feet, in the midst of a fine, level, fertile district, about the centre of the county of Antrim. It is flat on the top, which is watered by a never-failing spring. The sides are clothed with the greenest of grass, and to this day Slieb-mish is what it was in the days of St. Patrick—a pasture-ground for sheep. For the foregoing description of this famous mountain the writer is indebted to his father, Mr. Edward Murray.

[6] "But after I had come to Ireland I was employed in tending sheep, and I prayed frequently during the day. The love of God, and His faith and fear, increased in me more and more, and the spirit was stirred, so that in a single day I have said as many as a hundred prayers and at night nearly the same   Though I remained in the woods and on the mountain, even before dawn, I was aroused to prayer, in snow and ice and rain; and I felt no injury from it, nor was there any slothfulness in me, as I see now, because my soul was then fervent."—*Confessions of St. Patrick*

After Patrick had served Milcho for six years, he was one night favored with a vision, as he relates in his "Confessions." "You fast well', said the voice. "You will soon go to your own country. The ship is ready."

To Patrick this was welcome news.

"Then girding close his mantle, and grasping fast his wand,
He sought the open ocean through the by-ways of the land."

A ship, indeed, was about to sail, but he had much difficulty in obtaining a place on board. After a passage of three days he landed at Treguier, in Brittany. He was still, however, a long distance from his native place, and in making the journey he suffered much from hunger and fatigue. But he bravely triumphed over all obstacles—including the devil, who one night fell upon him like a huge stone—and reached home at the age of twenty-two, about the year 410.

The Saint now formed the resolution of devoting himself wholly to the service of God, and retired to the celebrated monastery of St. Martin at Tours, where he spent four years in study and prayer. After this he returned home for a time.

It was not long, however, before Patrick's future mission was shadowed forth by a vision. One night a dignified personage appeared to him, bearing many letters from Ireland. He handed the Saint one, on which was written: "THIS IS THE VOICE OF THE IRISH." While in the act of reading, he says, "I seemed to hear the voices of people from the wood of Fochut, [1] near the western sea, crying out with one accord: '*Holy youth, we implore thee to come and walk still amongst us.*'" Patrick's noble heart was touched. He "awoke, and could read no longer."

Saint and student that he was, Patrick now began to prepare himself with redoubled vigor for the vast work that lay before him. He placed himself under the guidance of St. Germain, the illustrious Bishop of Auxerre, who sent him to a famous seminary on the isle of Lerins, where he spent nine years in study and retirement. [8] It was here that he received the celebrated crosier called the *Staff of Jesus,* which he afterwards car-

---

[1] The village bearing the name of *Tocoill,* but little varied from the ancient name, *Fochut,* found in St. Patrick's biography, is yet to be seen on the west of Killala, not far from the Bay of Kilcummin.—*Archbishop McHale's Letters.*

[8] Lerins is an island in the Mediterranean, not far from Toulon. In 410, the very year in which St. Patrick escaped from captivity, a young noble, who preferred poverty to riches and asceticism to pleasure, made for himself a home. The island was barren, deserted, and infested by serpents—all the more reason for his choice. The barrenness soon disappeared, for labor was one of the most important duties of the monk; and it is scarcely an exaggeration to say that one-half of the marshes of Europe were reclaimed and made fruitful by these patient tillers of the soil.—*Sister Cusack, Life of St. Patrick.*

ried with **him in his** apostolic visitations through
Ireland. [9]

The learned and saintly priest returned to his
patron, St. Germain, and passed several years in
the work of the holy ministry and in combating
heresy.   In 430, however, St. Germain sent him
to Rome with letters of introduction to the Holy
Father, warmly recommending him as one in
every way qualified for the great mission of converting the Irish people.   A residence of six
years in the country, a perfect knowledge of its
language, customs, and inhabitants, and a life of
study, innocence, and sanctity—these were the

[9] In the "Tripartite Life of St. Patrick," written by St. MacEvin
in the sixth century, it is stated that the Saint received this staff from
the Lord Himself, who " said that it would be of assistance to him
in every danger and every difficulty."

Jocelin, in his "Life and Acts of St. Patrick," composed in
the twelfth century, exclaims: "Oh excellent gift, descending from
the Father of Light! . . . For as the Lord did many miracles
by the rod in the hand of Moses, leading forth the Hebrews out
of the land of Egypt, so by the staff which had been formed by His own hand was He pleased, through Patrick, to do many and
great wonders for the conversion of many nations.   And the
staff is held in much veneration in Ireland, and even unto this
day is called the Staff of Jesus."

This precious relic of the Saint was long honored with the
veneration of Catholic Ireland in the Church of the Holy Trinity
at Dublin ; but in the early years of the so-called Reformation—
that godless time of sacrilege and wild profanation—the Staff of
Jesus was stripped of its priceless ornaments and cast into the
flames by a fanatical Protestant.

high testimonials which Patrick bore from the Bishop of Auxerre to the Vicar of Christ.

Pope Celestine I. gave the Saint a kindly reception, and issued bulls authorizing his consecration as bishop. Receiving the apostolic benediction, he returned to France, and was there raised to the episcopal dignity.[10] The invitation, " Come, holy youth, and walk amongst us," rang ever in his ears. It armed his soul with energy. The new Bishop bade adieu to home and kindred, and set out for the labor of his life with twenty well-tried companions.

It is supposed that St. Patrick first landed on the coast of the county of Wicklow ; but the hostility of the natives obliged him to re-embark, and he sailed northward toward the scenes of his former captivity. He finally cast anchor on the historic coast of Down, and, with all his companions, landed in the year 432 at the mouth of the little river Slaney,[11] which falls into Strangford Lough. The apostolic band had advanced but a short distance into the country when they encountered the servants of Dicho, lord of that

[10] The " Tripartite Life " of the Saint states that he was consecrated Bishop by Pope Celestine himself. Various other writers say that he was consecrated in France. See Sister Cusack's elaborate " Life of St. Patrick," chap. vi., p. 210.

[11] The Slaney " rises in Loughmoney, and passes through Ra holp, emptying itself into Strangford Lough, between Ringbane and Ballintogher.—*Sister Cusack.*

district.   Taking the Saint and his followers for
pirates, they grew alarmed and fled at their approach.

The news soon reached the ears of Dicho, who
hastily armed his retainers and sallied forth to
meet the supposed enemy.[12] He was not long in
learning, however, that the war which Patrick
was about to wage was not one of swords and
bucklers, but of peace and charity ; and with true
kindness and Irish hospitality, Dicho invited the
apostle to his residence.

It was a golden opportunity.   Nor did the
Saint permit it to escape.   He announced the
bright truths of the Gospel.   Dicho and all his
household heard, believed, and were baptized.
The Bishop celebrated Holy Mass in a barn, and
the church which the good, kind-hearted chief
erected on its site was afterwards known as *Sabhall*[13]*-Patrick*, or Patrick's Barn.   Thus Dicho was
Patrick's first convert in Ireland.   The glorious
work was commenced.   In that beautiful isle the
cross was destined to triumph over paganism, and
ever more to reign on its ruins.

---

[12] " **Dicho** came and set his dog at the clerics.   Then it was that
Patrick uttered the prophetic verse, *Ne trades bestis*, etc., *et canis
obmutuit*.   When Dicho saw Patrick he became gentle."—*Tripartite Life of St. Patrick.*

[13] *Sabhall* (pronounced *Saul*) means a barn.   It afterwards became a monastery of Canons Regular.   *Saul* is now the name of the
parish.

The great missionary next set out to visit his old master, hoping to gain him over to the faith.   But when Milcho heard of the Saint's approach his hard heathen soul revolted at the idea that he might have to submit in some way to the doctrine of his former slave.   The old man's rage and grief, it is related, induced him to commit suicide.   "This son of perdition," says the ancient monk, Jocelin, "gathered together all his house-hold effects and cast them into the fire, and then, throwing himself on the flames, he made himself a holocaust for the infernal demons." [14]

At this time Laegrius, [15] supreme monarch of Ireland, was holding an assembly or congress of all the Druids, bards, and princes of the nation in his palace at Tara.   St. Patrick resolved to be present at this great meeting of chiefs and wise men, and to celebrate in its midst the festival of Easter, which was now approaching.

He resolved with one bold stroke to paralyze the efforts of the Druids by sapping the very centre of their power.   He resolved to plant the glorious standard of the Cross on the far-famed Hill of Tara, [16] the citadel of Ireland.   Nor did he fail.

---

[14] Milcho's two daughters were converted, and one of his sons was made a bishop by St. Patrick.

[15] This Laegrius (or Leary) was one of the sons of Niall of the Nine Hostages.

[16] The Hill of Tara is large, verdant, level at the top, and ex-

It was the eve of Easter when the Saint arrived at Slane" and pitched his tent.   At the same hour the regal halls of Tara were filled with all the princes of the land.   It was the feast of *Baal-tien*, or sun-worship; and the laws of the Druids ordained that no fire should be lighted in the whole country till the *great fire* flamed upon the royal Hill of Tara.   It so happened, however, that Patrick's Paschal light was seen from the king's palace. The Druids were alarmed. [18]   The monarch and

tremely beautiful; and though not very high, it commands extensive and most magnificent prospects over the great and fertile plains of Meath.   At Tara the ancient records and chronicles of the kingdom were carefully preserved; these records and chronicles formed the basis of the ancient history of Ireland, called the "Psalter of Tara," which was brought to complete accuracy in the *third century;* and from the "Psalter of Tara," and other records was compiled, in the ninth century, by Cormac MacCullenan, Archbishop of Cashel and Kign of Munster, the celebrated work called the "Psalter of Cashel.'   The triennial legislative assemblies at Tara, which were the parliaments of ancient Ireland, continued down to the middle of the sixth century; the last convention of the states at Tara being held, according to the "Annals of Tigearnach," A. D. 560, in the reign of the monarch Diarmot, who abandoned that royal palace A. D. 563.—*O'Hart, Irish Pedigrees.*

[17] Slane is on the left bank of the Boyne, in the county of Meath.

[18] "The Druids," writes the Abbe MacGeoghegan, "alarmed at this attempt, carried their complaints before the monarch, and said to him that, if he had not that fire immediately extinguished, he who had kindled it, and his successors, would hold for ever the sovereignty of Ireland; which prophecy has been fulfilled, in a spiritual sense."—*History of Ireland.*

his courtiers were indignant. The Apostle **was**
ordered to appear before the assembly on the day
following.

> " Gleamed the sun-ray, soft and yellow,
>> On the gentle plains of Meath ;
> Spring's low breezes, fresh and mellow,
>> Through the woods scarce seemed to **breathe :**
> And on Tara, proud and olden,
>> Circled round with radiance fair,
> Decked in splendor bright and golden,
>> Sat the court of Laeghaire—
>
> "Chieftains with the collar of glory
>> And the long hair flowing free ;
> Priest and Brehon, bent and hoary,
>> Soft-tongued Bard and Seanachie.
> Silence filled the sunny ether,
>> Eager light in every eye,
> As in banded rank together
>> Stranger forms approacheth nigh.
>
> Tall and stately—white beards flowing
>> In bright streaks adown the breast—
> Cheeks with summer beauty glowing,
>> Eyes of thoughtful, holy rest ;
> And in front their saintly leader,
>> Patrick, walked with cross in hand,
> Which from Arran to Ben Edar
>> Soon rose high above the land."

The Apostle preached before Laegrius and
the great ones of Tara. " The sun which you
behold," said he, " rises and sets by God's decree
for our benefit ; but it shall never reign, nor **shall**

its splendor be immortal. All who adore it shall miserably perish. But we adore the true Sun - - Jesus Christ." [19]

The chief bard, Dubtach, was the first of the converts of Tara; and from that hour he conse-crated his genius to Christianity. A few days after Conall, the king's brother, embraced the faith. Thus Irish genius and royalty began to bow to the Cross. The heathen Laegrius blindly per-severed in his errors, but feared openly to oppose the holy Apostle. The scene at Tara recalls to mind the preaching of St. Paul before the assem-bled wisdom and learning of the Areopagus.

A court magician named Lochu attempted to oppose St. Patrick. He mocked Christ, and de-clared that he himself was a god. The people were dazzled with his infamous tricks. The hardy impostor even promised to raise himself from the earth and ascend to the clouds, and before king and people he one day made the attempt. The Saint was present. "O Almighty God!" he prayed, "destroy this blasphemer of thy holy

---

[19] It was on this occasion that St. Patrick, when told by the Druids that the doctrine of the Trinity was absurd, as *three* could not exist in *one*, stooped down, and, pulling a shamrock, which has three leaves on one stem, replied : " To prove the reality and, pos-sibility of the existence of the Father, Son, and Holy Ghost, I have only to pluck up this humble plant, on which we have trod-den, and convince you that truth can be attested by the simplest symbol of illustration."—*Mooney*.

Name, nor let him hinder those who now return, or may hereafter return, to Thee." The words were scarcely uttered when Lochu took a down-ward flight. The wretch fell at the Apostle's feet, dashed his head against a stone, and immediately expired.

After a short stay at various points, St. Patrick penetrated into Connaught. In the county of Cavan he overthrew the great idol called *Crom-Cruach*,[20] and on its ruins erected a stately church. It was about this time that he baptized the two daughters of King Laegrius. The fair royal con-verts soon after received the veil at his hands.

The Apostle held his first synod in 435, near Elphin, during which he consecrated several bishops for the growing Church of Ireland. It was in the Lent of this year that he returned to *Cruach-Pat-rick*, a mountain in Mayo, and spent forty days, praying, fasting, and beseeching heaven to make beautiful Erin an isle of saints.[21]

[20] *Crom-Cruach* (which signifies the stooping monument) was the chief idol in Ireland. It was situated in the present barony of Tullyhaw, county of Cavan. According to the " Tripartite Life of St. Patrick," this " arch idol of Erin was made of gold and silver, surrounded by twelve other idols formed of bronze."

[21] According to the ancient " Tripartite Life " of the Saint, it was on this occasion that he obtained from God the privilege of judging the people of Ireland on the last day.

" Is there anything else you demand ? " asked the angel. " There is," said Patrick. " The day that the twelve royal seats

The most glorious success everywhere attended his footsteps. The heavenly seed of truth fell on good ground, and produced more than a hundred-fold. Nor did miracles fail, from time

shall be on the Mount, and when the four rivers of fire shall be about the Mount, and when the three peoples shall be there—namely, the people of heaven, the people of earth, and the people of hell—that I myself may be judge over the men of Erin on that day." "This thing cannot be obtained from the Lord," said the angel. "Unless this is obtained from Him, I shall never leave this mountain," answered Patrick. The angel went to heaven. Patrick began to pray. When evening came the angel appeared. Patrick enquired as to the success of his request. "It is granted," said the angel; "all creatures, visible and invisible, including the twelve Apostles, entreated, and they have obtained."—*Tripartite Life,* part ii.

"Jocelin adds," writes the Abbé MacGeoghegan, "that he (St. Patrick) collected all the serpents and venomous reptiles of the country upon this mountain and cast them into the ocean, to which he ascribes the exemption of this island from all venomous reptiles. Solinus, however, who had written some centuries before the arrival of St. Patrick in Ireland, makes mention of this exemption; and after him Isidore, Bishop of Seville, in the seventh century, and Bede in the eighth, speak of it without assigning any cause. It seems that Jocelin is the first who gave this account; thus it is probable that it proceeds from the climate, or the nature of the soil, rather than from any supernatural cause."—*History of Ireland.*

To the present writer's mind this subject stands thus :

(1) It is a *fact* that Ireland is exempt from venomous reptiles.

(2) This exemption is the result either of God's working through nature, or of God's working a miracle through the instrumentality of St. Patrick.

(3) But whether this exemption can be traced to some blessing

to time, to come to the aid of the newly-announced doctrine. He reached Tirawley at a time when the seven sons of Amalgaidh were disputing over the succession to the crown of their deceased father. Great multitudes had gathered together. The Saint made his voice heard. An enraged magician rushed at him with murderous intentions; but, in the presence of all, a sudden flash of lightning smote the would-be assassin. It was a day of victory for the true faith. The seven quarrelling princes and over twelve thousand persons were converted on the spot, and baptized in the well of *Aen-Adharrac.*[22]

St. Patrick, after spending seven years in Connaught,[23] directed his course northward. He entered Ulster once more in 442. His progress through the historic counties of Donegal, Derry, Antrim, and others was one continued triumph. Princes and people alike heard, believed, and

---

of nature or to the miracle of the Saint, it is equally the work of the Almighty; for God is equally the Creator of nature and the Creator and Father of the Saints.

It is, in truth, wonderful that Ireland, which has a milder climate and is under the same physical conditions as England and Scotland, is exempt from venomous reptiles, from which they are not.

[22] *Aen-Adharrac*, signifies the one-horned hill.

[23] Ireland is at present divided into four provinces—Ulster, Munster, Leinster, and Connaught, and these are subdivided into thirty-two counties.

embraced the truth. Countless churches **sprang**
up, new sees were established, and the Catholic
religion placed on a deep, lasting foundation.
The Apostle of Erin was a glorious architect, who
did the work of God with matchless thorough-
ness.

"From faith's bright camp the demon fled,
The path to heaven was cleared;
Religion raised her beateous head—
An Isle of Saints appeared."

The Apostle next journeyed into Leinster, and
founded many churches. It is related that on
reaching a hill distant about a mile from a little
village, situated on the borders of a beautiful bay,
he stopped, swept his eye over the calm waters
and the picturesque landscape, and, raising his hand,
gave the scene his benediction, saying: "This village,
now so small, shall one day be renowned. It shall
grow in wealth and dignity until it shall become
the capital of a kingdom." It is now the city of
Dublin.

In 445 St. Patrick passed to Munster, and proceeded at once to "Cashel of the Kings." Angus,
who was then the royal ruler of Munster, went
forth to meet the herald of the Gospel, and
warmly invited him to his palace. This prince
had already been instructed in the faith, and the
day after the Bishop's arrival was fixed for his baptism.

During the administration of the sacrament a very touching incident occurred. The Saint planted his crosier—the Staff of Jesus—firmly in the ground by his side; but before reaching it the sharp iron point pierced the king's foot and pinned it to the earth. The brave convert never winced, though the pain must have been intense. The holy ceremony was over before St. Patrick perceived the streams of blood, and he immediately expressed his deep sorrow for causing such a painful accident. The noble Angus, however, quietly replied that he had thought it was a part of the ceremony, adding that he was ready and willing to endure much more for the glory of Jesus Christ.

Thus, in less than a quarter of a century from the day St. Patrick set his foot on her emerald shores, the greater part of Ireland became Catholic. The darkness of ancient superstition everywhere faded away before the celestial light of the Gospel. The groves of the pagan Druids were forsaken, and the holy sacrifice of the Mass was offered up on thousands of altars.

The annals of Christianity record not a greater triumph. It is the sublime spectacle of the people of an entire nation casting away their heathen prejudices and the cherished traditions of ages, and gladly embracing the faith of Jesus Christ, announced to them by a man who had once been

a miserable captive on their hills, but now an Apostle sent to them with the plenitude of power by
Pope Celestine.

Nor is it less remarkable that this glorious revolution—this happy conversion of peerless Ireland—
was accomplished without the shedding of one drop
of martyr blood, except, perhaps, at the baptism of
Angus, when,

> " The royal foot transpierced, the gushing blood
> Enriched the pavement with a noble flood."

While St. Patrick was meditating as to the site
he should select for his metropolitan see, he was
admonished by an angel that the destined spot was
Armagh.   Here he fixed the seat of his primacy
in the year 445.   A cathedral and many other religious edifices soon crowned the Hill of Macha.
The whole district was the gift of King Daire, a
grandson of Eoghan.

The Apostle, having thus established the Church
of Ireland on a solid basis, set out for Rome to
give an account of his labors to Pope St. Leo the
Great.   The Holy Father confirmed whatever
St. Patrick had done, appointed him his Legate,
and gave him many precious gifts on his departure.

The ancient biographers give many a curious
legend and quaint anecdote in relation to our
great Saint.   Eoghan (Eugene, or Owen) was one

of the sons of King Niall of the Nine Hostages.
He was a bold and powerful prince, who acquired
the country called after him " Tir-Owen" (Tyrone),
or Owen's country.   His residence was at the famous
palace of Aileach in Innishowen.[24]

When Eoghan heard of St. Patrick's arrival in
his dominions, he went forth to meet him, received
him with every mark of honor, listened with humility
to the word of God, and was baptized with all his
household.   But he had a temporal blessing to ask
of the Apostle.

" I am not good-looking," said the converted but
ambitious Eoghan ; " my brother precedes me on
account of my ugliness."

" What form do you desire ?" asked the Saint.

" The form of Rioc,[25] the young man who is
carrying your satchel," answered the prince.

St. Patrick covered them over with the same

[24] Innishowen (*i. e.*, Owen's Island) is a peninsula forming a
portion of the present county of Donegal.   It became the patrimony of the O'Doherty family.   In the ancient "Tripartite Life"
of our Saint it is related that he gave a particular blessing to Innishowen.   It is of this historic district that a poet of our day
writes:

> " And fair are the valleys of green Innishowen,
> And hardy the fishers that call them their own—
> A race that no traitor nor coward have known.
> Enjoy the fair valleys of green Innishowen."

[25] Rioc was St. Patrick's nephew and an ecclesiastic of dignified
bearing and extremely beautiful countenance.

garment, the hands of each being clasped round the other. They slept thus, and afterwards awoke in the same form, with the exception of the ton. sure.

"I don't like my height," said Eoghan.

"What size do you desire to be?" enquired the kind-hearted Saint.

The prince seized his sword and reached up-wards.

"I should like to be this height," he said; and all at once he grew to the wished-for stature. The Apostle afterwards blessed Eoghan and his sons.[26]

"Which of your sons is dearest to you?" asked St. Patrick.

"Muiredhach,"[27] said the prince.

"Sovereignty from him for ever," said the Saint.

"And next to him?" enquired St. Patrick.

"Fergus," he answered.

"Dignity from him," said the Saint.

"And after him?" demanded the Apostle.

"Eocha Bindech," said Eoghan.

"Warriors from him," said the Saint.

---

[26] "From this Eoghan," writes O'Hart, "came (among others) the following families: *O'Kane, O'Daly, O'Hagan, O'Crean, O'Caro-lan*, etc."—*Irish Pedigrees*, p. 118.

[27] The ancestor, according to the old genealogists, of the **Murray** family; this old name is written *O'Muiredhaigh* in Irish.

"And after him ?"

"They are all alike to me," replied **Eoghan.**

"They shall have united love," said **the man of** God.

"My blessing," he prayed, "on the descend-ants of Eoghan till the day of judgment. . . . The race of Eoghan, son of Niall, bless, O fair Bridget ! Provided they do good, government shall be from them for ever. The blessing of us both upon Eoghan, son of Niall, and on all who may be born of him, if they are obe-dient." [28]

St. Patrick, it is told, had a favorite goat which was so well trained that it proved very serviceable. But a sly thief fixed his evil eye on the animal, stole it, and made a feast on the remains. The loss of the goat called for investigation; and the thief, on being accused, protested with an oath that he was innocent. But little did he dream of his accuser. "The goat which was swallowed in his stomach," says Jocelin, "bleated loudly forth, and proclaimed the merit of St. Patrick." Nor did the miracle stop here; for "at the sentence of the Saint all the man's posterity were marked with the beard of a goat." [29]

About ten years before his death the venerable Apostle resigned the primacy as Archbishop of

---

[28] "Tripartite Life," part ii.

[29] "Life and Acts of St. Patrick," chap. xlviii.

Armagh to his loved disciple, St. Benignus,[30] and retired to Saul, his favorite retreat, and the scene of his early triumphs. Here it was that he converted Dicho and built his first church. Here also he wrote his "Confessions," and drew up rules for the government of the Irish Church. When he felt that the sun of dear life was about to set on earth, that it might rise in brighter skies, and shine for ever, he asked to be taken to Armagh. He wished to breathe his last in the ecclesiastical capital of Ireland. But on the way an angel appeared to the blessed man, and told him to return—that he was to die at Saul. He returned, and at the age of seventy-eight, on the 17th of March, in the year 465, St. Patrick passed from this world.

He was buried at Downpatrick, in the county of Down; and in the same tomb were subsequently laid the sacred remains of St. Bridget and St.

---

[30] St. Benignus was of the race of the Cianachta—O'Connors or O'Kanes?—of Glen Gemhin, in the county of Derry. His parents, however, resided near the site of the present town of Drogheda; and when St. Patrick came that way he passed the night at their hospitable residence. Benignus, then a mere boy, grew intensely fond of the Saint. He was baptized, and followed the Apostle of Ireland until he became his immediate successor as Archbishop of Armagh. St. Patrick has had one hundred and eight successors in the See of Armagh. Those of the present century are: *Richard O'Reilly, Patrick Curtis, Thomas Kelly, William Crolly, Paul Cullen, Joseph Dixon, Michael Kieran, and Daniel MacGettigan.*

Columbkille. The shrine of the Apostle of Ireland was visited by Cambrensis in 1174, and upon it he found the following Latin inscription:

> *Hi tres Duno tumulo tumulantur in uno,*
> *Brigida Patricius, atque Columba Pius.*

> In Down three Saints one grave do fill,
> Bridget, Patrick, and Columbkille.[31]

[31] The shrine of St. Patrick, enriched by many precious offerings, was destroyed in the general profanation under Henry VIII. "I had a very pleasant ride to Downpatrick," says Rev. Dr. Ve-tromile, "where I went to see the church built by St. Patrick, for which I paid a shilling to the woman who kept the key. The church is Gothic, and has been nearly rebuilt by the Episcopalians. I asked the woman—a Protestant—if St. Patrick was a Protestant. She answered, 'No—a Catholic.' 'How, then, is it,' said I, 'that the church is in the hands of Protestants?' 'They took it from the Catholics,' she replied. 'Then,' I said, 'it should be given back to the Catholics.' 'If they fight for it they will get it,' she answered. The inside of the church is plain. I saw the place where the altar must have stood, the pulpit, etc. Then I went to see St. Patrick's grave, which is close to the church in the cemetery, now used by Protestants. There is nothing to distinguish the grave of Ireland's Apostle. It is only a mound without headstone or inscription, not so much as a cross; yet everybody knows it, and the path leading to it from the road is kept smooth by the frequent visits of the Irish, who go thither to pray; and there is a cavity over the grave made by the Irish taking away, in their devotion, the earth for a *memento*. I could not but think what a magnificent monument they would build up on the grave of their Apostle, were they but allowed to do so. Still, though St. Patrick's grave has no sign to mark it, after the lapse of nearly fifteen centuries, many of them passed in bitter persecution, in a part of Ireland inhabited by Orangemen, every one in Downpatrick, and

This illustrious Saint was a man of work, and prayer, and penance. To his last breath he ceased not to teach his people. His daily devotions were countless. It is related that he made the sign of the cross many hundred times a day. He slept little, and a stone was his pillow. He traveled on foot in his visitations till the weight of years made a carriage necessary. He accepted no gifts for himself, ever deeming it more blessed to give than to receive.

His simple dress was a white monastic habit, made from the wool of the sheep; and his bearing, speech, and countenance were but the outward expression of his kind heart and great, beautiful soul. Force and simplicity marked his discourses. He was a perfect master of the Irish, French, and Latin languages, and had some knowledge of Greek.

He consecrated three hundred and fifty bishops,[32] erected seven hundred churches, ordained five thousand priests, and raised thirty-three per-

thousands elsewhere, can point out the spot. It is shown from generation to generation by tradition, and herein Protestants have before their eyes a certain proof of the truth and reliability of tradition."—*Travels in Europe.*

[32] Bishops were far more numerous then than now, but the reason is obvious. In an age when communication between one part of the country and another was difficult and often impossible for a considerable period of time, it was necessary that there should be bishops in every locality.—*Sister M. F. Clare.*

sons from the dead. But it is in vain that we try to sum up the labors of the Saint by the rules of arithmetic. The wear and tear of over fourteen hundred years have tested the work of St. Patrick; and in spite of all the changes of time, and the malice of men and demons, it stands to-day greater than ever—a monument to his immortal glory.[38]

"It should ever be remembered," said the Nun of Kenmare, "that the exterior work of a saint is but a small portion of his real life, and that the success of this work is connected by a delicate chain of providences, of which the world sees

---

[38] After the Most Blessed Virgin, there is, perhaps, no saint in the calendar who has been chosen patron of so many churches in our country as has St. Patrick. The cathedrals of Erie, Newark Rochester, Harrisburg, and New York bear his noble name ; and there is scarcely a town or city from Maine to California that has not its St. Patrick's Church. The greatest and most beautiful church in the New World is St. Patrick's Cathedral, New York The style of architecture is the pure Gothic that prevailed in Europe in the thirteenth and fourteenth centuries. In 1858 the corner-stone was laid by Archbishop Hughes. The foundation is of immense granite blocks ; and all above the base course con-sists of fine white marble. The extreme length is 332 feet, extreme breadth, 174 feet. The two massive towers will each be 328 feet high. This magnificent edifice was dedicated to divine worship in May, 1879. The ceremony was grand and impressive. Among the many distinguished dignitaries who participated therein were His Eminence Cardinal McCloskey, Archbishop Gibbons of Bal-timore, and Archbishop Purcell of Cincinnati. The sermon—a noble effort—was delivered by Bishop Ryan, Coadjutor of St Louis.

little and thinks less, with this interior life. Men are ever searching for the beautiful in nature and art, but they rarely search for the beauty of a human soul, yet this beauty is immortal. Something of its radiance appears at times even to mortal sight, and men are overawed by the majesty or won by the sweetness of the saints of God; but it needs saintliness to discern sanctity, even as it needs cultivated taste to appreciate art. A thing of beauty is only a joy to those who can discern its beauty; and it needs the sight of angels to see and appreciate perfectly all the beauty of a saintly soul. Thus, while some men scorn as idle tales the miracles recorded in the Lives of the Saints, and others give scant and condescending praise to their exterior works of charity, their real life, their true nobility is hidden and unknown God and the angels only know the trials and the triumphs of holy human souls."

SAINT BRIDGET,

THE LILY PATRONESS OF IRELAND.

DIED A.D. 523.

"Bridget, enthroned in heaven above,
 Look on thy children dear ;
And help them to eternal life,
 In God's most holy fear."[1]

S T. BRIDGET, the holy Patroness of Ireland, was born at Faughart, [2] a village in the present county of Louth, soon after the light of faith began to illumine her lovely native isle. Her parents were Catholics and persons of rank. [3]

[1] Bridget is from the Irish, and signifies *strength*. The name is sometimes written Bridgit and Bride.

[2] Faughart is in no way remarkable except as the birthplace of the Saint. It is near the town of Dundalk. The ruins of St. Bridget's old church are still here. The situation is very picturesque, looking out on the bay of Dundalk, the scene of many a notable event in Irish history.— *Sister Cusack, Life of St. Bridget.*

[3] Her mother, Broeseach, was an O'Connor, and was of noble birth ; both her parents were Christians.— *Sister Cusack.*

Bridget's early life was surrounded by the supernatural. It is said that, when a child, angels
were her constant companions, and even aided
her in erecting a little altar, at which she amus-
ed herself.   On reaching girlhood, whatever she
touched or had charge of in the way of food
multiplied under her hand.   Once when her old
nurse was suffering from a burning fever the fair
young Saint cured her by making the sign of the
cross on some water, which was turned into mead
—then the common drink of the country.

She resolved to consecrate her virginity to
heaven, but met with much trouble on account of
her rare beauty and the opposition of her parents.
Many sought her hand.   But finding that the
eagerness of a multitude of suitors might, perhaps,   hinder her from devoting herself entirely
to God, she prayed that her beauty might be
changed to ugliness.   Her prayer was heard.
One of her eyes became greatly enlarged, and
her angelic face so altered that both parents
and suitors soon left her free to embrace her religious state.

Taking with her seven young ladies, Bridget
went to Bishop Maccelle, [4] a disciple of St. Patrick, and requested him to give them the veil.

---

[4] The celebrated Archbishop McHale is directly descended from
Bishop Maccelle, who received the profession of St. Bridget.—
Sister M. F. Cusack, Life of Daniel O'Connell.

He hesitated for a time, but the lovely Saint re-doubled her prayers. At length, seeing a pillar of fire over her head, he clothed her in the mantle of religion, and received her profession and that of her fair companions.

During the ceremony, as Bridget bent her head to receive the holy veil, she placed her hand on the wooden altar-step; and in a moment the dry wood became green and fresh, her eye was cured, and all the radiance of her former beauty re-turned.

On one occasion, as the Saint and her nuns were enjoying the hospitality of good Bishop Maccelle she begged him to give them some spiritual instruc-tion. He complied in a short discourse on the *Eight Beatitudes.* When he concluded she turned to her Sisters and said: " We are eight virgins, and eight virtues are offered to us as a means of sanctification. It is true that whoever practices one virtue perfectly must possess every other; yet let each of us now choose a virtue for special devotion."

The Sisters, through courtesy and respect, re-quested St. Bridget, as superioress, to take the first choice. She at once took the beatitude of "Mercy" as the beautiful virtue to which she especially wished to devote herself. It was, in truth, a happy choice —one in which she has had many followers in " the Isle of Saints and Sages."

Of the many convents founded by this illustrious lady, Kildare became the most renowned. "As it was erected under the shelter of the oak," writes the Nun of Kenmare, "it obtained the name of Cell of the Oak, or Kildare. The great plain of the Curragh was her pasture-ground, donated to her by some famous chief. Bishop Mel assisted her in her arrangements, and Ailill, the King of Leinster, gave her the wood for her building. This establishment was erected some time between the years 480 and 490."[5]

St. Bridget's whole life was love in action. The wants of others touched her pure, noble, and affectionate heart. A good mother once brought her little daughter to see the Saint. The girl was about twelve years of age, and had been born dumb. Not knowing her infirmity, however, the Abbess carressed her, asking her if she intended to be a nun. There was no reply. The mother explained her child's condition; but St. Bridget remarked that she could not let the girl's hand go until she received an answer. She repeated the question. "I will do whatever you desire," said the child, who, thus wonderfully cured, remained with her dear benefactress ever after.

---

[5] The little conventual building in Kildare was soon surrounded by a great city. We have said little, for such it was in its first beginnings, but it soon became a vast building and contained many hundred inhabitants.—*Nun of Kenmare.*

The holy Abbess took the most tender care of her religious. One of the Sisters was very ill and asked for some milk. But there was none. The Saint, however, ordered some water to be given to the patient. It was suddenly changed into rich, warm milk, and the miraculous draught cured the sick Sister.

During one of her journeys a man came to her and related his domestic troubles. His wife, he said, hated him for some unknown reason, and peace had fled from his home. The Saint gave the poor fellow some water, directing him to sprinkle it through the house in his wife's absence. He did so, and his wife's dislike was turned into the most tender affection—an affection that lasted for life.

On one occasion a leper came to the convent and asked to have his clothes washed; but as he was only master of what was on his back, it became necessary to provide him with clothing while this act of charity was in the course of accomplishment. St. Bridget desired one of her nuns to give the afflicted son of Adam a second habit which she did not use. But the nun was unwilling to obey, and as a swift punishment she was then and there struck with leprosy. At the end of an hour, however, she repented of her disobedience, and was cured by the intercession of the tenderhearted Saint.

Another nun, happy in possessing the true spirit
of obedience, provided the leper with clothing;
and when his tattered rags were washed and returned to him he was healed of his terrible disease. "Thus," exclaims the Nun of Kenmare,
from whose excellent work[6] we have gathered
these details—"thus was God glorified; for the
miracles of the saints are not for their own
glory."

> " Her only thought was heaven and God,
>   Her only joy was pure;
> She sought bright mansions in the skies,
>   And life for e'er secure."

Our Saint enjoyed the most intimate friendship of
St. Patrick. She foretold the date of his departure
from this world, was present at his holy death, and
supplied the winding-sheet—which she had long kept
for the purpose—in which his blessed remains were
wrapped.

One of the most touching and beautiful incidents in the life of St. Bridget was her meeting
with the young student, Nenedius. As she was
leaving her convent on the plains of the Liffey, she
met him running along with boyish impetuosity.
The holy Abbess requested one of her religious to
call him to her; but Nenedius was in such a hurry
that he could scarcely be prevailed upon to stay a
moment.

[6] " Life of St. Bridget."

The Saint enquired why he ran with such speed. "I am running to heaven," answered the boy.

"Would to God," said Bridget, "that I were worthy to run with you to that blessed place! Pray for me that I may one day enter there."

"O holy Virgin!" exclaimed Nenedius, "pray for me that I may persevere in the path that leads to heaven."

And the Saint prayed for the dear boy, telling him, in prophetic language, that on the day of her death she would receive the Holy Viaticum from his hands.

St. Nenedius—for he became a saint—took the most special care of that hand which would one day be so honored; and in the kindness and humility of his heart, which ardently hoped that the life of St. Bridget would be prolonged to extreme old age, he allowed many years to roll away before he was ordained priest. He left Ireland and wandered as a pilgrim in other countries. But at length he was raised to the sacred dignity of the priesthood, turned his steps homewards, and as he reached the shores of his native isle he was called to the bedside of Ireland's holy Patroness. She was preparing for heaven. Nenedius administered the Holy Sacraments to the dying Saint: and on the first of February, in the year 523,

St. Bridget, borne by angels, passed to the bosom of God.[1]

[1] St. Columbkille wrote a poem in praise of St. Bridget.   Its first stanza may be   rendered:

> "Bridget, the good and the virgin,
> Bridget, dear lady without sin,
> Bridget, the bright and God-given,
> May she lead us to beautiful heaven."

There are churches dedicated to divine worship under the patronage of St. Bridget in Buffalo, Rochester, Pittsburgh, Cleveland, Philadelphia, San Francisco, St Louis, New York, and countless other places in our country.

SAINT COLUMBKILLE

THE APOSTLE OF CALEDONIA.

DIED A. D. 597.

S T. COLUMBKILLE,[1] whose glory is em-
balmed in legend and history, was born at
Gartan, in the county of Donegal, Ireland, on December 7, A. D. 521.[2]   His father was
descended from the famous King Niall of the
Nine Hostages,[3] supreme monarch of Ireland at
the close of the fourth century.   Before the child's
birth his mother, who also belonged to a distinguished Irish family, had a dream which posterity

---

[1] Columbkille signifies *dove of the cell.*   The name is often
written *Columba.*

[2] The birth of our Saint was foretold by St. Patrick.   In blessing
Fergus, son of Niall, he said, referring to Columbkille :

> " A youth shall be born of your race,
> Who will be a sage, prophet, and poet—
> A glorious, bright, clear light,
> Who will not utter falsehood."
> —*Tripartite Life of St. Patrick.*

[3] So named because of the hostages taken from nine powers,
which he subdued and made tributary.

263

has accepted as a graceful and poetical symbol of her son's career.

An angel appeared to the lady, bringing her a veil covered with flowers of rare beauty and wonderful variety of colors; but all at once she saw it carried away by the wind, and rolling out as it fled over plain and wood and mountain.

"Woman," said the bright spirit, "you are about to become the mother of a son who will blossom for heaven, who will be reckoned among the prophets of God, and who will lead numberless souls to the celestial country."

St. Bute, one of those holy monks whose lives light up the pages of Erin's ancient history, died on the day of Columbkille's birth. He spoke of the event. "To-day," said the departing old saint, "a child is born, whose name is Columb-kille. He shall be glorious in the sight of God and men."

The good priest who baptized the child was his first instructor. It is recounted that from his earliest years Columbkille was accustomed to heavenly visions. Often, when his guardian angel appeared to him, the happy boy would ask if all the angels in heaven were as young and shining as he.

Later on the same sweet spirit invited him to choose among all the virtues those which he would like best to possess. "I choose," said the youth, "chastity and wisdom." And immediately three young girls of dazzling beauty appeared and threw themselves on his neck, embracing him. The pious youth frowned and repulsed them with indignation.

" What !" they exclaimed, "do you, then, not know us ?"

" No," he replied, "not the least in the world."

" We are three sisters,'' said the lovely visitors, "whom our Father betroths to you."

" Who is your Father ?" enquired Columbkille.

" Our Father," they gracefully answered, "is God.''

" Ah !" said he, "you have indeed an illustrious Father. But what are your names ?"

" Our names," replied the sisters, "are Virginity, Wisdom, and Prophecy. We come to leave you no more, but to love you with a love pure and everlasting."

Columbkille passed into the great monastic schools, which were nurseries not only for the clergy of Ireland, but also for young laymen of all conditions. Here manual labor was joined to study and prayer. Like all his young companions, he had to grind over night the corn for the next day's food; but when his turn came the work was so well and quickly done that his companions suspected him of having been assisted by an angel. On completing his course of studies and monastic training he was ordained priest by his reverend master, the Abbot St. Finnian, founder of the renowned monastic school of Clonard.

A remarkable incident is related of the royal Saint's student career at Clonard, when he was only a deacon. A famous old bard named Gemman came to live near the monastery. Columbkille, who was at all times in life a poet and passionate admirer of Irish poetry, determined to join the bard's school, and to share his labors and his studies. One day the two were reading together, at a little distance apart, out of doors. A young girl ran towards them, pursued by a robber. She hoped, no doubt, to find safety in the authority of the venerable bard. Scarcely, however, had the poor girl reached the spot than her hard-hearted pursuer, running up, struck her with his lance, and she fell mortally wounded.

Gemman called to his pupil for assistance. "How long," he exclaimed in accents of horror, "shall God leave unpunished this crime which dishonors us?"

" Only for this moment," replied the indignant young monk. " At this very hour, as the soul of this innocent creature ascends to heaven, the soul of the murderer shall go down to hell!" The words were hardly uttered when the wretched assassin fell dead.

Soon, far and wide, Columbkille's name became famous. As he was closely allied to the reigning monarch of all Ireland, and, indeed, eligible himself to the same high office, it was very natural that his influence increased with his years.[4] Before reaching the age of twenty-five he had presided over the erection of a crowd of monasteries. As many as thirty-five in Ireland honored him as the founder. Of these the chief were Derry and Durrow.

The young Columbkille was especially attached to Derry, where he habitually lived. He superintended with care not only the discipline and studies of his community, but also external matters—even so far as to watch over the preservation of the neighboring forest. He would never permit an oak to be cut down. Those that fell by natural decay, or were struck down by the wind, were alone made use of for the fire which was lighted on the arrival of strangers, or distributed to the neighboring poor. The poor had a first right in Ireland—as everywhere else—to the goods of the monks; and the monastery of Derry

---

[4] In the MS. life of St. Columbkille by O'Donnell it is asserted that the Saint, in the year 544, being a prince of the royal family, was offered the crown of Ireland, and that Dermod MacCerball, his competitor, succeeded only because our holy abbot preferred the cowl to a diadem.—*Butler.*

This was two years before he was ordained priest.

fed a hundred applicants every day with the most careful regularity.[5]

Derry was the spot that Columbkille loved best. In the poem attributed to his old age he says so touchingly :

> " Were all the tribute of Scotia mine,
> From its midland to its borders,
> I would give all for one little cell
> In my beautiful Derry.
>
> " For its peace and for its purity,
> For the white angels that go
> In crowds from one end to the other
> I love my beautiful Derry."

Columbkille, it may be noted, was as much a

[5] The Saint fed a hundred men daily, but his steward, or dispenser, did not quite appreciate the liberality of his master. He had a fixed time for giving the dole of food, and any one who came late was peremptorily dismissed. A poor man came one day late, and was, as usual, sent away. The next day he came in time, but was told there was nothing for him. For many days he came, but each time he met with some repulse. He then sent a message to Columba to tell him that he advised him for the future to put no limit to his charity while he had alms to give, except what God set on the number of those who came for it. Columba was struck by the message, and came down to the gate of the monastery, not waiting even to put on his cloak. He hastened after the beggar ; but when he had gone some distance he found not the poor man, but Christ, who had taken the form of a beggar. Then, as he fell down and adored his Lord, he obtained from Him a royal alms—new lights, new graces, new and yet more wonderful powers of miracle and prophecy.—*Sister Cusack, Life of St. Columba.*

bard as a monk during the first part of his life; and he had the roving, ardent, and somewhat quarrelsome character of the race. He had a passion for traveling, but a still greater one for books. It must be said, in truth, that his intense love of books brought him into more than one misadventure. The poet-monk went everywhere in search of rare works, which he would borrow or copy; but occasionally he met with refusals, which he sharply resented.

At the time of which we write there was in Ossory a holy recluse, very learned doctor in laws and philosophy, named Longarad. Columbkille paid him a visit and asked leave to examine his books. The uncourteous old scholar gave a direct refusal. Columbkille was indignant.

"May your books," he said, "no longer do you any good—neither you nor those who come after you—since you have taken occasion by them to show your inhospitality." The curse was heard, according to the legend. As soon as Longarad died his books became unintelligible. "They still exist," wrote an author of the ninth century, "but no man can read them."

But another event in the career of our Saint leads us to that turning-point in life which for ever changed his destiny and transformed him from a wandering poet-monk and ardent student into a glorious missionary. While visiting his old master, the Abbot Finnian, Columbkille found means to make a secret and hurried copy of the abott's Psalter by shutting himself up at night in the church where it was deposited, and illuminating his work by the light which escaped from his left hand while he wrote with the right.

Finnian, however, discovered what was going on by means of a curious wanderer, who, attracted by the singular light, looked in through the key-hole. But the poor fellow's curiosity met with swift punishment. While his face was pressed against the door he had his eye suddenly plucked out by a crane, one of those familiar birds that were permitted by the Irish monks to seek a home in their churches.

The abbot, for some reason or other, was much displeased, and declared that Columbkille had taken an unwarranted liberty with his book. He even claimed the copy when it was finished, on the ground that a copy made without permission ought to belong to the owner of the original. But the poet-monk refused to give up his work, and the question was referred to the king at Tara.

King Diarmid, at that time supreme monarch of Ireland, was related to Columbkille, but he pro-nounced against his kinsman. Diarmid's decision was given in a rustic phrase which has become a proverb in Ireland : "To every cow its calf, and, there-fore, to every book its copy." [6]

Columbkille vigorously protested. "It is an unjust sentence," he exclaimed with indignation. All parties were hot and prepared for an open rupture. The occasion soon came. A young prince, son of the king of Connaught and a hostage at Tara, had a dispute, during a game of hurling, with the son of one of Diarmid's officers. It ended in a quarrel, and the prince killed the youth by striking him with his hurley. He fled at once for sanctuary to our Saint, who was standing in the king's presence.

But King Diarmid—contrary to all precedent—refused to respect the undoubted right of Columb-kille to protect his client, and he ordered the un-happy prince to be torn from the very arms of his protector and immediately executed.

The noble, fiery nature of the Saint revolted at this last outrage. "I will denounce your wicked judgment to my family and my friends," said he to the king, "and the violation in my person of the immunity of the Church. My complaint shall be heard and you will be swiftly punished. No longer shall you see my face in your province until the Almighty Judge has subdued your pitiable pride. And as you have humbled me to-day before your

---

[6] *" Le gach boin a boinin, le gach leabhar a leabhran."*

friends and nobles, God will humble you on the batt-tle-day before your enemies!"

Diarmid attempted to retain him by force, but, evading his guards, the poet-monk escaped by night from Tara and hastily directed his steps to his native Tyrconnell.   As he pushed along on his lonely way his agitated soul found utterance in the "Song of Trust": [7]

> " Alone am I upon the mountain,
> O God of Heaven! prosper my way,
> And I shall pass more free and fearless
> Than if six thousand were my stay.
> My flesh, indeed, might be defended,
> But when the time comes life is ended.
> If by six thousand I was guarded,
> Or placed on an islet in a lake,
> Or in a fortress strong protected,
> Or in a church my refuge take,
> Still God will guard His own with care,
> And even in battle safe they fare.
> No man can slay me till the day
> When God shall take my life away;
> And when my earthly time is ended
> I die—no matter how defended." [8]

The "Song of Trust" may be reckoned among the most authentic relics of the ancient Irish tongue.—*Montalembert.*

[8] St. Columbkille was the author of many hymns and poems, both in Irish and Latin. See "The Prose and Poetry of Ireland," pp. 25-38, and the "Life of St. Columba," by Sister M. F. Clare.

One of his celebrated Latin hymns is the *Altus.* The following is the first stanza as translated by the Nun of Kenmare:

> " Ancient of days
> Father most high,

Columbkille arrived safely in his native province. His words like a trumpet-blast, aroused

> Who art and shall be
> As the ages go by,
> With Christ and the Spirit,
> In glory supernal,
> Who art God evermore,
> Unbegotten, eternal;
> We preach not three Gods,
> But the unity, One,
> The Father, the Spirit,
> And co-equal Son."

The *Noli, Pater* is also a famous Latin hymn from the gifted
pen of our Saint. Colgan says that two graces are believed to be
granted to the recital of this hymn: (1) that those who recite it
should be preserved from the effects of thunder and lightning;
(2) that those who recite it at night before going to rest and in
the morning when they rise shall be preserved from all adversity.

THE NOLI, PATER.

> "Father, keep under
> The tempest and thunder,
> Lest we should be shattered,
> By Thy lightning's shafts scattered.
> Thy terrors while hearing,
> We listen, still fearing,
> The resonant song
> Of the bright angel throng,
> As they wander and praise Thee,
> Shouts of honor still raise Thee.
>
> To the King ruling right,
> Jesus, lover and light,

the powerful clans of Ulster; nor was it hard to procure the aid of the king of Connaught, the father of the executed young prince. The combined forces marched against Diarmid, who met them at Cul-Dreimhne.[9] The battle was short. Diarmid's army was routed, and he fled, taking refuge, at Tara. According to the historian Tighernach, the victory was due to the prayers and hymns of Columbkille, who for days had fasted and appealed to heaven for the punishment of royal insolence.

"As to the manuscript," says Montalembert, "which had been the object of this strange conflict of copyright elevated into a civil war, it was afterwards venerated as a kind of national, mili-

> As with wine and clear mead,
> Filled with God's grace indeed,
> Precursor John Baptist's words
> Told of the coming Lord,
> Whom, blessed for evermore,
> All men should bow before,
> Zacharias, Elizabeth,
> This Saint begot.
> May the fire of thy love live in my heart yet
> As jewels of gold in a silver vase set."
> —*Nun of Kenmare's translation.*

[9] Cul-Dreimhne is north of the town of Sligo. The "Annals of the Four Masters" state that "three thousand was the number that fell of Diarmid's people. Only *one* man fell on the other sid

tary, and religious palladium. Under the name
of *Cathac*, or *Fighter*, the Latin Psalter transcribed by Columbkille, and enshrined in a kind of porta-
ble altar, became the national relic of the O'Donnell clan. For more than a thousand years it was
carried before them to battle as a pledge of victory, on the condition of being supported upon the
breast of a cleric free from all mortal sin. It has
escaped as by miracle from the ravages of which
Ireland has been the victim, and still exists, to the
great joy of all learned Irish patriots." [10]

Columbkille was victorious; but victory is not
always peace. He soon felt the double reaction
of personal remorse and the condemnation of
many pious souls. In the Synod of Teilte, held
in 562, he was accused of having occasioned the
shedding of Christian blood. Though absent, he
was excommunicated. But our poet-monk knew
not that timidity which draws back before accusers or judges. He suddenly presented himself
to the synod, which had struck without hearing
him. Nor did he fail to find a defender in that
assembly.

When Columbkille made his appearance the
famous Abbot Brendan arose, met, and embraced

---

[10] This precious relic is now preserved in the museum of the
Royal Irish Academy, Dublin. For a minute description of it
see O'Curry's "Lectures on the MS. Materials of Ancient Irish
History," p. 327.

him. " How can you," exclaimed the members of the synod, "give the kiss of peace to an excommunicated man?"

" You would do as I have done," answered the noble Brendan, "and you would never have excommunicated him, had you seen what I see—a pillar of fire which goes before him, and the angels that are his companions. I dare not distain a man predestined by God to be the guide of an entire people to eternal life."

The synod gracefully withdrew the sentence of excommunication, but Columbkille was charged to win to Christ, by his preaching, as many pagan souls as the number of Christians who had fallen in the battle that he had occasioned.

The soul of the Saint was troubled. The voice of an accusing conscience touched his manly heart. He wandered from solitude to solitude, from monastery to monastery, seeking masters of Christian virtue, and asking them anxiously what he should do to obtain the full pardon of God for the blood of those who had fallen on the field of Cul-Dreimhne. At length he found a holy monk named Abban, to whom he poured out the troubles of his sad soul. To Columbkille's earnest enquiries Abban assured him that those killed in the battle enjoyed eternal repose; and, as his *soul-friend*, or confessor, he condemned him to perpetual exile from Ireland.

It is now that the second and grandest part of the Saint's life commences. He took a loving leave of his warlike kindred, to whom he was intensely attached, and directed his course towards Scotland. The new scene of his toils was to be among its pagan inhabitants. Twelve of his devoted monks accompanied him; and thus, at the age of forty-two, Columbkille bade a last farewell to his native land.

The bark of the holy exiles of Erin put in at that little isle which our Saint immortalized, and which took from him the name *I-Colm-Kill*, now, perhaps, better known as *Iona*.[11] On that small spot, surrounded by foaming, sombre seas, over-shadowed by the bare and lofty peaks of other islands, and with a wild, romantic scenery greeting the eye in the far-off distance, Columbkille, poet, prince, monk, and missionary, founded the *first* monastery in Scotland, and began the gigantic labors of a new life more than heroic, more than apostolic. Over thirteen hundred years ago this became the monastic capital and centre of faith learning, and Christian civilization in North Britain.

In the midst of his community the Saint in-

[11] Iona is only three miles in length by two in breadth, flat and low, bordered by gray rocks which scarcely rise above the level of the sea. Its highest hill is only 320 feet above the ocean.—*Montalembert.*

habited, instead of a cell, a sort of hut built of
planks and placed upon the most elevated spot
within the monastic enclosure.   Up to the age of
seventy-six he slept there upon the hard floor with
a stone for his pillow.

This hut was at once his study and his oratory.
It was there that he gave himself up to those prolonged prayers which excited the admiration, and
almost the alarm, of his disciples.   It was there
that the princely Abbot retired after sharing the
outdoor labor of his monks, like the least among
them, to consecrate the rest of his time to the
study of Holy Scripture and the transcription of
the sacred text.[12]

It was in the same hut that he received with unwearied patience and gentle courtesy the hundreds
of visitors of high and low degree who flocked to
see him.   Sometimes, however, he was obliged to
complain mildly, as of that indiscreet stranger who,
desirous of embracing him, awkwardly overturned
his ink on the border of his robe.

But who shall describe his labors as a great
missionary?   For over a third of a century he

[12] For Columbkille the work of transcription remained until his
last day the occupation of his old age, as it had been the passion of
his youth.   It had such an attraction for him, and seemed to him
so essential to a knowledge of the truth, that three hundred copies
of the Holy Gospel, written by his own hand, have been ascribed to
him.— *Montalembert, Monks of the West,* vol. ii.

traversed the wild regions of Caledonia—regions hitherto inaccessible even to the Roman eagle. At his preaching and miracles the fierce pagan Picts" bowed beneath the cross.

Skimming Loch Ness with his little skiff, the Saint soon penetrated to the chief fortress of the Pictish king, the site of which is still shown upon a rock north of the town of Inverness. Brude was the name of the hardy and powerful ruler. At first he refused to receive the Catholic missionary, and gave orders that the gates of the

---

[13] Butler ("Lives of the Saints," vol. vi.) thinks that the Picts were the original inhabitants of Scotland. Bede ("Eccles. Hist.") tells us that they spoke a language different from their Celtic neighbors. The original Scots were an *Irish* colony that conquered a portion of Caledonia and settled there. Ireland, it must be remembered, was called *Scotia* in early ages, and its inhabitants *Scots*. King Niall of the Nine Hostages, monarch of Ireland, was the first that gave the name of *Scotia Minor*, or " Little Scotia," to Scotland. Before that " Scotland" went by the name of Alba. The Scots (or Irish) and the Picts lived as good neighbors till about the year 840, when Kenneth II., King of the Scots, defeated the Picts. About the year 900 the Scots became masters of the rest of the country, and from that time all North Britain took the name of *Scotland*, or land of the Scots. At a somewhat later period Ireland gradually lost the name of Scotia, which was thus wholly transferred to the neighboring country that she had conquered and colonized. Such, in brief, was the origin of the name Scotland. Nearly all the great old Scottish families—as the MacDonalds, Campbells, Murrays, etc.—are lineal descendants of the ancient Irish that colonized and became masters of North Britain.

fortress should be closed on the unwelcome visitors.

But the dauntless Columbkille was not alarmed. "He went up to the gateway," says Montalembert, "made the sign of the cross upon the two gates, and then knocked with his hand. Immediately the bars and bolts drew back, the gates rolled upon their hinges and were thrown wide open, and the Saint entered like a conqueror. The king, though surrounded by his council, was struck with panic ; he hastened to meet the missionary, addressed to him pacific and encouraging words, and from that moment gave him every honor." Thus obstacles vanished at the very glance of the illustrious Irish Abbot.

He accomplished the conversion of the entire Pictish nation, and destroyed for ever the authority of the Druids in that last refuge of Celtic paganism. Before he closed his glorious career he had sown their forests, their defiles, their inaccessible mountains, their savage moors and scarcely-inhabited islands with churches, schools and monasteries. Out of the many monasteries which he founded in Scotland—over which Protestantism afterwards passed its devastating hand —the remains of fifty-three are to be seen to this day.

No pen can describe the great, gentle, loving heart of Columbkille. It is told that a poor man

once sheltered him under his roof for the night. In
the morning the Saint enquired what worldly goods
his host possessed. He was informed that the whole
capital was five cows, poor and small; "but," added
the man, "if you bless them they will increase."
The Saint requested the cows to be driven into his
presence. It was done. "Your cattle," said he,
"will increase to one hundred and five, and you
shall be blessed with many good children." It happened just as he predicted.

One morning at Iona the Abbot hastily called a
monk. He told him to prepare at once for a voyage
to Ireland. A good young lady named Mangina,
he explained, had fallen in returning from Mass and
broke. her thigh-bone. "She is now," said he,
"calling on me earnestly, hoping that she may receive some consolation from the Lord."

He then gave the monk a piece of blessed bread
in a little casket of pine wood, and ordered him to
have it dipped in water, and to let the water be
poured on the injured limb. All was done as com,
manded, and the injured member was instantly
healed. On the cover of the casket the Saint wrote
the words *twenty-three years*, and to a day Mangina
lived twenty-three years after her cure.

On another occasion he suddenly stopped while
reading, and said with a smile to his monks: "I
must now go and pray for a poor little woman who
is in the pains of childbirth, and who suffers like a

true daughter of Eve.   She is down yonder in Ireland, and reckons upon my prayers ; for she is my
cousin and of my mother's family."   Whereupon
the great priest hastened to the church, and when
his prayer was ended returned to his spiritual sons,
saying : " She is delivered.   The Lord Jesus, who
deigned to be born of a woman, has come to her aid,
and this time she will not die." [14]

Another incident is suggestive of Columbkille's
great veneration for the sign of the cross.   A certain youth was carrying home a vessel of new
milk, and on passing the door of the Abbot's little

---

[14] " Prophecies," as they are called, of St. Columbkille have
been published at various times and places during this century.
They are all silly fictions.   No man who respects truth, the memory
of the Saint, or his own intelligence, can give any credit to such
vile forgeries.   The pious and learned O'Curry fully discusses this
subject in one of his matchless " Lectures."   " It is remarkable,"
he says, in concluding, " that no reference to any of these long,
circumstantially-defined prophecies can be found in any of the many
ancient copies of the Saint's life which have come down to us. . . .
I feel it to be a duty I owe to my country, as well as to my creed as
a Catholic, to express thus in public the disgust which I feel
with every right-minded Irishman in witnessing the dishonest exer-
tions of certain parties of late years in attempting, by various publications, to fasten these disgraceful forgeries on the credulity of
honest and sincere Catholics as the undoubtedly inspired revelations
of the ancient saints of Erin. . . .   It is time that this kind of de-
lusion should be put an end to.   Our primitive saints never did, according to any reliable authority, pretend to foretell political events
of remote occurrence."—*Lectures on the MS. Materials of Ancient
Irish History,* p 410.

cell, where, as usual, he was writing, he asked a blessing on his burden. But when the man of God made the sign of the cross, a strange commotion seemed to move the contents of the vessel; the lid was suddenly flung off, and the greater part of the milk was scattered around.

The youth laid down the pail, and, kneeling, he began to pray. The Saint, however, desired him to rise. " To-day you have acted unwisely," he said, "in not making the sign of the cross of our Lord on your vessel before you poured in the milk. It was this omission that caused the demon to enter there, but, being unable to bear the sign of the cross, he has now fled away." Columbkille then asked him to bring the vessel near, that he might again bless it; and no sooner had he done so than "the benediction of his holy hand" so increased the little milk which remained that the pail was once more filled to the brim.

Towards his last days a celestial light was occasionally seen to surround him as a garment. And once as he prayed his face was first lit up with beatific joy, which finally gave expression to a profound sadness. Two of his monks saw the singular change of countenance. Throwing themselves at the feet of the venerable Abbot, they implored him, with tears in their eyes, to tell them what he had learned in his prayer.

" Dear children," said he, with gentle kindness,

" I do not wish to afflict you.   But it is thirty years to-day since I began my pilgrimage in Caledonia.   I have long prayed to God to let my exile end with this thirtieth year, and to call me to His heavenly country.   When you saw me so joy-ous, it was because I could already see the angels who came to seek my soul.   But all at once they stopped short down there upon that rock at the farthest limits of the sea which surrounds our island, as if they would approach to take me and could not.

"And, in truth, the blessed spirits could not, because the Lord had paid less regard to my ardent prayer than to that of the many churches which have prayed for me, and which have ob-tained, against my will, that I should still dwell in this body for four years.   That is the reason of my sadness.   But in four years I shall die with-out being sick; in four years, I know it and see it, they will come back, those holy angels, and I shall take my flight with them towards the Lord."

Dear old Saint ! his last day on earth came.   It was a Saturday in sunny June.   Drawn in a car by oxen, the venerable Abbot passed through the fields near the monastery, and blessed his monks at their labor.   Then, rising up in his rustic chariot, he gave his solemn benediction to the whole island —a benediction which, according to local tradi-tion, was like that of St. Patrick in Ireland, and

drove from that day all vipers and venomous creatures out of Iona.[15]

He then took his way to the granary of the
monastery and gave it his blessing, remarking at

[15] After the death of St. Columbkille, Iona became the most
famous sanctuary of the Celts. It was the burying-place of kings,
princes, and nobles. Seventy kings were buried at the feet of our
Saint.

Even Shakespeare, in his great tragedy of "Macbeth," does
not forget to put the following dialogue into the mouths of his
characters:

> "ROSSE. Where is Duncan buried?
> MACDUFF. Carried to Colmes-Kill,
> The sacred storehouse of his predecessors,
> And guardian of their bones."

The ravages of the Danes first dimmed the light of Iona. They
sacked its famous monastery in 801, and killed sixty-eight people,
as is recorded by the "Annals of the Four Masters," vol. i. p. 411.
For safety the sacred remains of Columbkille were transferred to Ireland towards the close of the same century.

The ruin and plunder begun by the pagan Danes was completed
by Protestant fanaticism in the dark days of the so-called Reformation. All the sacred edifices of Iona were pillaged by a horde
of brutal ruffians. It was a desert in the eighteenth century.
"The three hundred and sixty crosses which covered the soil of the
holy island" had been thrown into the sea. "We are now tread-
ing," wrote Dr. Samuel Johnson when he visited this historic spot,
"that illustrious island which was once the luminary of the Cale-
donian regions, whence savage clans and roving barbarians derived the benefits of knowledge and the blessings of religion." Iona
now belongs to the Duke of Argyll. It has a population of about 350
souls—all Presbyterians! See "The Monks of the West," appendix,
note i.

the same time to his faithful attendant, **Diarmid:**
"This very night I shall enter into the path of
my fathers. You weep, dear Diarmid; but console yourself. It is my Lord Jesus who deigns to
invite me to rejoin Him. It is He who has revealed to me that my summons will come to-
night."

The holy Abbot departed from the store-house.
On the road to the monastery he was met by a
good and ancient servant, the old white horse,
which came and put his head upon the shoulder of
his kind master, as if to take a last leave of him.
"The eyes of the old horse," says one of the
Saint's biographers, "had an expression so pathetic that they seemed to be bathed in tears."
But carressing the faithful brute, he gave it a
blessing.

He now retired to his cell and began to work
for the last time. It was at his dearly-beloved employment —transcribing the Psalter. When the
great old man had come to the thirty-third Psalm,
and the verse, "*Inquirentes autem Dominum non
deficient omni bono,*" he paused. "I must stop," he
said; "Baithen [16] will write the rest."

After some time spent in earnest prayer, he entrusted his only companion with a last message for
his spiritual sons, advising them, like the Apostle
of old, "to love one another."

[16] Who became the Saint's successor.

As soon as the midnight bell had rung for the Matins of the Sunday festival, the noble old Saint arose from his bed of stone, entered the church, and knelt down before the altar. Diarmid followed him, but as the church was not yet lighted he could only find him by groping and crying out in sad tones: "My father, where are you?" He found Columbkille lying before the altar, and, placing himself at his side, he raised the Abbot's venerable head upon his knees.

The whole community soon arrived with lights, and wept as one man at the sight of their dying chief and father. Once more the dear Saint opened his eyes, and turned them toward his children on each side with a look full of serene and radiant joy. Then with Diarmid's aid he raised, as best he could, his right hand to bless them all. His hand dropped, the last sigh came from his lips, and his face remained calm and sweet like that of a man who in his sleep had seen a vision of heaven. And thus died, or rather passed away, at the age of seventy-six, on the 9th of June, in the year 597, the glorious St. Columbkille, Irish prince, poet, monk, and missionary—a man whose beautiful name and shining deeds will live for ever and for ever."

"This great Saint has not been forgotten in the New World. There are churches in Newark, Cleveland, St. Louis, Boston, New

" The countenance of Columbkille," says his an‑ cient biographer, St. Adamnan, " resembled that of an angel.   In conversation he was brilliant ; in work, holy ; in disposition, excellent ; and in coun‑ cil, distinguished.   Though he lived on earth, his manners were those of heaven.   Every hour of his life was passed in prayer, reading, writing, or some useful occupation."

York, and various other places, dedicated to divine worship under the patronage of St. Columbkille.

SAINT GREGORY THE GREAT,

POPE, AND DOCTOR OF THE CHURCH.

DIED A. D. 605.

OURAGE, it has been said, is a necessary virtue in all the followers of Jesus Christ. The ancient faith is the religion of courage and of combat ; and we find a happy illustration of this principle in the life of our great Saint.

Gregory[1] was born at Rome of pious, wealthy, and noble parents, about the year 540. Gordian, his father, was a senator, but after the birth of the Saint, he bade adieu to the world, and died one of the seven cardinal deacons of the Eternal City. His mother, Sylvia, also consecrated herself to heaven in the religious state.

Gregory went through a long and brilliant course of studies. Shortly after reaching manhood he was appointed chief magistrate of Rome by the Emperor Justin the Younger. The death of his father left him master of an immense for-

---

[1] Gregory is from the German, and signifies *watchful.*

tune, with which he built six monasteries, and transformed his own stately residence into a seventh.[1] He himself took the monastic habit in 575.[2]

In this retirement Gregory became so wholly absorbed in prayer, fasting, and the study of the sacred sciences that he contracted a painful weakness of the stomach. He fell into swoons if he did not eat often. But what gave him the greatest sorrow was his inability to fast even on Easter Eve. He consulted a monk of eminent sanctity in relation to this affliction. Both prayed to heaven, and Gregory was happily cured.

While yet a simple monk this illustrious Saint projected the conversion of England. He happened one day to take a walk through the Roman market, and the sight of several young slaves exposed for sale attracted his attention. He was so struck with their fair forms and beautiful countenances that he stopped and made enquiries as to

[1] This mansion once the residence, and now the convent, of St. Gregory, is another interesting monument by which Mount Cœlius is adorned. Living in one of the most disastrous epochs in Roman history, this Holy Pontiff has, by his piety, his munificence, his zeal, and his learning, earned the veneration of the Catholic Church. No English traveler, at least, should leave unvisited the monument of this illustrious Pontiff, to whom his nation was once so much indebted.—*Archbishop MacHale*, letter liv.

[2] He belonged to the Order of St. Benedict

their country and religion. The slave-dealer informed him that they came from an island called Britain,
and that they were heathens.

"What evil luck," cried Gregory, heaving a
deep sigh, "that the Prince of Darkness should
possess beings with an aspect so radiant, and that
the grace of those countenances should reflect a
soul void of the inward grace! But of what nation
are they?"

"'They are Angles," was the reply.

"Truly they are well named," said the great-
souled monk, " for these Angles have the faces of
angels; and they must become the brethren of the
angels in heaven. From what province have they
been brought?"

"From Deïra."

"Still good," he continued. *"De ira eruti*—they
shall be snatched from the ire of God, and called to
the mercy of Christ. And what is the name of the
king of their country?"

"Alle."

"So be it," said Gregory; "he is right well named, for they shall soon sing the *Alleluia* in his kingdom."

He bought the captive youths and took them to
the palace of his father—now his own monastery.
"The purchase of these three or four slaves," says
Montalembert, "was thus the origin of the redemption of all England."

From that hour Gregory formed the grand de sign of bringing over the Anglo-Saxons to the Catholic Church; and towards its completion he con secrated a persevering courage, devotion, and pru dence which the greatest men have not surpassed. At first he sought and obtained permission from the Pope to go as a missionary to England; but when the news of his departure spread through Rome the populace overwhelmed the Sovereign Pon tiff with reproaches.

"Holy Father," they cried out, "what have you done? In allowing Gregory to go away you have in jured Rome, you have undone us, and offended St. Peter."

The Pope reconsidered his action, and de spatched messengers to recall Gregory. The Saint was overtaken on the third day, and obliged, though with much reluctance, to return to the Eternal City.

Pope Pelagius II. died at the beginning of a dreadful pestilence, and Gregory was unanimous ly chosen to succeed him in 590. He opposed his own election by every means in his power; and when he saw all his efforts fail he fled in disguise, and lay concealed in woods and caverns for three days. During this time the people of Rome prayed and fasted. A pillar of light pointed out our Saint's wild abode. He was thus discovered, and no longer resisted the clear will of Heaven.

He was consecrated on the 3d of September, in the midst of great acclamations.

Writing to one of his friends, the new Pontiff says: "I remember with tears that I have lost the calm harbor of my repose, and with many a sigh I look towards the firm land which I cannot reach. If you love me, assist me with your prayers."

Sad and sombre was the state of the Church at that period. Plague and famine desolated Rome. The Eastern churches were wretchedly divided, and shattered by the Nestorians and other heretics worse than heathens. In the west of Europe, Spain was overrun by the Arian heresy, and England was buried in paganism. But Gregory was a man of vast genius and unquailing courage. It was in the midst of such unhappy circumstances that he carried out the spiritual conquest of England.

In obedience to the command of the Vicar of Christ, St. Augustine and his forty companions set out for the distant land of the Angles. When the travelers reached Lerins—that Mediterranean isle where, a century and a half before, St. Patrick had prepared himself for the conversion of Ireland—they were frightened by the tales they heard in relation to the Anglo-Saxons. These people, it was told, were a nation of wild beasts and cannibals. The monks gathered around their leader and besought him to return to the Pope, with the request that they might be relieved from a journey so perilous and toilsome.

Augustine departed for Rome. He told all to Gregory, but that man of hardy, apostolic spirit would not listen to such demands. He seized his pen and wrote those timid "fishers of men" a letter that revived their drooping courage.

" It were better," wrote the great Pope, "not to begin that good work at all than to give it up after having commenced it. . . . Forward, then, in God's name ! . . . The more you have to suf. fer, the brighter will your glory be in eternity. May the grace of the Almighty protect you and grant me to behold the fruit of your labors in the eternal country ! If I cannot share your toil, I shall none the less rejoice in the harvest, for God knows that I lack not the good will."

Augustine and his band of missionaries tra. versed France, crossed the Strait of Dover, and stepped ashore on the same spot where over six hundred and fifty years previously Julius Cæsar had erected the Roman standard. The new con- querors, like Cæsar, arrived under the ensigns of Rome; but it was of Rome the Eternal, not Rome the imperial. They came to restore the law of the Gospel which the fierce Saxon had drowned in blood. They came to imprint the immortal seal of the Catholic faith on the soil of England.

" The history of the Church," says Bossuet, "contains nothing finer than the entrance of the holy monk Augustine into the kingdom of Kent with forty of his companions, who, preceded by the cross and the image of the great King, our Lord Jesus Christ, offered up their solemn prayers for the conversion of England." [4]

When the success of Augustine's mission reached Gregory, it filled his great heart with joy inexpressible. He writes to the Patriarch of Alexandria :

[4] Ethelbert, the noble King of Kent, was baptized on Whitsunday, 597, and a crowd of Saxons followed his example. "The first of the converts," writes Montalembert, "was also the first of the benefactors of the infant Church." Ethelbert transferred his own palace in the town of Canterbury to St. Augustine. He also gave him a piece of ground for the foundation of a monastery. The charter of the new monastery has been brought to light in our age. It is " the oldest authentic record of the religious and political history of England." Here is the text and signatures of the ancient document:

" I, Ethelbert, King of Kent, with the consent of the venerable Archbishop Augustine and of my nobles, give and concede to God, in honor of St. Peter, a certain portion of the land which is mine by right, and which lies to the east of the town of Canterbury, to the end that a monastery may be built thereon, and that the proprieties hereinafter named may be in full possession of him who shall be appointed thereof. Wherefore I swear and ordain, in the name of Almighty God, who is the first and sovereign Judge, that the land thus given is given for ever—that it shall not be lawful either for me or for my successors to take any part of it whatsoever from its possessors ; and if any one shall attempt to lessen or to annul our gift, that he be in this life deprived

" The bearer of your letters found me sick and leaves me sick. But God grants me gladness of heart to temper the bitterness of my bodily suffering. The flock of the Holy Church grows and multiplies. The spiritual harvests gather into the heavenly garners. . . . You announced to me the conversion of your heretics, the concord of your faithful people. . . . I make you a return in kind, because I know you will rejoice in my joy and that you have aided me with your prayers.

" Know, then, that the nation of the Angles, situated at the extremest *angle* of the world, had till now continued in idolatry, worshipping stocks

of the Holy Communion of the Body and Blood of Christ, and at the day of judgment cut off from the company of the saints.

" ✠ I, Ethelbert, King of the English, have confirmed this gift by my own hand with the sign of the holy cross.

" ✠ I, Augustine, by the grace of God, Archbishop, have freely subscribed.

" ✠ I, Eadbald, son of the king, have adhered.

" ✠ I, Hamigisile, Duke, have approved.

" ✠ I, Hocca, Earl, have consented.

" ✠ I. Angemundus, Referendary, have approved.

" ✠ I, Graphio, Earl, have said it is well.

" ✠ I, Tangisile, *regis optimas*, have confirmed.

" ✠ I, Pinca, have consented.

" ✠ I, Geddi, have corroborated."

This venerable document bears the date of January 9, 605. See Montalembert's " Monks of the West," vol ii. p. 160, and Palgrave's "Rise and Progress of the British Commonwealth," vol. ii. pp. 215-18.

and stones. God inspired me to send thither a
monk of my monastery here to preach the Gospel to them. This monk, whom I caused to be
ordained bishop by the French bishop has penetrated to this nation at the uttermost ends of the
earth, and I have now received tidings of the
happy success of his enterprise. He and his companions have wrought miracles that seem to come
near to those of the Apostles themselves, and more
than ten thousand English have been baptized by
them at one time." [5]

This great Pope was the father of the poor.
So as to spare them confusion in receiving alms,
he relieved their necessities with much sweetness
and amiability. He called the old men among
them his fathers. He often entertained them at
his own table. He kept by him an exact list of
the Roman poor, and provided liberally for the
wants of each. At the beginning of every month
he distributed corn, wine, cheese, fish, beef, and
other articles of food. He appointed officers in
every street to attend to the daily wants of the

[5] This celebrated Pope sent England its *first* library, in 601. It
consisted chiefly of religious works, but it may be noted that
in the collection was *a copy of Homer.* In the library of the
college of Corpus Christi, Cambridge, a Latin MS. of the four
Gospels is yet preserved which, according to an old tradition, is
the copy brought from Rome by St. Augustine in 596. We should
not forget that it was St. Augustine and his monks that first taught
the English how to read.

needy sick, and before eating himself he always
sent some delicacy from his table to the homes of
poverty. On one occasion a beggar was found
dead on the corner of some out-of-the-way street.
The news struck Gregory to the heart with sorrow, and it is said that he abstained from celebrating Mass for several days, deeming himself
guilty of negligence in not seeking the poor with
more care and energy.[6]

A lady of distinction, being troubled with scruples, wrote to our illustrious Doctor, saying that
she could never be at ease till he would obtain
from God by revelation an assurance that her sins
were forgiven.

" You ask," replied Gregory, "what is both
difficult and unprofitable. It is difficult, because
I am unworthy to receive any revelation. It is
unprofitable, because an absolute assurance of
your pardon does not suit your state till you can
no longer weep for your sins. You ought always
to fear and tremble for them, and wash them away
by daily tears. Paul was taken up to the third
heaven, yet trembled lest he became a reprobate.
Security is the mother of negligence."

[6] The grave cares of the pontificate did not prevent Gregory
from indulging in practices of the most ardent charity. Every
day he invited twelve paupers into his palace and personally
waited upon them at table, and, according to the legend, that
humility was rewarded by his one day seeing an angel make the
thirteenth of the company at that table.—*Artaud.*

He was a man of unceasing toil and activity. It is truly incredible how much he wrote,[7] and, during the fifteen years that he governed the Church, what great things he achieved for the glory of God, the good of the faith, the reformation of manners, the relief of the poor, the comfort of the afflicted, the establishment of ecclesiastical discipline, and the progress of piety and religion. But our astonishment redoubles when we remember that during all this time his life was a daily battle with bad health.[8]

It was this illustrious Pontiff who ordered that blessed ashes should be placed on the heads of the faithful at the beginning of Lent.[9] He instituted processions on the Feast of the Purification of the Most Blessed Virgin, and the recitation of the Lit-

[7] Gregory was the author of a prodigious number of excellent works. Among these is his incomparable book "On the Pastoral Charge." He wrote it shortly after he became Pope. It treats of the duties and obligations of pastors. It is a volume that has been highly praised by popes and councils. Alfred the Great translated it into Anglo-Saxon, and sent a copy to each of the bishops in his kingdom. This great Pope also reformed the Sacramentary, or Missal and Ritual of the Church.

[8] This holy Pope had labored many years under a great weakness of his breast and stomach, and was afflicted with slow fevers and frequent fits of the gout, which once confined him to his bed two whole years.—*Butler.*

[9] Up to the time of Celestine III., created Pope in 1191, it was the custom to place the holy ashes on the head of the Pope as they are now placed on the heads of the faithful, and to repeat the well-

any of the Saints on the feast of St. Mark, on account of the growing virulence of the plague which
had carried off his august predecessor.

The disease always ended in a fit of sneezing or
of yawning, and the Pope ordered that " *God
bless you* " should be said to those who sneezed,
and that the sign of the cross should be made on
the lips of those who yawned. It was at the end
of this dreadful plague that the antiphon *Regina
cæli lætare* was introduced into the chants of the
Church.[10]

Our great Saint was the first who used the
phrase, *to speak ex cathedra.* He was also the first
who ordered that pontifical bulls or diplomas
should be dated from the incarnation of our Divine Redeemer. Through a sentiment of humble modesty—ever the companion of real greatness—he styled himself in all his letters " *ser-*

known formula : " Remember, man, that thou art dust, and unto
dust thou shalt return." But, under Urban VI., elected Pope in
1378, a different custom was introduced, which obtains to this day—
namely, that of strewing the ashes upon the head of the Holy Father
without saying a word.—*Artaud.*

[10] Many persons affirm that St. Gregory the Great instituted what
is known as the " Gregorian Chant." But the learned Dominic
M. Manni, in his " Dissertation on the Discipline of the Ancient
Ecclesiastical Chant," printed at Florence in 1756, proves that
Gregory did not invent that chant, but reduced it to a more fitting
form and rendered it more easy to be studied. A chant similar to
the " Gregorian " was known in the time of Pope Hilary, who
was raised to the Pontificate in 461.—*Artaud.*

vant of the servants of God.'' The custom over twelve centuries has consecrated this beautiful title. It is used in our own day by Leo XIII.

Extraordinary men commissioned by Heaven to begin works which are to be truly great and enduring seldom live to old age. Gregory the Great, whose pontificate had left a bright and lasting impression on the memory of Christendom and a peerless example in the annals of the Church, filled the chair of St. Peter only fifteen years. He died on 12th of March in the year 605.[11]

---

[11] The first Catholic colonists of Maryland named the Potomac after St. Gregory. "Never have I beheld a larger or more beautiful river," writes the venerable missionary, Father White, S. J. "In comparison with it the Thames is a mere rivulet."—*Relatio Itineris in Marylandiam.*

SAINT BEDE, O. S. B.,

FATHER OF THE CHURCH.

DIED A.D. 735.

———

HE early history of the Catholic Church in England is crowned by one of those great figures that stand out above the sea of ages, and triumph over the forgetfulness as well as over the systematic contempt of scoffing and frivolous generations.

The name of Bede,[2] after having been one of the brightest and most popular in Christendom, still remains invested with an imperishable fame. He is the type of that studious and learned life which, in the eyes of many, sums up the entire mission of the monk.

To have seen him pray, says an ancient writer, one would think that he left himself no time to study; and when we look at his books we admire

[1] O. S. B., the Order of St. Benedict, of which he was a member.
[2] Bede is from the Anglo-Saxon and signifies *prayer*.

that he could have found time to do anything else but write.

Our Saint [8] was born in the North of England, at a village near the mouth of the Tyne, in the year 673. The little Bede, at the age of seven, was confided by his relatives to the care of Abbot St. Benedict Biscop, who had just completed his monastery of Wearmouth. But the great abbot soon transferred the charge and education of his young pupil to his assistant, Ceolfrid. The latter, with twenty companions, had founded the house of Yarrow.

No sooner, however, had they settled down in their new home than a cruel epidemic swept over the establishment. Death carried away all the choir monks. The Abbot Ceolfrid and his favorite pupil, the young Bede, then in his thirteenth year, alone remained. But the two continued to celebrate as best they could, with tears and sorrow, the entire canonical service until the arrival of a new body of monks.

It is truly touching to think of these two heroic souls. One was already a mature and illustrious man, the other an obscure child predestined to fame. Together they sang the praises of God in

[8] The title of Venerable, which was given to him only in the ninth century by a kind of universal consent, did not then, as now, imply an inferior position to that of saint or blessed in the celestial hierarchy.—*Montalembert.*

their lonely, plague-stricken cloister—together they awaited the future with lofty faith and unconquerable courage.

The life of Bede was entirely passed in the monastery of Yarrow, which he immortalized by his virtues and his vast learning. From a pupil he soon rose to be a master of the highest rank. At the age of thirty he was elevated to the sacred dignity of the priesthood. Many were his duties. It was his pleasure, as he himself tells us, "to learn, to teach, and to write." He gave daily lessons to six hundred monks. And until his last illness he had no assistant in his literary labors.

" I am my own secretary," he said; "I dictate, I compose, I copy all myself." [4]

This great genius, this cheerful and unwearied worker, was the author of forty-five different books. Many of these are comments on Holy Scripture, but he handled all the sciences and every branch of literature. [5]

---

[4] In King Alfred's version Bede is styled Mass-Priest, because it was his employment to sing every day the conventual Mass. He tells us that the holy abbot and founder, St. Benedict Biscop, like the rest of the brethren, used to winnow the corn and thresh it, to give milk to the lambs and calves, and to work in the bake-house, garden, and kitchen. Bede must have sometimes had a share in such employments, and he was always cheerfully obedient and indefatigable. —*Butler.*

In his scientific essay, "De Rerum Natura," it is worth noting

He taught princes and advised prelates, but such was his love of simplicity that he would never accept the dignity of Abbot.[6] When consulted as to abuses in church or state, his words were wise, noble, and weighty. He always wrote with manly independence.

In a letter to his pupil Egbert,[7] Bishop of York, he says: "Beware, dear bishop, of the crime of those who think only of drawing earthly lucre from their ministry. It is said that there are many villages in our Northumberland, situated among inaccessible hills or woods, where the arrival of a bishop to baptize, and teach the faith and the distinction between good and evil, has never been wit-

that this Father of the Church, in the eighth century, teaches that the earth is *round*.

The Protestant Bayle greatly admired the learning of our Saint. According to Bayle, he surpassed Gregory the Great in eloquence and copiousness of style, adding that there is scarcely anything in all antiquity worthy to be read which is not found in Bede.

[6] He declined the abbatial dignity which was pressed upon him. Malmesbury gives us a letter of Pope Sergius, by which, with many honorable expressions, he was invited to Rome, that Pope desiring to see and consult him in certain matters of the greatest importance. This must have happened about the time that he was ordained priest. Bede out of modesty suppressed this circumstance. What hindered his journey hither we know not; but we have his word for it that he lived from his childhood in his monastery without traveling abroad—that is, without making any considerable journey. —*Butler.*

He was a prince, and brother of the King of Northumberland.

nessed, yet where no one is exempt from payment of the bishop's dues. Thus there are bishops who, far from evangelizing their flock without reward, as our Lord wills, receive, without preaching, the money which He has forbidden them to accept even while preaching."

In this great soul the Christian virtues were naturally united to that thirst for knowledge, that love of study, that vivifying desire for work, that noble thoughtfulness of things human and divine, which makes Bede such an interesting figure in early English history—that history of which he himself was the father and founder.[8]

But the most beautiful part of his life was the hour of his happy departure from this world. It was a scene sublime. His last days were devoted to the translation of the Gospel of St. John into Anglo-Saxon. Even his illness did not interrupt the work, which he continued with the aid of a young secretary. As the venerable monk dic tated he would sometimes pause and say: " Make haste to learn, for I know not how long I may remain with you, or if my Creator may shortly call me."

[8] Bede wrote his famous work called the " Ecclesiastical History of the English Nation " in the year 731. It is dedicated to a pious and learned king of Northumbria. " This work," says Montalembert, " has made Bede not only the father of English history, but the true founder of history in the Middle Ages."

Edmund Burke styles Bede the " Father of English learning."

On the eve of the Ascension the translation was nearly finished. "Beloved father, there is still one chapter wanting," said the young secretary. "Would it fatigue you to speak any more ?'

" I am still able to speak," answered Bede. " Take your pen, make it, and write rapidly.' The other obeyed.

At noon he sent for the priests of the monastery and bade them a last farewell, requesting each of them to say Masses for his eternal repose. Thus passed his last day until the evening.

" Most dear master," said his companion tenderly, "there remains but one verse to write."

"Write quickly," answered Bede. In a few minutes the work was completed, and the young monk exclaimed: "It is now finished."

" You say truly, it is finished," said the dying Saint. " Dear child, hold my head in your arms, and turn me, that I may have the pleasure of looking towards the little oratory where I was wont to pray." Thus, lying on the floor of his cell, he sang, "Glory be to the Father, and to the Son, and to the Holy Ghost," and as he murmured the last of these divine names his beautiful soul passed to the bosom of God. [9]

---

[9] The monastic sanctuary towards which the dying look of Bede was turned still remains in part, if we may believe the best ar-

His death occurred at the age of sixty-two, on the evening of the 26th of May, in the year 735.

" Remember," writes the famous monk Alcuin to the religious community of Yarrow, many years after, "remember the nobility of your fathers, and be not the unworthy sons of such great ancestors; look at your books, at the beauty of your churches and monastic buildings. Let your young men learn to persevere in the praises of God, and not in driving foxes out of their holes, or in wearing out their strength running after hares. What folly to leave the footsteps of Christ and run after the trail of a fox! Look at Bede, the noblest doctor of our country. See what zeal he showed for knowledge from his youth, and the glory which he has received among men, though that is much less important and less dazzling than his reward before God. Stir up, then, the minds of your sleepers by his example. Study his works, and you will be able to draw from them, both for yourselves and others, the secret of eternal beauty."

thæologists, and his memory has survived the changes of time. An old oaken chair is still shown which he is supposed to have used. It is the only existing relic of this great Saint. His tomb was first at Yarrow, but his relics were removed to Durham in the eleventh century. They were an object of veneration to the faithful up to the general profanation under Henry VIII., who pulled down the shrine and threw the bones on a dunghill, along with those of all the other holy apostles and martyrs of Northumberland.—*Montalembert.*

SAINT BERNARD,

ABBOT OF CLAIRVAUX AND DOCTOR OF THE CHURCH.

DIED A. D. 1153.

T. BERNARD,[1] the glory of the twelfth century and one of the great men of all time, was born in 1091 at the castle of Fontaines, near Dijon, France. He belonged to an eminent family. Tecelin, his father, was lord of Fontaines. He was a good man, and a noble knight of gentle manners. The Saint's mother, Elizabeth, was a truly Christian lady, who considered her children as sacred deposits committed to her charge by Heaven. Though of a very delicate constitution, she never trusted them to the care of strangers, but wisely and tenderly nursed them herself.[2]

The little Bernard was especially dear to his pious mother, as she had a vision of his future greatness and sanctity. In the sunshine of her

---

[1] Bernard is from the German and signies *bold as a bear.*

Our Saint was the third of a family of seven, six sons and one daughter.

eye he unfolded like a beautiful flower. With the simplicity of a good, gentle child he secretly imitated her actions—prayed like his mother; gave bread to the poor, like his mother; behaved kindly to every one, like his mother; spoke little, like his mother, and wept over his faults with the pure, crystal tears of boyhood.

From his earliest years he showed a wonderful inclination for study. There was something quick and bright in the precocious intelligence which shone forth in his eye, and in the refined and expressive features of his gracious countenance. His kind, open heart diffused over his face and person the innocent joy and smiling grace so lovely in childhood. At this time his figure was slender, his hair golden, and his complexion very fair.

Bernard gave a striking proof both of his patience and his delicacy of conscience in one of his childish illness. A woman offered to cure him of a headache which had long baffled all remedies; but the keen-sighted boy, having caught sight of some superstitious object, in her hand, divined her intention, sprang out of bed, and chased her from the room with a cry of indignation, because she had sought to cure his malady by the hateful arts of magic.

Our Lord, it seems, rewarded the piety of this heroic act. The pain instantly left the child, and he rose full of joy and health. Some years now passed by, and Bernard grew in age and grace before God and man.

The promising boy was sent to Chatillon, on the Seine, to pursue a complete course of studies in the college of that town. He made rapid progress. He soon learned to read and write Latin with ease and elegance ; he cultivated poetry, and even became too passionately fond of literature. He was, however, a wise, practical student, who was not misled by the mere tinsel and glitter of knowledge. He sought knowledge with a practical end in view; and any other intention would be unworthy of a Christian.[3]

But in the pursuit of learning he never lost sight of virtue. The charm of early innocence was not destroyed, as too often happens, with the progress of years and education. In him, as time rolled away, the head was not a gainer at the expense of the heart, nor was love overlaid by intellect.

Whilst Bernard's mental gifts developed, faith

---

[3] As the great Saint afterwards said himself: "There are some who wish to learn only for the sake of learning, and this curiosity is ridiculous; others wish to learn only to be considered learned, and this vanity is blamable; others wish to learn only to traffic with their learning, and this traffic is ignoble. When, then, is learning good? It is good, says the prophet, *when it is put in practice;* and he is guilty, adds the Apostle, who, having a knowledge of the good which he should do, does it not."

took deeper root in his soul. He enjoyed the in‹
ward sweetness of a perpetual spring. It was
the blossoming period of life. There are few men
who have no recollection of that mysterious time
when the pure young soul opens and produces the
first flower of love. Happy when its sweet perfume rises aloft towards heaven!

At this age every young man is a poet. He is a
poet because he loves, and because poetry is the
natural language of all who love. But poetry
does not express itself in words alone. It lives in
the pensiveness of silence; it lives sometimes in
tears; it kindles the eyes; it gives birth to sighs
and dreams. We love and know not what we
love—we catch faint glimpses of it, we invoke it, we
seek it everywhere amid the shadows and reflections
of truth and beauty. But our ideal is not upon
earth; and hence that mixture of love, and hope,
and sorrow which fills the soul with feelings unde-
finable.

The young Bernard passed through the various
stages of that poetical period of life. Alas! it is
of short duration. The flower must fall before
the fruit can appear; and between the fall of the
flower and the maturity of the fruit there is in the
spiritual as in the natural life a long, uncertain in-
terval—a time of toil and heavy, anxious labor,
which sometimes drags on even to the end of our
earthly course!

Bernard was in this second period when he **left** Chatillon to return to his father's house.   He **was** then just nineteen, shining outwardly with all **the** brightness of youth and genius.   His rank as **a** young nobleman, his prudence and natural modesty, his gift of conversation, his affability and sweetness of temper, made him beloved by every one.   But these very advantages had their dangers.   He no longer felt within him the transports of his first fervor.   His piety seemed to have lost its sweetness.   For him the springtime was past.   Shadows were gathering around his precious soul.

Purity, with him as with most other young people, was the first virtue on trial.   Protected hitherto by innocence and modesty, it had suffered no assault;   but the charms of the world, into which he had just entered, excited his senses, and strongly allured a heart full of simplicity and only too open to outward impressions.   He battled bravely, however, against this weakness of fallen human nature;   and God mercifully came to his aid and blessed him with victory.   Truly there is no king like him who is king of himself.

Meanwhile, he was struck to the heart by a **new** affliction.   It put an end to his home happiness.   His mother, like a fruit ripe for heaven, **was** snatched away by death.   The good and **gentle** lady bade adieu to this world, fortified **by the**

sacraments, and surrounded by her family and
by many distinguished ecclesiastics.[4]

The temptations of the world and the loneliness
that seemed to surround his steps after the death
of his mother deeply touched the heart of Bernard.   Sometimes he seriously pondered the matter over, and began to think of forsaking his
home and retiring to Citeaux, where God was
served with great fervor.   Grace touched his
heart.   One day, as he was going to see his brothers, who were then with the Duke of Burgundy
at the siege of Grancei Castle, he stepped into a
church on the roadside, and, in great anxiety of
soul, prayed that God would direct him and show
him the way in which he should go.

At that moment a deep calm fell upon his
troubled soul, the breath of heaven rekindled the
lamp of his spiritual life, and the young nobleman, all on fire with love, consecrated himself for

---

[4] "She was often seen," writes an ancient author, "alone, and
on foot, on the road from Fontaines and Dijon, entering the
houses of the poor, distributing food and medicine, carrying all
kinds of succor and consolation to the afflicted; and what was
most admirable in her beneficence was that she so practised it
as to preserve the utmost possible concealment.   She did all her
good works in person, without the assistance of her servants;
and of her it might be said with truth, that her left hand knew not
the bounty of her right."

It may be remarked that this was a Catholic lady of the so-
called "dark ages"; but we confess that to our mind she was
a noble, large-hearted, and very *enlightened* woman.

ever to God, and joyfully took upon him the yoke
of Him who is meek and humble of heart. He resolved to embrace the Cistercian Rule.[5]

Many years after this change Bernard loved to
recall its circumstances. "I am not ashamed to
confess," he would say to his monks at Clairvaux,
"that frequently, and especially at the beginning
of my conversion, I have experienced great hardness and coldness of heart. I sought Him whom
my soul desired to love—Him upon whom my
frozen heart might rest and gather warmth; and as
no one came to help me, and to melt the thick ice
which bound all my interior senses in its chain, my
soul became more and more languid, weak, and be-
numbed, giving way to grief, and almost to despair,
and murmuring inwardly, 'Who can endure such
cold?' Then all at once, at the first sight, perhaps, of some spiritual person—or, perhaps, at the
mere remembrance of the dead or the absent—the
Spirit of God began to breathe upon these frozen
waters; they flowed again, and my tears served me
for food day and night."

Bernard's friends and brothers endeavored to
dissuade him from entering the religious state;

[5] The Cistercians were founded by St. Robert in 1098. He
adopted the rule of St. Benedict, and established the house of
Citeaux—hence the name Cistercian. The Trappists—now the
most austere order in the Church—are a reformed branch of the
Cistercians.

but he so graciously pleaded his cause as to draw them all over to join him in his noble undertaking. One of the saint's uncles, named Gauldri, a veteran warrior, came to the same resolution. One by one his brothers made choice of the narrow way. And Hugh of Maçon, a very rich, noble, and distinguished man, and an intimate friend and school-fellow of St. Bernard, shed tears when he heard of his design; but two interviews induced him to become his companion.[6]

The saint's companions were now thirty[7] in number, all assembled in a house at Chatillon, engaged in the work of preparing themselves for the final consecration to heaven. In truth, there was something very extraordinary in this union of so many persons of high distinction bent on one supernatural object. It gives a true idea of Bernard's immense sway over his fellow-men. His burning words of love and power, like a living chain, bound them together and linked them to his own great heart.

[6] "This same Hugh," says a writer of that day, "afterwards became Abbot of Pontigny and Bishop of Auxerre—a church which he still rules in such a manner as to prove that he has the merit as well as the dignity of the episcopate."

[7] Several of those whom Bernard gained to God being married persons, their wives, who entered into their views, retired into a Benedictine convent, near Dijon, the same to which Hombeline, St. Bernard's sister, afterwards went.—*Ratisbonne.*

On the day appointed for the execution of their design, Bernard and his four brothers went to the castle of Fontaines to bid a last farewell of their father, and to beg his blessing. It was a scene of sorrow. The pearly tears of the gentle young Hombeline mingled with the sobs of the aged Tecelin.[8]

As Bernard and his brothers left the castle-yard they saw their youngest brother, who was at play with other children of his own age. Guido, the eldest, embraced him, saying: "Adieu, my little brother Nivard. Do you see this castle and these lands? Well, all will be yours—yours alone."

"What!" exclaimed the child, with more than a child's thoughtfulness, "are you going to take heaven for yourselves and leave earth for me? The division is not equal." He soon after followed his brothers.

The thirty now journeyed together on foot, under the guidance of their beloved leader, who marched at their head. On reaching the famous monastery of Citeaux, this holy company prostrated themselves at the gate and begged of the abbot, St. Stephen,[9] to be allowed to join the

---

[8] For the consolation of the reader we hasten to say that towards the close of his life the venerable Tecelin rejoined his sons, and died, full of days, in the arms of St. Bernard.

[9] St. Stephen Harding, who was an Englishman. The rules of

monks in their penitential lives. The good abbot received them with open arms,[10] and gave them the habit. This was in 1113. St. Bernard was then twenty-three years of age.

From the moment of his entrance on the monastic life St. Bernard's chief care was to realize in himself the advice he had given to others. "If you begin," said he, "begin well."

"Bernard, Bernard," he would say to himself, "why did you come here?" He studied to mortify his senses, and in all things to die to himself. This practice, by continual repetition, became a custom, and custom was almost changed into nature ; so that, his soul being always occupied on God and the things of God, he seemed not to perceive what passed around him. After a year's novitiate he knew not whether the top of his cell was covered with a ceiling, nor could he tell

the monks of Citeaux were extremely rigorous. "These holy monks," says an ancient chronicler, "wished to live unknown and forgotten in their deep solitude. Their austerities seemed beyond human endurance. They were half naked, exposed to the most piercing cold of winter and the most burning heat of summer. To their continual labor they joined the most painful exercises : vigils, almost throughout the night, the Divine Office, spiritual lectures, long prayers, and other devout practices, succeeded each other without any intermission."

[10] Perhaps the prophetic eye of St. Stephen beheld the pope, the cardinals, the fourteen bishops, and the thousands of monks whom the chief applicant at the convent gate was to add to his order.

whether the church had more than one window, though it had three.

But man may stumble, even in climbing to the mountain heights of sanctity. It was so with our Saint. His affection for his mother had induced him to make a vow to recite the Seven Penitential Psalms daily for the repose of her soul.

"Once," says an ancient writer, "whilst still in his novitiate, he went to rest without having accomplished the duty which he had prescribed for himself. The next day Stephen, his spiritual father, being inwardly enlightened, said to him: 'Brother Bernard, to whom did you give the care of reciting your seven psalms yesterday?'

"At these words Bernard, astonished that a practice which he had kept secret should be known, burst into tears, and, throwing himself at the feet of his venerable guide, confessed his fault, and humbly begged pardon for it."

On finishing the year of novitiate, he and his companions made their profession. Bernard was now a monk. In all monastic exercises his ardor was extraordinary. He was unable, however, to reap the corn so as to keep up with the rest, and his superior appointed him other work; but he earnestly begged of God that he might be enabled to cut the grain, and soon equalled the best hands. As he toiled away his soul lived continually in God's holy presence.

It was to him a season of abundant grace and rapid progress. "He avows," says an ancient author, "that it was principally in the fields and woods that he received by prayer and contemplation the understanding of the Scriptures; and he is in the habit of saying pleasantly to his friends that he never had any other master in this study but the beech-trees and the oaks of the forest."

Bernard's constitution was feeble and delicate, but his fasts and mortifications were rigorous. At length he fell ill. He could neither eat nor sleep, and was often tormented by long fainting-fits. Thus he hastened the ruin of his health by the excess of his austerities; and, indeed, he had reason in after-years to regret his want of due discretion in the use of penitential practices.

He was a great lover of poverty in his habit, cell, and all others things, but he was none the less a lover of cleanliness. He termed dirtiness a mark of sloth or a pitiable vanity. His diet was coarse bread softened in warm water. He had a great aptitude for contemplation, and found every place suitable for that exercise.

But he omitted no opportunity of speaking for the good of his neighbor, and adapted himself with wonderful tact and prudence to the circumstances of all with whom he conversed—the rich or the poor, the learned or the ignorant. "When you speak," he would say, "do not hurry your words." And though his writings are warmed by the breath of his holy unction, yet they convey not the grace and fire of the winged words that flew from his burning lips.

The mother-house at Citeaux [11] soon became too narrow to shelter the numerous earnest souls that sought safety and salvation within its sanctified precincts. New foundations became necessary. St. Stephen Harding, therefore, appointed Bernard Abbot, and ordered him to go with twelve monks [12] and to establish a new house in the diocese of Langres.

[11] Citeaux offers at the present time but a melancholy spectacle. We visited this desert in the month of October, 1839, and this visit wrung our heart. Modern industry—more pitiless than the Vandals of past ages—has sought to drive from the place the slightest remembrance of the monks who civilized and sanctified it. Upon the ruins of the abbey rises a sugar manufactory of beet-root, which has since fallen into ruins; and a wretched play-house supplies the place of the monks' library—perhaps even of their church! The cell of St. Bernard, which was still in existence twenty years ago, has also been sacrificed to the *utility* of a manufactory. They showed us its remains. A castle, or rather a villa, painted yellow, contrasted strangely with the tombstones and loose bones which we tread under our feet. We examined with great care old plans of the immense enclosure, which included more than two hundred acres, without counting the fields, farms, court-yards, and other dependencies of the monastery ; but now it is not easy even to recognize the site—three villages have been constructed out of the remains.—*Abbé Ratisbonne.*

[12] Among the twelve were Bernard's brothers, his uncle Godfrey, and several relations.

Our Saint was then only in his twenty-fifth year; and it was a subject of general surprise that a young man of such delicate health, and who had no experience in worldly affairs, should be chosen as the head of so perilous an enterprise. But his virtue had shone forth in so remarkable a manner that St. Stephen—better versed than others in the hidden ways of Providence—did not hesitate to uphold this choice, the consequences of which were so happy for the Church.

The holy company set out on their journey, and singing psalms, with their young Abbot at their head, they took their way across a wild, uncultivated country. At length they reached a swampy valley. It was once the haunt of robbers, was surrounded by a dense forest, and was called the "Valley of Wormwood." Here they halted. It was to be the future home of St. Bernard, who gave it the name of Claire-Valée—which in time took the form of *Clairvaux*—for it was, indeed, to become a furnace of divine light.

The thirteen hardy monks at once bent themselves to the work of clearing off a spot of earth, and, with the assistance of the country people, built themselves little cells. At first they had much to suffer. On one occasion the distress was so extreme that even the very salt failed them. But their holy Abbot was a light in darkness, and proved himself equal to all difficulties.

"Guibert, my son," said Bernard to one of the monks, " take the ass, and go and buy salt in the market."

" My father," replied Guibert, " will you give me money to pay for it ? "

" Have confidence," said the man of God. "As to money, I do not know when we shall have any; but there is One above who keeps my purse and who has the care of my treasures."

At this Guibert smiled, and, looking at the Abbot, ventured to say: " My father, if I go empty-handed I fear I shall return empty-handed."

" Go," still replied Bernard, " and go with con. fidence. I repeat that my treasure will be with you on the road, and will furnish you with what is necessary."

This was enough. The monk saddled his ass, received the Abbot's blessing, and started on his way to the market, which was held near a castle called Risnellus.

" Guibert," continues the simple chronicler who relates the foregoing, " had been more incredulous than he should have been ; nevertheless, the God of all consolation procured him ar unexpected success, for not far from the neighbo ig town he met a priest, who saluted him and asked him whence he came. Guibert confided to him the ob. ject of his mission and the extreme poverty of his monastery. The recital so touched the heart of the charitable priest that he furnished him abundantly with all sorts of provisions."

The happy monk returned in haste to Clairvaux, and, throwing himself at Bernard's feet, related what had happened to him on the road.

"I told you, my son," said the Abbot gently, "that there is nothing more necessary to the Christian than confidence in God. Never lose it, and it will be well with you all the days of your life."

Clairvaux, at the time of its foundation, may be compared to the grain of mustard-seed spoken of in the Gospel. Nothing, in fact, could have been weaker, humbler, and more miserable than this heavenly seed when it was first cast into the field of the Church. It long vegetated without any development. It had to struggle against the most violent storms and tempests; but the principle of life contained within it rendered the work of God indestructible, and after many profound humiliations it made a sudden spring and grew into vast proportions.

In the year 1118,[13] William of St. Thierry, one

---

[13] It was towards the end of this year that Bernard had the happiness of seeing his old father, who, by a movement of grace, came to join his sons and share their destiny. Tecelin took the religious habit, and not wishing that any difference should be

of the most learned men of his age, visited the wonderful valley. "On coming down from the mountain," he writes, "and entering Clairvaux, the presence of God was visible on all sides, and the silent valley published, by the simplicity and humility of the dwellings, the humility and simplicity of those who inhabited them. Then, penetrating further into this holy place, so full of men, where none were idle, but all occupied at some kind of work, there was to be found at mid-day a silence like that of midnight, interrupted only by manual labor and the voices which sang the praises of God. The harmony of this silence and the order maintained was so imposing that even worldly strangers —struck with reverence—not only feared to utter an idle or wicked word, but even to indulge a thought which was not serious and worthy the holy retreat."

Such was this illustrious school of Christian wisdom under the direction of the Abbot Bernard !

The Saint, on account of indiscreet austerities, was often afflicted by severe bodily illness. In truth, he was frequently on the very verge of the tomb ; but such trials only ennobled his nature and increased his merits. To common souls,

made between him and the other monks, he humbly practised all the exercises of the Order, and shortly after closed his noble career by the happy death of the just.— *Ratisbonne.*

however, sickness is an occasion of weakness. **It** relaxes the springs of the spiritual life. But to strong souls it is, on the contrary, an exercise of courage and patience—a means by which the Christian overcomes himself, tames his inferior nature, and learns to imitate the patience of Him who suffered in order to leave us a golden example.

It was about this period that St. Bernard began to compose his works.[14]

---

[14] St. Bernard's first work was his treatise on the "Twelve Degrees of Humility." "Humiliation," he writes " is the road to humility, as weakness in suffering tribulations and injuries produce patience. If you do not exercise humiliations, you cannot attain to humility."

He wrote numerous pious and learned works. His volume "On the Errors of Abelard," and another "On Consideration," addressed to Pope Eugenius III., are his masterpieces. His "Sermons" are admirable. The style is smooth, elegant, and poetical. This great Doctor was the most illustrious orator of his age. His funeral oration on the death of his brother Gerard is a most eloquent and affecting composition ; and his two eulogies on the Irish archbishop, St. Malachy, are worthy of all praise. The "Letters" of St. Bernard amount to over four hundred and forty.

"St. Bernard, in his writings," says Butler, " is equally tender, sweet, and violent ; his style is sublime, lively, and pleasant ; his charity appears even in his reproaches, and shows that he reproves to correct—never to insult. This gives such an insinuating turn to his strongest invectives that it gains the heart, and instils both awe and love ; the sinner whom he admonishes can only be angry with himself, not with the reprimand or its charitable author. He had so diligently meditated on the Holy Scrip-

The fame of his greatness soon spread to distant parts; and his ability, holiness of life, and rare capacity for business drew to him a large number of persons, who made him the umpire of their differences. Priests and laymen alike came to consult him; and princes, prelates, and even kings had recourse to this man of God, as to an oracle. Thus his light began to shine as the dawn of the morning.

Henry, Archbishop of Sens, was one of the first who opened his heart to the holy Abbot of Clairvaux. His life had hardly been in harmony with his responsibilities and exalted profession; and he wrote to our Saint, asking for some instructions on the duties of the episcopate. Bernard's humility was alarmed.

"Who am I," he exclaimed, "that I should dare to teach a bishop? And yet how can I dare to refuse him? The same reason inclines me to grant and to refuse. There is danger on both sides; but, no doubt, there is most in disobedience."

He then despatched to the Archbishop of Sens, under the form of a letter, a work on the duties of bishops. It is a production of great merit. In one paragraph he thus pointedly addresses the archbishop:

tures that almost in every period he borrows something from their language, and diffuses the marrow of the sacred text with which his own heart was filled."

"As to you, bishop of the Most High, whom do you desire to please—the world or God? If the world, why are you a priest? If God, why are you a worldly priest? We cannot serve two masters at once. To desire to be a friend of the world is to declare one's self the enemy of God. If I please men, said the Apostle, I shall not be the servant of Jesus Christ." [15]

Some time after this St. Bernard was declared Archbishop of Rheims, by the election of the clergy and the acclamations of the faithful; but his refusal of this dangerous post was most firm and decided. He was obliged, however, to have recourse to the authority of Rome, that he might not be forced to yield to the earnest desires of the ancient and noble church of Rheims.

He opposed the election of unworthy persons to the episcopacy and other ecclesiastical dignities with the zeal of an Elias. This made the Saint many malignant enemies, who spared neither slander nor invectives. Their commonplace topic was that a monk ought to confine himself to his cloister. To this Bernard boldly answered that a monk was a soldier of Christ as well as other Christians, and that he ought to defend the truth and honor of God's sanctuary.

[15] The remarkable conversions of innumerable great princes, prelates, noblemen, and ladies, wrought by St. Bernard, form too long a list to find even mention in this sketch.

He often put priests in mind of the strict obligations they incurred in relation to the Church revenues which they enjoyed. "You may imagine," he
wrote to the dean of Languedoc, "that what belongs to the Church belongs to you while you of-
ficiate there. But you are mistaken. Though it be
reasonable that he who serves the altar should live
by the altar, yet it must not be to promote his pride
or his luxury. Whatever goes beyond bare nourishment and plain, simple clothing is sacrilege and
rapine."

In this respect his own conduct was a bright
model. A great famine desolated the surrounding country in 1125, and in order to relieve the
poor he often left his monks destitute of all provisions.

One day, as St. Bernard was going to visit the
Count of Champagne, he met a sad procession which
was leading an unhappy wretch to execution. The
great Abbot was touched with compassion. He
darted into the crowd, and took hold of the cord
which bound the criminal.

"Trust this man to me," he said. "I wish to
hang him with my own hands." And holding the
cord, he led the unfortunate fellow to the palace of
the Count of Champagne.

"At this sight the terrified ruler exclaimed:
'Alas! reverend father, what are you doing? You
do not know that this is an infamous wretch who

has deserved hell a thousand times. Would you save a devil?"

"No," replied the Saint gently; "I do not come to ask you to leave this unhappy man unpunished. You were about to make him expiate his crimes by a speedy death. I desire that his punishment should last as long as his life, and that he should endure the torments of the cross to the end of his days."

The prince was silent. But St. Bernard took off his tunic, clothed the criminal with it, and brought him to Clairvaux, where "this wolf," says the chronicle, "was changed into a lamb." He was called Constantine. He persevered in the practice of good works for more than thirty years, and at last died at Clairvaux in a most edifying manner.

Our Saint kept up a vast correspondence not only with princes, prelates, kings, and popes, but with women of rank who sought his holy direction, or others whom he had converted to a devout life. From these epistles, which breathe the spirit of wisdom and tenderness, we have room but for one short extract. It is from a letter addressed to a young lady of great virtue named Sophia.

"You are most happy," writes the Abbot of Clairvaux, "to have distinguished yourself from those of your rank, and to have raised yourself above them by the desire of solid glory, and by a generous contempt of that glory which is false. By this distinction you are more illustrious than by the splendor of your birth.

" Let other women borrow foreign beauty when they find themselves deprived of that which was once their own. They show clearly that they are deficient in the true and interior beauty, because they adorn themselves with such care to please madmen.

"As to you, my daughter, consider as unworthy of you a beauty which is derived from the skins of beasts or the labor of worms. The true beauty of anything resides in itself, and depends not upon anything apart from itself. Chastity, modesty, silence, humility—these are the ornaments of a Christian virgin.

" Oh ! how many graces does chaste modesty shed over the countenance. How much more love-ly are these charms than pearls and jewels ! As for you, your treasures depend not on the body, which withers and corrupts—they belong to the soul, and they will share its immortality."

St. Bernard had fled from the world. The life of one hidden with Christ was his choice. The reigning desire of his soul was to live and die un-known to men, amid the daily duties of a Cister-cian monk. He would have sung the office, toiled in the fields, prayed, and read the Holy Scriptures and the works of the Fathers, and when he was ripe for heaven would have passed peacefully away to his eternal reward. Thus has many a brave monk lived and died, while the dull, dizzy world dreamed not of the hidden saints who were warding from it the just anger of Almighty God. But such was not to be the destiny of the great Abbot of Clairvaux.

We can, however, merely glance at his public life. He was the chief figure of his time, and around him clusters the history of the twelfth century.

He first stands before us as the valiant and successful defender of the Holy See and the Vicar of Christ. On the death of Pope Honorius II., in 1130, Innocent II. was chosen to fill the chair of St. Peter by the majority of the cardinals. At the same time, however, a faction endeavored to invest the proud and powerful Cardinal Peter di Leone with that supreme dignity. He took the name of Anacletus. He was a worldly, ambitious man, and succeeded in getting into his hands the strongholds about the city of Rome. Innocent was obliged to fly to Pisa.

It was a most deplorable contest. But God always raises up an extraordinary man for extraordinary occasions. A council of French bishops was held near Paris, and St. Bernard was invited to attend. His voice rang loud and clear in favor of Innocent, who was thus recognized by the council, and soon after came into France. The Saint also brought over Henry I. of England, who was at first inclined to favor the anti-pope. He passed from city to city, from nation to nation, and at the sound of his voice they became reconciled to the Holy See.[16]

Among the most obstinate adherents of the anti-pope were the people of Milan. St. Bernard was sent to the city. He wrought miracles, and was received as a man from heaven. Of him, as of Cæsar, it may be said, "He came, he saw, he conquered"; but how different was the victory! Milan was at once reconciled to Innocent.

The Milanese were so charmed with the holy Abbot of Clairvaux that one day the faithful, headed by the clergy, came in procession to his abode, and wished to conduct him by force to the archiepiscopal throne, then vacant. Resistance was in vain; but the Saint made use of an expedient.

"To-morrow," said he, " I shall mount my horse and abandon myself to Divine Providence. If the horse takes me outside of the walls of your city, I shall consider myself free from any engagement; but if he remains within the city, I will be your Archbishop."

The following morning he mounted his horse,

[16] The death of the anti-pope in 1138 opened the way to the peace of the Church.

and, riding at full speed, he departed in haste from the walls of Milan.

Our Saint next found a fitting sphere for the exertion of his zeal in maintaining the purity of the Catholic faith. He stood the bold and watchful sentinel of the Church. He entered the lists against the famous but unhappy Peter Abelard,[17] some of whose writings had been condemned, in 1121, by the Council of Soissons. The vanity of Abelard made him imagine that he could explain the most profound mysteries of religion by the mere light of reason. He seemed ignorant of nothing but himself, and, of course, fell into many errors. It was then that St. Bernard broke silence, and pursued the innovator with invincible energy. He thus wrote to the Pope:

"It is to you, Most Holy Father, that we turn when the kingdom of God is in danger or suffers any scandal, especially in what touches the Faith. This is the privilege of the Apostolic See, since to Peter alone it was said, *I have prayed for thee that thy faith fail not.* We must claim, then, of the successor of St. Peter, the fulfilment of the words

---

[17] Peter Abelard was born in 1079, near Nantes, in France. He was "a man as extraordinary for the splendor of his erudition as for the romance of his life—the father of the sophistry of the Middle Ages, and the patriarch of modern rationalism." He always, however, professed a sincere respect for the Church, and it has been said with truth that "his errors were rather in his language than in his mind"

which follow: *When thou shalt be converted, strengthen thy brethren.* Now is the time to fulfil these words, to exercise your primacy, to signalize your zeal, and to do honor to your ministry.

"A man[18] has arisen in France who, from an ancient doctor, is turned into a modern theologian; who, having sported from his youth up with the art of dialectics, now, in his old age, gives forth to us his reveries on Holy Scripture; who, imagining himself to be ignorant of nothing that is in heaven or on earth, decides all questions without hesitation; who, ready to give a reason for everything, pretends, against all the rules of faith—and of reason itself—to explain even that which is above reason.

"This is the sense which he gives to these words of the wise man: *He who believes lightly is a fool!* He says that to believe lightly is to put faith before reasoning; although the wise man is not speaking of the faith we owe to God, but of the too easy credence we give to the words of men. After all, Pope Gregory taught that Divine Faith loses all merit when it is based upon human reason.

"Mary is praised because she prevented reason by faith; Zachary is punished for having sought

---

[18] Abelard. He thus begins this letter: " Brother Bernard, Abbot of Clairvaux, presents his most humble duty to Pope Innocent, his much-beloved Father."

in reason for a support to faith. But quite differ-
ently speaks our theologian. In the very first lines
of his extravagant theology he defines faith to be
an opinion—as if the mysteries of our faith de-
pended upon human *reason*, instead of being supported, as they are, on the immutable foundations
of truth!

"What! do you propose to me as doubtful that
which is of all things most certain? St. Augustine
did not speak thus. *Faith*, said he, *is not a conjecture or opinion formed within us by the labor of our
reflections. It is an interior conviction, and an evident
demonstration.* Let us, then, leave these question-
able opinions to the peripatetic philosophers, who
make it a rule to doubt of everything, and who, in
fact, know nothing.

"But let us hold to the definition of the Doctor
of the Gentiles. *Faith*, says that Apostle, *is the
foundation of the things we hope for, and a certain
proof of those we see not.* It is, then, a foundation,
and not an opinion—not a deduction. It is a certainty and not an estimation."

Abelard was silenced and confounded by the
thunder of St. Bernard. He wrote an apology for
his errors, retired to the monastery of Cluni, and
died an edifying death in 1142."

[19] Philosophical disputes, when they deeply agitate the minds of
men, are never isolated contests; they attest the intellectual
life of an age, and characterize its tendency. Thus the mere

In 1147 Pope Eugenius III. appointed St. Bernard to preach the second Crusade. This the eloquent Abbot performed with incredible success in all the chief provinces of France. He afterwards did the same in the principal cities of Germany.[20]

The Abbot of Clairvaux spoke as one having authority, and numberless miracles marked his footsteps " This morning, after Mass," says an

enunciation of the questions raised in St. Bernard's time gives the lie to the long-cherished opinion that the Middle Age was a time of ignorance and barbarism. The many rich monuments which that age has left to our own testify, on the contrary, its intellectual vigor ; and the twelfth century especially is distinguished by its subtilty of thought, as well as by the sublimity of its leading idea. The philosophical and profoundly Christian idea which ruled all the science of the Middle Age was faith as the source of light. Faith was the common centre of all branches of human knowledge ; and from this living source the waves of light and truth were seen to flow in harmony and order. But the development of this idea coincided with the most critical period of the development of the human mind. The nations of Christendom had arrived at that era when imagination, exhausted by prodigious efforts, begins to fade away before positive reason—an age of maturity which has its perils as well in the intellectual as in the physical order. . . . . In the twelfth century this double tendency—that of the Christian idea which sought to enlighten science by faith, and that of the rationalizing idea which sought to explain faith by human arguments—was clearly brought out and formed two distinct schools, the one impersonated by St. Bernard, the other represented by the too celebrated Abelard. —*Ratisbonne*.

[20] For more about the Crusades see the life of St. Louis.

ancient writer, "I presented to him a girl who had a withered hand. He cured her on the spot."

While at Sarlat, a town in which many errors contrary to faith had been spread, the man of God blessed with the Sign of the Cross some loaves which were brought to him for that purpose. "By this," said he, "shall you know the truth of our doctrine, and the falsehood of that which is taught by the heretics. Such as are sick among you shall recover their health by tasting of these loaves."

Geoffrey, Bishop of Chartres, who stood near the Saint, having some doubts on the point, said:

"That is, if they taste with a right faith they shall be cured."

"I say not so," replied St. Bernard. "*Assuredly* they that taste shall be cured, that you may know by this that we are sent by authority derived from God, and preach His truth." A great number of sick persons were cured by tasting the bread.

The true greatness of this apostolic man never shone with a brighter lustre than in the hour of sorrow and humiliation. One of his biographers relates a characteristic anecdote. "A certain cleric," said he, "having come to Clairvaux, demanded of St. Bernard in an imperious tone why he would not admit him into his community.

" 'What good is it,' he exclaimed, 'for you to recommend perfection in your books, when you will not afford it to those who are seeking for it?' adding in an angry tone, 'If I had your books in my hands I would tear them to pieces!'

" ' 'I think,' replied the Saint, 'that you have not read in any of those books that it is impossible for you to become perfect at home; for, if I recollect what I have said, it is a change of manners, not a change of place, that I have advised in all my books.'

"On which, this man, transported with rage, struck him so rudely on the cheek that it grew red and swelled. Those who were present at this sacrilegious action, unable to contain their fury, were about to fall upon the hardened wretch; but the Saint stopped them, and besought them, in the name of Christ, not to touch him, but to let him depart without molestation.'

From the beginning of the fatal year 1152 the illustrious Abbot of Clairvaux experienced a return of his old maladies, and suffered from long fainting-fits; but his mind, ever calm and powerful, ruled his feeble limbs, and he was still able to use them within the monastery in the service of heaven. While enduring the most acute sufferings, he wrote with a trembling hand to the Abbot of Bonneval, one of his dearest friends. It was his last letter.

" I have received," said the kind and venerable old man, "with much gratitude, the marks of affection which you have sent me ; but henceforth nothing can give me pleasure.   What joy can a man taste who is overwhelmed with suffering?   I have no moment of respite, except when I go entirely without food.   I can say with Job that sleep has departed from me, lest the insensibility of sleep should hinder me from feeling my sufferings.

" My stomach can no longer endure any food, and yet it causes me pain when I leave it altogether empty.   My feet and my legs are swelled with dropsy ; but, that I may conceal nothing from your heart, which interests itself in all that concerns me, I must confess, though, perhaps, somewhat imprudently, that amid all these evils my soul sinks not; the spirit is ready in a weak frame.

"Pray to our Lord, who desires not the death of sinners, to keep me at my departure out of this world, and not to delay this departure.   It is time for me to die.   Aid with your prayers a man devoid of all merit, that in this momentous hour the tempter may not triumph over me.   In this my extremity, I have yet desired to write to you with my own hand, to show you how much I love you, and that when you recognize my handwriting you may also recognize my heart; but I should have been much better pleased to have spoken than to have written."

Silence and sorrow now mingled in the cloisters of Clairvaux. The monks surrounded the couch of their great father, contemplating, with a holy fear, the last shining of that bright star whose light was about to disappear from the horizon of this world, to rise more grand and glorious in the land of triumphant souls. The Saint himself seemed like some ripe and perfect fruit bound to this life by a slight thread, which the least motion might break. He received the Sacraments of the Church, and, while awaiting his last hour, we find him lovingly employed in comforting his children.

"I know not," said he, casting a glance toward heaven, "to which I ought to yield—the love of my children which urges me to stay here, or the love of my God which draws me to Him."

These were his last words. The tolling of the bells, accompanying the funeral chants intoned by the deep voices of seven hundred monks, interrupted the profound silence of the valley, and announced to the world the death of the incomparable St. Bernard. It was about nine in the morning, on the 20th of August, 1153. The Saint was sixty-three years of age. For forty years he had been consecrated to Christ in the cloister, and for thirty-eight he had exercised the office of Abbot. He left behind him seven hundred monks at Clairvaux,[21] and one hundred and sixty monasteries, founded in different nations of Europe and Asia.[22]

---

[21] The French Revolution, towards the close of the last century, placed its unholy hand on the old home of St. Bernard. For about ninety years Clairvaux has been used by the government of France as a penitentiary. It now contains over 2,000 convicts, who are employed in various industrial pursuits, chiefly in weaving cotton fabrics.

[22] There are many churches in our country dedicated to divine worship under the name and patronage of St. Bernard.

SAINT LAWRENCE O'TOOLE,

ARCHBISHOP OF DUBLIN.

DIED. A.D. 1180.

S T. LAWRENCE[1] was the youngest son of Maurice O'Toole, a rich and powerful prince of Hy-Murray, in Leinster, Ireland. He was but ten years of age[2] when his father delivered him as a hostage to Dermot, King of Leinster. The cruel king treated the boy with great inhumanity.

O'Toole, however, being informed of the ill-treatment and poor health of his son, obliged Dermot to place him in charge of the Bishop of Glendalough. The good prelate carefully grounded him in the principles of religion, and, at twelve years of age, the little Saint was sent back to his father.

Soon afterwards Prince O'Toole and his sons visited Glendalough. He told the bishop that it was his intention to devote one of his sons to the Church, and proposed casting lots in order to find

---

[1] Lawrence is from the Latin, and signifies *crowned with laurel.*
[2] St. Lawrence seems to have been born about the year 1131.

Little Lives of the Great Saints.

out which. The young Lawrence was startled at
such a foolish thought, and more than glad to find
so favorable an opportunity for the accomplishment
of his desires.

" There is no need to cast lots," he exclaimed.
"It is the wish of my heart to have no other portion than God in the service of the Church."

On hearing this his father placed him once more
under the care of the venerable bishop, who
rejoiced in having charge of one so young, and noble, and promising.

The soul of Lawrence expanded in the holy
cloistered shades and amid the romantic beauties
of Glendalough. [8] His mind was stored with
knowledge, and he grew in age, and grace,
and wisdom.

---

[8] Glendalough—the valley of the two lakes—is one of the most
remarkable spots in Ireland. It is about twenty-three miles from
Dublin, in the county of Wicklow. The long valley is surrounded by high mountains, whence the water falls over many
craggy rocks, and feeds the two lakes and rivers below. Here
are to be seen to this day the ruins of many ancient churches and
monasteries.

" The walls of the Seven Churches," says Conyngham, "and a
belfry roofed with stone, still stand as monuments of the ancient
greatness and glory of Glendalough. Several old crosses and
monuments, with curious carvings and inscriptions in Irish, are
yet found among the ruins. The whole scenery of the valley
is picturesquely wild and imposing, with its bold, precipitous cliffs
and mountains, relieved by pleasant green valleys, rushing
streams, and placid lakes."—*Lives of the Irish Saints.*

At the age of twenty-five he was chosen Abbot of the monastery of Glendalough. The Saint governed his large community with rare virtue and prudence. When a great famine desolated the country, his charity was boundless. Nor did he cease to aid the poor and the unhappy when the resources of the abbey were exhausted. He even distributed a treasure which his father, Prince O'Toole, had left with him as a deposit.

But other trials were not wanting to test his goodness. Some false monks, whose eyes could not bear the brightness of his virtue, the holiness of his conduct, and the manly zeal with which he opposed their disorders, slandered his reputation. The young Abbot remembered that Christ had His calumniators, and that the disciple is not better than his Master. He looked up to Heaven, and fought his enemies with silence and patience.

On the death of Gregory, first Archbishop of Dublin,[4] our Saint was unanimously chosen his successor. He was then about thirty years of age; and, much against his own wishes he was consecrated in 1162 by Gelasius, Archbishop of Armagh.

In this exalted position he carefully watched over himself and the large flock committed to his charge. He was an unwearied toiler in winning

---

[4] Dublin became and archiepiscopal see in 1152. The four metropolitan sees of Ireland are Armagh, Dublin, Cashel, and Tuam.

souls to Christ. Before all shone the light of his example. His words were powerful, because they were enforced by sweetness and lofty virtue.

The Saint's spirit of prayer and penance was admirable. He always assisted at the midnight office with the Regular Canons of his cathedral ; and often when the world was buried in slumber he might be seen for hours whispering aspirations to heaven before some lonely crucifix.

He never ate flesh-meat. He fasted on all Fridays. He wore a rough hair-shirt, and often used the discipline. Every day he entertained thirty poor persons at table; and countless others partook of his charity at home. In him all found a tender father ever ready to aid them in their temporal and spiritual necessities.

For the renewal of his interior spirit, this great Irish Archbishop made frequent retreats at Glendalough—that holy and picturesque spot in which he had first learned the beauty of the narrow way that leads to heaven. On such occasions he usually retired to a famous cave at some distance from the monastery. This wild abode overhung the south side of the lake. It was hewn out of a solid rock three hundred feet above the water. Six hundred years before the days of St. Lawrence it had listened to the sighs and prayers of St. Kevin, the religious founder of Glendalough.[*]

[*] Several legends are preserved about St. Kevin in connection

But the quiet, holy career of Lawrence was about to be disturbed by an unhappy event that fills many a dark page in history. The land was rent by discord. A band of English freebooters invaded Ireland. The tocsin of strife sounded louder than ever, and the rage of contending hosts marked the beginning of a long, gloomy period of appalling misfortunes for the " Isle of Saints and Sages." Our own age has not seen its termination ! [*]

When Dublin was besieged by the faithless Dermot and his English allies, the city soon felt its weakness, and St. Lawrence O'Toole was sent at the head of a deputation to make terms with the enemy. But while the venerable Archbishop was

with this singularly wild retreat. One is that he fled there from a maiden who passionately loved him, and who had followed him from place to place, for he was a man of comely appearance and fine proportions · but

> " Ah ! little the good Saint knew
> What that wily sex can do."

In his rocky bed in the cliff he at last thought himself safe from her intrusion ; but in the morning, as he awoke, " Cathleen's eyes of most unholy blue " were looking down upon him. He impulsively started up and pushed her from him, and she fell over the beetling rock into the lake below. Whatever truth there is in this legend, it has afforded Moore a subject for one of his most pathetic lyrics —*Conyngham.*

[*] For an account of the English invasion of Ireland, see Abbé MacGeoghegan's " History of Ireland," chap. xvi.

engaged in negotiations with the leaders at their headquarters, a number of treacherous officers were secretly examining the city walls. A weak point was discovered. One thousand picked soldiers entered with fury, sword in hand; and no pen can picture the scenes of carnage that followed. Old and young were butchered without mercy, and crimes the most revolting were committed.

The Saint did everything that man could do to save his unhappy people. Fearless of danger, he passed from quarter to quarter; but, alas! often the most he could achieve was to procure a decent burial for the slain.

About seven months after this dreadful disaster, the death of Dermot, and other favorable circumstances, induced the noble-hearted Archbishop—who was none the less a patriot because he was a Saint—to urge a grand union of the Irish princes for the utter extermination of the fierce and lawless invaders. With this object he flew from province to province. He implored them to forget their foolish animosities and combine against the foreign foe. But in vain were the pleadings of sanctity and eloquent patriotism. A few years passed, and history records that Roderick O'Connor, the last king of Ireland, signed a treaty with Henry II. by which he promised to hold his title from the English monarch. The Saint himself was

one of the witnesses to this document, which bears
the date of 1175.

In the same year Lawrence was obliged to go
over to England, to see Henry II. in relation to
some affair relating to his diocese. He was nearly
killed while at Canterbury. As he was ascending
the steps of the cathedral altar to say Mass, a sacrilegious ruffian conceived the scheme of making the
Saint another St. Thomas ; and, rushing at him, he
struck him on the head with a heavy club. The
Archbishop fell to the floor. The people were
horror-struck, and thought he was murdered. But
he soon recovered and called for water, which he
blessed. No sooner was the ghastly wound washed
with the holy water than the blood ceased flowing,
and the Saint celebrated Mass.

In 1179 the Third General Council of Lateran
was held at Rome. St. Lawrence and six Irish
bishops assisted at that august assembly. Pope
Alexander III. greatly admired the wisdom and
learning of the Archbishop of Dublin, and appointed him Legate of the Holy See in Ireland.

Meanwhile a misunderstanding had arisen between Roderick O'Connor and Henry II. Between
the bickering rulers, St. Lawrence undertook to
negotiate, and with that object he made another
journey to England. "Blessed are the peacemak-
ers," says Christ. But the English monarch would
not hear of peace, and immediately after the

Saint's arrival, he sailed for Normandy. Lawrence followed the rude, ill-tempered king[7] into France. In a second interview his charity and prudence triumphed over Henry's wild passion and brutal selfishness. He granted everything, and left the whole negotiations to the discretion of the great Archbishop.

But the earthly pilgrimage of the Saint was drawing to its termination. On the way home he was seized by a fever. He retired to the monastery of Eu, on the borders of Normandy. "This is my resting-place," he said as he reached the entrance. He prepared for death and received the last Sacraments.

[7] Of Henry II. the English historian Lingard writes : " His temper could not brook contradiction. Whoever hesitated to obey his will, or presumed to thwart his desire, was marked out for his victim, and was pursued with the most unrelenting vengeance. His passion was said to be the raving of a madman, the fury of a savage beast ! We are told that in its paroxysms his eyes were spotted with blood, his countenance seemed of flame, his tongue poured a torrent of abuse and imprecation, and his hands were employed to inflict vengeance on whatever came within his reach ; and that on one occasion, when Humet, a favorite minister, had ventured to offer a plea in justification of the King of Scots, Henry, in a burst of passion, called Humet a traitor, threw down his cap, ungirt his sword, tore off his clothes, pulled the silk coverlet from his couch, and, unable to do more mischief, sat down and gnawed the straw on the floor."—*History of England.*

What a picture of the *first* of that long line of English tyrants who have tried, for seven hundred years, to lord it over Ireland!

When the abbot suggested that he should make a will, Lawrence answered with a smile: "Of what do you speak? I thank God I have not a penny left in the world."

A little before the light of this world faded from his eyes, the thought of dear, unhappy Ireland made him exclaim: "O foolish and senseless people! what are you now to do? Who will cure your misfortunes? Who will heal you?" He died on the 14th of November, 1180, and was canonized in 1226. St. Lawrence O'Toole is the last canonized saint of Ireland.[8]

[8] Though seven centuries have elapsed since his holy life." writes Dr. Conyngham, " and though Irish soil has been freely nurtured with the blood of Irish martyrs by the so-called Reformers, yet we have not one Irish saint canonized since Ireland ceased to be a nation. This is a mournful and significant fact. When Irish sanctity was recognized and honored abroad as well as at home, Ireland was an independent nation, respected among the proudest nations of the earth. Since she lost the priceless jewel of freedom, not all the sanctity of her children ; not all their munificence in endowing churches, monasteries, and convents ; not all the Christian charity and holy zeal displayed by the pious inmates of the religious houses in feeding the hungry and instructing the ignorant, down to the time of their suppression at the Reformation ; not all the blood of the faithful shed by Henry's infamous successors; not all the tortures inflicted on priest and layman during the enforcement of the 'Penal Laws,' ever procured the honor of canonization for a native of Ireland since Ireland ceased to be a nation."--*Lives of the Irish Saints.*

There is a church in St. Louis under the patronage of St. Lawrence O'Toole ; and we have no doubt there are others in various parts of this republic.

SAINT ELIZABETH,

PRINCESS OF HUNGARY.[1]

DIED A.D. 1231.

T. ELIZABETH[2] was born at Presburg, Hungary, in the year 1207. Her father, Alexander II. of Hungary, was a brave, religious monarch, and her mother, Queen Gertrude, was a woman of lofty soul, great piety, and a lineal descendant of Charlemagne.

From the very cradle Elizabeth gave proofs of her sublime destiny. At three years of age she expressed her compassion for the poor and sought by gifts to soothe their misery. Thus the virtues of her future life were foreshadowed in infancy. Her first act was an almsdeed; her first word was a prayer.

Some years before our Saint's birth, Herman, Duke of Thuringia, had a son born, whom he named Louis. The duke obtained a promise

----

[1] By birth she was Princess of Hungary ; by marriage she became Duchess of Thuringia.

[2] Elizabeth is from the Hebrew, and signifies *worshipp* / *of God* or *consecrated to God.*

from the King of Hungary that the little Elizabeth should be given in marriage to his son; and
to confirm the engagement, it was agreed, at
Herman's earnest request, that the princess, when
four years of age, should be sent to his court, and
there brought up under the care of a virtuous
lady.

The day arrived; a brilliant cavalcade of lords and
noble ladies came for Elizabeth. The child was
clothed in a silk robe embroidered with gold.
King Alexander said to Lord de Varila: "To your
knightly honor I confide my sweetest consolation."
The good queen, with tears streaming down her
face, also commended her dear little one to his care.
"I willingly take charge of her," said the noble
knight; "I shall always be her faithful servant."
He kept his word.

Great rejoicing greeted the child in her new
nome, and at four years of age, she was solemnly
affianced to Louis, who was then eleven. Ever after they were companions. She called him *brother*
and he called her *sister*. This was in the good old
Catholic times, when simplicity was still honored
as a virtue.[1]

---

[1] "A touching and salutary custom," writes the Count de Montalembert, "existed in Catholic ages and families—to bring up
together those whose after-lives were destined to be united; a
blessed inspiration which mingled in the mind of man the pure name
of sister with the sacred name of wife, so that none of the young

Elizabeth was a sweet and lovely child ; even in her sports she thought of God. When successful in games of chance, all her winnings were distributed among poor girls, of whom she imposed the duty of saying a certain number of *Paters* and *Aves.*

As she grew up she increased in piety and virtue. She loved prayer, and often stole into the palace chapel to offer up her soul to heaven. She was very devout to her guardian angel, and had a special love for St. John the Evangelist.

This noble girl practised many self-denials. "As the lily among thorns," says one of her ancient biographers, "the innocent Elizabeth budded and bloomed in the midst of bitterness, and spread all around her the sweet and fragrant perfume of patience and humility."

She was educated with Agnes, sister to the young duke. On their first appearing together at church the two were dressed alike, and wore golden crowns set with jewels. There was a majestic crucifix in the house of God, and on seeing the sacred image Elizabeth took off her crown

heart's freshness was lost, but the fond and varying emotions of brotherhood served to prepare for the grave and arduous duties of marriage. Thus all that was ardent and impetuous in the soul was calmed down and sanctified ; thus the purest and closest relations of life were from childhood joined in an earnest and only love, providing for after-years the remembrance of the sweetest and most holy affections."—*Life of St. Elizabeth.*

and laid it on a bench, at the same time bowing down her graceful person to adore the Almighty.

The vain, worldly Duchess Sophia, who ac-companied the young ladies, was offended. "What ails you, Lady Elizabeth?" she said rudely. "What new whim is this? Do you wish that every one should laugh at you? Young ladies should hold themselves erect, and not throw themselves on the ground like fools or old women. Is your crown too heavy? Why do you re-main stooped like a peasant?"

"Dear lady," answered the gentle Saint, "do not blame me. See before my eyes the image of my sweet and merciful Jesus, who was crowned with thorns. I am but a vile creature. My crown would be a mockery of His thorny wreath." And the lovely girl wept as she uttered those earnest words.

She then knelt humbly as before, and contin-ued her devotions, leaving the dutchess and Agnes to speak just as they pleased. Having placed a fold of her mantle before her face, it was soon wet with tears. The other two, in order to avoid a contrast that would be far from elevating them in the eyes of the people, were obliged to follow her example, and to draw their veils over their faces, "which it would have been much more pleasing to them *not* to do," adds the old chronicler.

Elizabeth had now many enemies and few

friends in the lordly home of her betrothed. The good Duke Herman, who loved her tenderly, had passed away to a better world. The duchess-mother, who governed during her son's minority, despised her, and used every effort to oblige her to take the veil in some convent.

From the unamiable Agnes she suffered daily insult. " My Lady Elizabeth," said she to her on one occasion, "if you imagine that my brother Louis will marry you, it is a great mistake; or, if he does, you must become quite a different person from what you are now!" Thus, in the midst of luxury and boundless wealth, this sweet, simple girl bore her heavy cross in silence and patience.

She had, however, one *true* friend. Louis was yet young; but, in spite of the hostile feelings of his mother and sister, his affection for Elizabeth grew day by day. He loved her with "a love that was more than love." He loved her beauty, her innocence, her piety, her modesty, her simplicity. He consoled her in moments of sadness. At such times he whispered his pure, undying affection. When he returned from journeys or hunting-parties, he always brought her some little love-gift—a pair of beads, a crucifix, a purse, a gold chain, or something else. She called him " my dear brother," and he addressed her as " my sweet sister."

When eighteen years of age, Louis proclaimed his intention of marrying his betrothed, and, at the same time, imposed silence on her enemies.   He did this with such manly decision that no one dared to make any opposition.

The marriage was celebrated in 1220, with great rejoicing, at the castle of Wartburg.   The young duke was twenty years of age, the dear St. Elizabeth but thirteen.

Louis was not unworthy of his bride so holy and beautiful.   The purity and greatness of his soul were reflected in his manly, graceful person. Though modest as a girl, he was as brave as a lion. In short, his whole character was summed up in the motto which he had happily chosen from boyhood: "*Piety, purity, justice towards all.*"

As to Elizabeth, she recompensed her husband with the love of all that was good and lovely.   The old biographers picture her great personal attractions—her black hair, her sweet-looking countenance, her bright eyes, which beamed with tenderness, her figure of unrivalled grace, and her simple, winning ways.

Louis and Elizabeth were never so happy as when in each other's company.   Even after marriage they preserved the custom of calling each other *brother* and *sister*.   "So entire was the union of their souls," says Montalembert, "that they

could ill endure being separated even for the short-
est time. Thus when the duke's hunting excur-
sions were not too distant, he always took his dear
Elizabeth with him, and she was happy to accompany him, even though she had to travel over
rugged roads and dangerous paths, and to brave
storms; but neither hail, nor snow, nor floods,
nor excessive heats could hinder her from going, so
anxious was she to be near him who never kept her
from God." [4]

Nothing, in truth, could be more imposing even
to worldly souls than the sight of so much virtue
in these young persons. United by a holy concord, full of purity and humility before God, full
of charity and good will towards men, loving
each other with a love that drew them both to
God, they offered to heaven and earth a sight the
most edifying.

Elizabeth chose for her confessor a holy and
very learned priest named Conrad; and under
the direction of this wise spiritual guide, she
walked the narrow way of virtue, and even reached
the lofty summits of sanctity.

She went on this earthly pilgrimage with her

[4] "Duke Louis saw," says one of the old chroniclers, "that
she loved God with her whole heart, and that thought comforted
him; and she, confiding in the piety and wisdom of her husband,
did not conceal from him any of her penitential exercises, well
knowing that he would never interfere between her and her Saviour."

eyes ever fixed on heaven. Her mortifications were many and rigorous. She wore a hair-shirt next her skin. Every Friday and every day in Lent she used the discipline in memory of Christ's sufferings.

But piety did not make her sad or gloomy. She was the most cheerful at festivals. "She played and danced sometimes," says St. Francis de Sales, "and was present at assemblies of recreation without prejudice to her devotion, which was so deeply rooted in her soul that, like the rocks about the Lake of Rietta, which grew greater by the beating of the waves, her devotion increased amid the pomps and vanities to which she was exposed by her condition."

The pure heart of this holy princess overflowed with love and mercy for her unhappy fellow creatures. Her generosity was boundless, for she saw Christ in every poor person. She delighted in paying secret visits to various abodes of misery, the bearer of money, provisions, and words of cheer; and her fair, graceful form might often be seen on such missions of charity, as she glided along the winding, rugged paths that led from the ducal

---

[5] St. Elizabeth said of those who, in praying, wore a sad or severe countenance: "They seem as if they wished to frighten our good God. Can they not say to him all they please with cheerful hearts?"— *Montalembert.*

castle to the cabins scattered over the surrounding valleys.

One day, accompanied by a favorite maid of honor, she was descending a narrow pathway, carrying under her mantle bread, meat, eggs, and other food for the poor, when suddenly she was met by her husband, Duke Louis, who was returning from a hunting-party. He was astonished to see his dear Elizabeth toiling along such a rough road under the weight of a burden.

"Let us see what you carry," said he, at the same time drawing aside the mantle which she held closely clasped to her bosom.

Only red and white roses—the most beautiful he had ever seen—met his eye, and this astonished him, as it was no longer the season of flowers. Seeing that Elizabeth was troubled, he sought to console her by his caresses, but he ceased at once on seeing over her head a luminous appearance in the form of a crucifix. The good duke then desired her to continue her route without being disturbed by him, and he returned to Wartburg, reflecting on what God did for her, and carrying with him one of those wonderful roses, which he preserved all his life.[6]

As the castle of Wartburg was built on a steep rock which the weak and infirm poor were unable

[6] At the spot where this meeting took place he erected a pillar, surmounted by a cross, to consecrate for ever the remem-

to climb, our Saint erected a hospital at the foot of the elevation for their reception and entertainment. Here she daily often fed them with her own hands, made their beds, and attended them in the heat of summer, when the air of the place seemed unsupportable to all who were strangers to her heroic charity.

During a frightful famine that desolated the country, she extended her generous aid to every part of her husband's dominions. Sometimes a miracle smiled on her holy toil. One day as she carried a quantity of food to a group of mendicants, she saw with uneasiness that she had not a sufficiency to give some to each, and that every moment more applicants arrived. The sweet Saint, however, began to pray interiorly, as she handed around the food, and found that, according as she gave pieces away, they were replaced by others, so that after giving each of the multitude a share there was still some left!

Through motives of religion, Duke Louis took the cross to accompany the Emperor Frederick Barbarossa on the Sixth Crusade. ' The news of

brance of that which he had seen hovering over the head of his wife.—*Montalembert.*

Those who would possess one of the most charming biographies ever written should get Montalembert's *Life of St. Elizabeth.*

⁷ " The name and idea of *Crusade*," says Montalembert, "were alone sufficient to make the hearts of all nations beat with ardor.

this step overwhelmed St. Elizabeth with sorrow,
for her attachment to her husband was something
inexpressibly tender and beautiful.

" Dear brother," she said, as the pearly tears
rolled down her lovely cheeks, "if it be not against
God's will, remain with me."

" Allow me to set out," said Louis, "for I have
made a vow to God."

All at once the spirit of heroic self-denial shone
out, and she said earnestly: "May He in His
goodness watch over you. May all happiness
attend you for ever. Go, then, in the name of
God !"

But the moment of parting was extremely pain-

These great and holy expeditions exercised over souls an influence so powerful that no valiant knight or pious and fervent
Christian could resist it. The remembrance of the almost fabulous
exploits of Richard *Cœur de Lion*, forty years before, still
lived in the minds of the chivalry and the people. The brilliant
and unhoped-for success of the Fourth Crusade dazzled all Eu
rope. People saw the destruction of that ancient empire of By
zantium, which never did else than betray the Christians who
were fighting for the faith, but which still occupied an immense
place in the veneration of Christendom, and from the ruins of
which was destined to rise a new empire, founded by a few French
knights and some Venetian merchants. . . . The whole of the
thirteenth century was penetrated with an earnest desire to rescue
the tomb of Christ, and to bow down the power of the East before the Cross. This feeling was extinguished only at the death of
St. Louis."

For further information about the Crusades see the life of St. Louis,
King of France.

ful. All trembling with emotion, the princess clung to her husband; and it was only after a desperate effort in conquering his heart that his tongue could find expression. "Elizabeth," said the noble Crusader, "look at this ring that I take with me. On the sapphire is engraven the Lamb of God with His banner. Let it be to your eyes a sure and certain token of all that concerns me. He who brings you this ring, dearest and most faithful sister, and tells you that I am still alive, or that I have died, believe all that he shall say. May God bless you, my sweetest treasure! Adieu; remember our happy life, our fond and holy love, and forget me not in your prayers."

And Duke Louis rode away, leaving his wife bathed in tears, for she had a gloomy foreboding that she would never see him again.

A few months passed by, and, alas! the faithful ring was on its way back to the castle of Wartburg. Duke Louis was no more. A fatal fever had carried him away, and at the early age of twenty-seven he died like a saint and hero.[8]

---

[8] He received the last sacraments from the Patriarch of Jerusalem. "Then," writes Montalembert, "he requested all his men, in the names of God and our Lady to remember him if they survived the dangers of their holy undertaking—to bring back his remains to Thuringia, to inter them at Reynhartsbrunn, where he had chosen his burial-place, and also never to forget him in their prayers. Some time before he expired, Louis saw a number of doves flying into the room and fluttering around his bed 'Look,

When the sad news reached the youthful princess,' she murmured a prayer and fell to the floor,
stricken with grief.   Truly the shadow of the cross
had fallen along the pathway of that bright and
beautiful spirit!   For the first time Elizabeth really
saw the frown of adversity; for the first time perhaps,
she felt with sensible vividness that in the day of
trial virtue is the only solid comfort.   Heaven was
about to complete her many good works and sacrifices, and to give a rounded loveliness to a life so
precious and sublime.

Envy, jealousy, and malignity — all welled up
and concealed during her husband's lifetime — now
broke loose against the virtuous princess.   Calumny grew loud and barefaced.   It was asserted,
among other things, that she had squandered the
puplic revenue on the poor , and that as she was
unfit to govern during the minority of her little

took,' he exclaimed, 'at these snow-white doves!'   The bystanders thought he was delirious, but, in a moment after, he said:
' I must fly away with those beauteous doves.'   In saying these words
he slumbered in the Lord, quitted this mortal pilgrimage to enter
the eternal country, there to take his place among the heavenly host,
on the third day after the Feast of the Nativity of the Blessed Virgin
(September 11, 1227), having just attained his twenty-seventh year."
—*Life of St. Elizabeth.*

"Many miracles," says Butler, "are related to have been wrought
by him, in the history of Thuringia and in that of the Crusades."—
Lives of the Saints, vol. xi.

9 St. Elizabeth was only twenty years of age at the time of her husband's death.

son Herman, the reins of power should be handed over to her brother-in-law, Henry. Justice and honor fled from the heart of this ambitious man. The wild passions of the mob were appealed to by fiery speeches, and Elizabeth was brutally turned out of the castle of Wartburg. Not a voice was raised in her favor.

It was midwinter, and the cold was very severe. This daughter of a royal race descended on foot— her eyes wet with tears—along the rugged, narrow pathway that led to the city. She herself carried her new-born babe, and the three other children followed with her two faithful companions.

This incident, so shocking to human nature, restored the Saint's tranquillity. She sought shelter at a poor inn, and was not rejected—though the hard-hearted Duke Henry had issued a proclamation forbidding any one to receive herself or her children. When she heard the midnight bell ringing for Matins at the Franciscan monastery which she had founded not many years before, she immediately arose and went to church. After assisting at the office, she desired the Fathers to sing a solemn *Te Deum* to thank God for His mercies in visiting her with such afflictions.

For some time after this the troubles of the princess were countless. She could find no place to lodge. A poor priest offered her a room in his little house ; but her enemies were on hand and drove her forth. At length she found a refuge from her uncle the Bishop of Bamberg.

A change, however, soon came about. The voice of justice was heard. A spirited remonstrance from some of the chief nobles of Thuringia brought the usurping Henry to his senses, and he even promised to restore Elizabeth her rights and all her possessions. She returned for a short time to the castle of Wartburg, but the piety of her life was not pleasing to her worldly relations.

The Saint left the lordly residence where she had spent so many years, and retired to Marburg, in Hesse. The revenues of this city were granted to her to provide for her maintenance. Here she retired to a house of her own, and, under the guidance of her director, Conrad, she labored only for heaven. She was a member of the Third Order of St. Francis. [10] Tattlers she detested. She spoke little, and her words were marked by modesty and reserve. She gave her rich dowry to the poor, and supported herself by spinning.

Her father, the King of Hungary, sent an am-

---

[10] Butler says that "she imitated the state of nuns, though, by the advice of her confessor, she remained a secular, that she might better dispose of her alms for the relief of the poor."

bassador to invite her home. "Say to my dearest father," she remarked, "that I am more happy in this contemptible life than he is in his regal pomp, and that, far from sorrowing over me, he ought to rejoice that he has a child in the service of the King of Heaven. All that I ask of him is to pray and to have prayers offered for me, and I will ceaselessly pray for him as long as life is left me."

It pleased the Almighty that a halo of glory and majesty should surround the close of this noble lady's earthly pilgrimage. One day she met a deaf and dumb boy, and asked him a question. He at once got the use of speech. On another occasion she saw a blind man walking near a church. She questioned the poor fellow, and learned that he would like to see the sunlight and the house of God. The sweet Saint told him to kneel and pray, and she prayed with him. Immediately he saw. The light of this world dawned on his eyes for the first time as he exclaimed: "May God be ever blessed !"

Three days before she died she was warned to prepare for her departure. Elizabeth put all her affairs in order, and devoutly received the last sacraments from Conrad, her faithful friend and confessor. "O Mary! come to my assistance," she exclaimed, and falling into a gentle slumber, her pure and beautiful spirit passed away, on the 19th of November, 1231. She was only twenty-four years of age."

[11] Many miracles were wrought at the tomb of St. Elizabeth, and their authenticity was carefully examined into by Siffrid, Archbishop of Mentz. "Pope Gregory IX.," writes Butler, "after a long and mature discussion, performed the ceremony of her canonization on Whit-Sunday, 1235, four years after her death. Siffrid, upon news hereof, appointed a day for the translation of her relics, which he performed at Marburg in 1236. The Emperor Frederick II. would be present, took up the first stone of the Saint's grave, and gave and placed on the shrine with his own hands a rich crown of gold. St. Elizabeth's son, Herman, then Landgrave, and his two sisters, Sophia and Gertrude, assisted at this august ceremony, also the Archbishops of Cologne and Bremen, and an incredible number of other princes, prelates, and people, so that the number is said to have amounted to *above two hundred thousand persons.*"—*Lives of the Saints,* vol. xi.

St. Elizabeth had four children—a son, Herman, and three daughters. Herman in due time became ruler of Thuringia, but died young. The eldest daughter married the Duke of Brabant; the other two entered the religious state, and each became abbess of her community.

There are churches in New York, Philadelphia, St. Louis, and various other places in the United States bearing the name of the dear St. Elizabeth.

SAINT LOUIS,

KING OF FRANCE.

DIED A. D. 1270.

S̲T. LOUIS[1] is one of the very few names in history that recall the great saint, the perfect hero, the able statesman, the skilful general, and the illustrious monarch. Such a noble combination of rare qualities we find in the beautiful character of this king of France.

Louis was born at Poïssey[2] on the 25th of April, 1215. His father was Louis VIII. and his mother, Blanche, a princess of Castile. She was

---

[1] Louis is from the German, and signifies *bold warrior*. The English usually write it *Lewis*.

[2] Poïssey was both the place of his birth and of his baptism; "and because," says Butler, "he had been there raised to the dignity of a Christian by the grace of baptism, he afterwards honored this place above others, to show how much he esteemed this spiritual dignity above that of his temporal crown. He made it his favorite place, took singular pleasure in bestowing charities and doing other good actions there; and in his familiar letters and private transactions, several copies whereof are still extant, he signed himself *Louis of Poïssey.—Lives of the Saints*, vol. viii.

a woman of extraordinary beauty, virtue, and ability.

This good mother never allowed the Saint to suckle any other breasts than her own. With the most careful care she attended to every part of his education. She taught him to be pure in thought, word, and action.

"My dear son," she would often say to the little Louis, "I love you with all the tenderness of a mother; but I would rather a thousand times see you fall down dead at my feet than that you should ever be guilty of one mortal sin."

These golden words as the King himself relates, made a deep and lasting impression on his mind.

Louis was an excellent student. He became a perfect master of the Latin tongue, a good public speaker, and a writer of grace and dignity. He was thoroughly instructed in the art of war, the best maxims of government, and all the accomplishments of one destined to rule a great kingdom. He was also a good historian, and often read the Fathers and Doctors of the Church.

He came to the throne while a mere boy. His father, Louis VIII., died in 1226; and Queen Blanche was declared regent for her son, then only twelve years old. Fearing seditions, she hastened the coronation of Louis. The ceremony was performed at Rheims by the Bishop of Soisson.

The toscin of rebellion now sounded in various parts of the kingdom ; but the rebels soon found they had made a mistake. Queen Blanche and the young Saint headed the army of France, and the leaders of revolt were speedily brought to terms. The whole period of the king's minority, however, was disturbed by some form of rebellion.

Modesty, the most amiable of virtues, diffused its radiance over the royal Saint's character. He loved music and singing. But if any one, in song or speech, let slip a word in the least indecent before him, he was for ever banished from the king's presence.

When the time came to choose a fair companion, he sought the most worthy, and was rewarded with the hand of Margaret, eldest daughter of the Count of Provence. She was a lady of surpassing wit, beauty, and virtue. Louis met her at Sens, where they were married in May, 1234. God blessed the Saint and his lovely bride with a constant union of hearts and a family of noble, virtuous children. [2]

This good King never thought himself so happy

---

[2] This great Saint and great King, showing the ring he always wore, whereon he had engraven these words, GOD, FRANCE AND MARGARET, said with such exquisite simplicity: *Hors cet and n'ai point d' amour*—"I have no love beyond this ring."—*Montalambert.*

as when enjoying the conversation of learned and religious men.   But he knew how to observe times and seasons with a becoming liberty.   Once when a certain monk started a grave religious subject at table, he gently turned the discourse to another topic, saying: "All things have their time."   On such occasions his words were cheerful without levity or impertinence, and instructive without stiffness or austerity.

His piety was admirable.   He allotted several hours in the day to the recitation of the divine office and other prayers, and when he appeared at the foot of the altar it was with surpassing humility and recollection.   But his devotions never made him forget any part of the care which he owed to the state.   He knew well that the piety must be false which neglects any duty that we owe to others or to ourselves.   The same lofty motive that animated him in the churches made him most diligent in every branch of his high charge.   It was his greatest support in all secular employments.

He scarcely allowed himself any time for amusement.   His temperance and mortification were such that he practised both with extreme austerity, amid the dainties of a royal table.   It was observed, that he never touched any fruit when it was first served in season.   He had the happy ingenuity of often abstaining from delicacies and of practising many self-denials without attracting notice. He wore a hair-shirt, often used disciplines, and went to confession two or three times a week.

Thus this great king made the exercise of penance easy and familiar, and kept his senses and inclinations ever under the rule of reason and good government. "There is no king," said an ancient saint, "like him who is king of himself."

But his severity was all towards himself. Virtue did not make him morose. He was the soul of kindness, and very agreeable in conversation. The inward peace of his mind, and the joy which overflowed his pure heart from the continued thought of God's holy presence, enhanced the natural sweetness and liveliness of his temper. Coming from his closet or from the church, he appeared in a moment conversing upon business, or at the head of his army, with the countenance of a hero fighting battles, enduring the greatest fatigues and daring the most trying dangers.

He was scrupulously faithful in keeping his word and in observing all treaties. In negotiations this gave Louis vast advantage over his adversaries, who often by frivolous evasions eluded their most solemn oaths and engagements. The reputation of his rare and inflexible integrity soon made all parties rejoice to put their affairs into his hands and to have him for their arbiter. Joinville assures us that the king's head was the best and wisest in his council. In sudden emergencies his clear, powerful mind readily resolved the most knotty difficulties.

Frederick II., the wicked and faithless Emperor of Germany, though he often broke his engagements with Louis, as well as with other powers, could never provoke him to war, so dexterous was the Saint in maintaining both his honor and his interests without appealing to the sword.

In truth, being exempt from those passions which commonly blow the coals, he had a happy advantage in the pursuit of justice and necessary defence. While his foresight and magnanimity kept him ever in readiness, his love of peace and the nobility of his nature inclined him rather to sacrifice some petty consideration than to see the spilling of one drop of Christian blood.

St. Louis was the author of several excellent laws; justice flourished in his reign, and the people loved him as a wise and tender father. He forbade usury, and restrained the Jews from its practice. He ordered that every one convicted of blasphemy should be marked upon the lips— some say on the forehead—with a red-hot iron. He even caused this sentence to be carried out on a wealthy citizen of Paris, a man of great consideration; and when some of the courtiers mur mured at this seeming severity, he said that he would rather undergo the punishment himself than omit anything which might put a stop to a crime so horrible.

The father of our Saint had ordered in his will that the price of his jewels should be laid out in founding a monastery. St. Louis very much increased the sum, and the structure was truly royal and magnificent. It was the Abbey of Royaumont. Out of devotion, he sometimes worked with his own hands in building the church. This was afterwards one of the places to which he often retired to breathe the air of holy solitude.

He founded the Chartreuse at Paris, and built many other religious houses and hospitals.[*]

In 1239 St. Louis received a remarkable present from the Emperor of Constantinople. It was the crown of thorns that had pressed the sacred head of Jesus Christ. He sent two Dominican Fathers to bring this precious treasure into France. He met it himself five leagues beyond Sens, attended by his whole court and a great number of clergy. He and his brother Robert, walking in their bare feet, carried it into Sens, and afterwards in the same manner into Paris. This holy crown was

[*] Felibien remarks that it is incredible what a number of churches St. Louis built; and that, though they are all Gothic, they are costly and finely wrought.—*Butler.*

deposited by the king in the royal chapel of St Nicholas.

St. Louis was obliged to declare war against Henry III. of England, whom he defeated in 1242. The English king concluded a peace by promising to pay a stated sum of money in five years.

At this time the restless barbarians of Asia were raising a great commotion. A band of Saracen desperadoes, in the mountains of Phœnicia, was under the command of a leader called the "Old Man of the Mountains." These ruffians were sworn to take the life of all who opposed the spread of Mahometanism.

The chief's word was their sole law, and they carried out his will with reckless energy in any part of the world. The "Old Man" fixed his evil eye on St. Louis, and sent two resolute soldiers disguised into France. They had strict orders to assassinate the Saint. But the Almighty watched over His servant. The king was warned of the diabolical scheme, had the fanatical wretches arrested, and courteously sent them back to their master in the mountains.

Hordes of Tartars, under the fierce and roving successors of Genghis-Khan, spread desolation through Hungary, Poland, and Bohemia. Europe was filled with terror. Queen Blanche expressed her fears; but St. Louis calmly viewed the situation. "Madame," said he, "what have we to fear ? It these barbarians come to us, we shall either conquer or shall die martyrs." The haughty leader of the Tartars went so far as to send a letter to the Saint commanding him to deliver up his king. dom. But the brave ruler of France took no notice of such insolence.

A violent illness brought the King to the very brink of the grave in the year 1244. In vain, it seemed, was Heaven solicited for the preservation of his life. For some days he lay as one dead. Then a piece of the true Cross and other relics were applied to his person. He slowly recovered. By his first words he expressed his resolution to take the cross as a Crusader, and, calling for the Bishop of Paris, who was present, Louis desired him to re. ceive his vow and put the badge of the cross on his shoulder.

His wife and his mother fell weeping at his feet, and conjured him not to think of such a vast and per. ilous enterprise. But it was all to no purpose : he received the red cross. He wrote to the sadly-oppress. ed Christians of Palestine that he would make all haste to their assistance.

Four years, however, were required to com. plete the preparations for this expedition. He proclaimed his mother, Blanche, regent of the kingdom. Queen Margaret declared that she would accompany her husband, and bravely she kept her word. Accompanied by the flower of

his nobility, Louis sailed for Cyprus in the sum.
mer of 1248. Thus, in brief, began the *sixth* Crusade.[5]

[5] The Crusades were military expeditions undertaken by the
Catholics of Europe for the purpose of delivering the Holy Land,
and particularly the sepulchre of our Blessed Redeemer, from the
oppressive dominion of the Turks. As early as 637, Jerusalem
fell into the hands of the Saracens, who for political reasons permitted the Christians to visit the Holy City. In 1065 the ferocious
Turks obtained possession of Jerusalem, and from that date the
Christian inhabitants were exposed to every kind of insult and
outrage. From religious motives pilgrims were induced to visit
the spots made sacred by the sufferings of Christ; but on reaching Palestine, after traveling thousands of miles amid dangers
and hardships, they were only allowed to enter the city of Jerusalem on the payment of a certain sum of money, and, if they succeeded in gaining admittance, they were exposed to all the rigors
of Mahometan brutality. Some were even condemned to death,
and others loaded with chains and compelled to draw a cart or
plough.

Catholic Europe could not quietly stand this sad condition of
things. The first Crusade was preached by Peter the Hermit,
a French priest, in 1095. The Pope blessed the undertaking.
Thousands hastened to enroll their names for the sacred expedition,
and as a mark of their engagement a cross of red material
was worn on the right shoulder; hence the word's *Crusade* and *Crusader*.

"There does not exist in the annals of history," says Balmes,
"an event so colossal as the Crusades. . . . In the Crusades,
we see numberless nations arise, march across deserts, bury
themselves in countries with which they are unacquainted, and
expose themselves to all the rigors of climates and seasons: and
for what purpose? To deliver a tomb! Grand and immortal
movement, where hundreds of nations advance to certain death—,
not in pursuit of a miserable self-interest not to find an abode

Louis invaded Egypt, and took the strong city of Damietta. But calamity soon frowned. Disease seized his hardy veterans. The French gallantly advanced from the sea-coast towards the capital of Egypt, and strove to surmount the unseasonable inundation of the Nile which opposed their progress.

It was in vain the fearless king did all that a hero and great commander could accomplish. Disease, the waters of the Nile, and the hosts of Mahomet conquered. Louis was made prisoner and loaded with chains. The greater part of his nobles were captured. All who could not redeem their lives by service or ransom were inhumanly massacred, and a circle of Christian heads decorated the worse than pagan walls of Cairo.

The true hero is at all times a hero. It was so with our Saint. Though in chains and battling with disease, he every day recited the Breviary with his two chaplains. Daily he had the prayers of Mass—except the words of consecration—read

in milder and more fertile countries, not from an ardent desire to obtain for themselves earthly advantages, but inspired only by a religious idea, by a jealous desire to possess the tomb of Him who expired on the cross for the salvation of the human race! When compared with this, what becomes of the lofty deeds of the Greeks chanted by Homer? Greece arises to avenge an injured husband; Europe to redeem the sepulchre of a God."—*European Civilization*, p. 243.

to him, that he might the better join in **spirit**
with the Church in her Sacrifice.

In the midst of insults he preserved an **air of**
calm, majestic dignity which awed the rude infidels by whom he was surrounded. Never did
he appear so great as in those dark days of trial
and adversity.

The sultan demanded $450,000 for the king's
ransom and that of the other prisoners. Louis
answered that a ruler of France ought not to redeem himself for money ; but he agreed to give
the city for his own freedom, and the sum of
money for the ransom of all the other prisoners.
The sultan, charmed with such noble generosity,
at once gave him his freedom, and remitted a
fifth part of the amount demanded. A truce was
concluded for ten years. It comprehended the
Christians of Palestine.

After many perils the Saint journeyed to Palestine. The very sight of his piety was a moving
sermon. On one occasion he converted forty
Mahometans to the true faith. Fasting, and on
foot, he visited Nazareth. He adored the secret
judgments of God and referred all to his greater
glory.

While rebuilding Cæsarea, and strengthening
some strongholds still in the hands of the Christians, Louis received the sad news that his **mother,**
the noble Queen Blanche, was no longer in **this**

world. He burst into tears. "O Lord!" he exclaimed, throwing himself at the foot of the altar
in his chapel, "I thank Thee for having preserved
to me so long the best of mothers. Truly
there was nothing among creatures on earth that I
loved with such tenderness. Thou takest her from
me. It is Thy almighty will. May Thy holy name
be for ever blessed!"

The great King showed his deep affection
for his mother by having the holy sacrifice of the
Mass offered up in his presence every day to
the end of his life for the eternal repose of her soul.

Taking on board his queen, family, and officers,
the Saint now sailed for France. After an
absence of almost six years he made his public
entry into Paris.

Shortly after Henry III. of England visited
St. Louis. The English monarch was deeply
edified. The Saint assured this royal friend that
he felt infinitely more happy that God had given
him patience in suffering than if he had conquered
the whole world.

St. Louis was a man of unceasing labor. Every hour and every action of life were for the
honor and glory of God. He founded the celebrated college of the Sorbonne. He established
a large hospital for poor blind men. Every
day one hundred and twenty paupers dined at a
table provided for them near his own palace. He

often served them in person. He kept lists of reduced gentlemen, distressed widows and young
women, whom he regularly relieved in all parts of
his dominions.

Sixteen years had passed away since he
had last battled for the tomb of Christ, and again
the cries of the oppressed Christians in the
East found a willing echo in the kind, heroic heart
of Louis. He made two spiritual retreats as a preparation, and with a splendidly-equipped force
sailed for Africa in the summer of 1270. It
was his design to begin the war by taking
Tunis. The siege proved disastrous. The French,
scorched by oppressive heat and decimated by
deadly fevers, fought and died like brave men in
the burning sands of a foreign climate.

The pestilence seized the king. He called his
eldest son, Philip, to his bedside. He gave him
instructions wise and beautiful. Among other
things he said : " My son," I recommend you
above all to love God. Be ready to suffer
everything rather than commit a mortal sin.
When you are sick or afflicted return thanks to
Heaven. Bear it bravely. Be persuaded that you
deserve to suffer much for having so poorly served God, and that all tribulation will be your gain.

" Confess your sins often. Choose a wise
and pious spiritual father. Be bountiful. Be com-
passionate. Be kind to the poor. Punish all

who speak ill of God or His saints.   In the ad-
ministration of justice be upright and severe.
Ever have a great respect for the Church and the
Pope.

" To the utmost of your power oppose all blasphemy, oaths, games of chance, impurity, and
drunkenness. Never lay any heavy burdens on
your people. Take care to have many Masses
said for the repose of my soul.   Give me a
share in all your good works. I bless you, and may
Jesus Christ ever bless and protect you, my
beloved son !"

The great King had a majestic cross erected so
that he might keep his eyes fixed on it in his sufferings. " Into thy hands, O Lord ! I commend my spirit," he whispered, and expired in his
camp at the age of fifty-five, on the 25th of August,
in the year of 1250. ⁶ Twenty-five years after he
was solemnly canonized by Pope Boniface VIII.

⁶ The brother of St. Louis, Charles, King of Sicily, whose de-
lays had thrown this expedition into the heats, arrived with his
fleet a few minutes after the death of our Saint. The Christian army again defeated the Moors and Saracens in two great battles, and on the 30th of October concluded a peace with the
infidels on the following conditions: that all prisoners should
be released and the Christian slaves set at liberty; that Christians
should be allowed to build churches and to preach the faith in the
territories of these Mahometans, and that the Mahometans
should be allowed to embrace it; that the king of Tunis should
pay a yearly tribute of five thousand crowns to the king of
Sicily, and that the king of France and his barons should receive

St. Louis [7] was the last and greatest in the line of glorious heroes that drew the sword in defence of the tomb of Jesus Christ. He possessed a rare combination of personal accomplishments, and even of apparently opposite qualities, which made him not only superior to his age, but in truth one of the most extraordinary men that ever wore a crown. His heroic virtue shone brighter in his afflictions than it could have done amidst the most splendid triumphs. A fearless knight, a resolute warrior, and a true Catholic, he was as willing to risk his life as to bow his head to the will of Almighty God. He was a lover of danger, and penance, and humiliation. He was the indefatigable champion of justice, of the weak and the oppressed. He was the sublime personification of Christian chivalry in all its purity and grandeur.

210,000 ounces of gold to defray their expenses in this war—which was a larger sum than St. Louis had paid for his ransom. Such was the issue of the *eighth* and *last* of the Crusades which were undertaken for the recovery of Palestine, and which employed Europe for almost two hundred years.—*Butler.*

[7] One of the great cities of America bears the name of St. Louis. The cathedrals of St. Louis, New Orleans, and many other churches of our country are dedicated to divine worship under the patronage of the royal Saint. St. Louis University is the oldest Catholic institution of learning in the Mississippi Valley, with the rank and privileges of a university. It was founded in 1829 by the Jesuit Fathers. Among its founders was the celebrated Indian missionary, Father De Smet, who helped to build it with his own hands, and who was its first treasurer.

SAINT THOMAS AQUINAS, O. S. D.,

DOCTOR OF THE CHURCH, AND PRINCE OF CHRISTIAN PHILOSOPHERS.

DIED A. D. 1274.

T. THOMAS[1] AQUINAS, commonly styled the *Angelic Doctor*, was born at Belcastro, Italy, in the year 1226. He belonged to a noble family, which was allied by marriage with several of the royal houses of Europe. His father was Count Landolpho of Aquin, and his mother, Theodora, a daughter of the Count of Theate.

From his cradle Thomas seemed to be a favored child. He preferred books to any other playthings. If he cried, an old volume would at once pacify the little warbler. But the calmness of his countenance, the evenness of his temper, and the winning modesty of his manners were visible marks of the bounty of Heaven.

When but five years of age his father placed him under the care of the Benedictines of Monte Cas-

---

[1] Thomas is from the Hebrew, and, according to some writers, signifies *a twin;* others say that it signifies *profundity.*

sino.[2] These good monks laid the **foundation of** learning and religion in the soul of little **Thomas.** With joy they beheld the rapidity of **his progress,** his great mental gifts, and his happy **inclination to** virtue.

He was only ten years of age when the abbot of Monte Cassino advised Count Landolpho to send his son to some university. Thomas left the quiet solitude of the monastery and was sent to the University of Naples. It was a great change. The boy suddenly found himself surrounded by disorder and wild young men. But he was wise beyond his age. He guarded his eyes. He was the soul of modesty. He shunned bad company. And while others engaged in foolish or sinful diversions, Thomas made a good use of his time among his books, or retired to some church to pay a visit to the Blessed Sacrament.

[2] "This mighty abbey," writes Vaughan, "placed upon the mountain-side and looking down on the teeming plain of Aquino, about six miles from Rocca Secca, even in those days could be looked upon as an antiquity. Once a bushy grove, full of the impure worship of lascivious gods, in the sixth century St. Benedict laid the foundation of its history. When St. Thomas went there it had already thrice been jolted to the ground by earthquakes, over and over it had been besieged by barbarians, it had been clean destroyed by the Lombards and burnt to cinders by the Saracens; but it sprang up as often as cast down, and in the early days of St. Thomas was the most distinguished school of letters in the land."—*Life and Labors of St. Thomas of Aquin.* vol. i.

The Saint studied philosophy under a famous Irishman named Peter of Hibernia, and so astonishing was his progress that it is said he could repeat the lessons more clearly than they had been explained by his master. But his chief care was to advance in the science of the saints. He prayed much. He walked in the holy presence of God. He was a doer of good deeds. His humility, however, concealed them as much as possible. The many alms which self-denial enabled him to bestow upon the poor were given in such a manner that his left hand scarcely knew the bounty of the right.

Having formed an acquaintance with a Father of the Order of St. Dominic—a learned and holy man —Thomas resolved to consecrate himself to God in the same Order. His father, Count Landolpho, was informed of this design and was highly displeased.[2] He threatened and promised, but the future Doctor of the Church listened only to the call of Heaven   The student earnestly asked to be admitted into the Order, and in 1243 he received the habit in the convent at Naples. He was then seventeen years of age.

When the news of this event reached the ears of his mother, she at once set out for Naples. Thomas asked to be removed to another convent,

---

[2] The old count, however, finally consented, and died soon after.

that he might be spared the pain of an interview.
His wish was granted.   He was on the road to Paris
when he was arrested by order of his brothers,
who held commands in the emperor's army 'in
Tuscany.

They endeavored to tear off his religious habit,
but Thomas made a manly resistance. He was
now conducted to the family seat at Rocca Secca.
His mother was overjoyed, for Thomas had been
arrested at her express command. She made no
doubt about overcoming her son's resolution to
be a Dominican. She urged him to throw
off the religious dress, but he respectfully declined. She did not, however, despair of chang-
ing his views and inducing him to embrace another profession. But her hopes were illusory.
In vain did she urge her parental authority; in
vain did she shed tears, entreat, and caress.
Thomas was deeply grieved that he was the cause
of such pain to his mother, but nothing human
could shake his heroic resolution. He was as firm
as the granite hills on the subject of his religious
vocation.

The Countess was much disappointed, and at
length had recourse to very harsh measures in
order to force her son into compliance with her
wishes, so worldly and unreasonable. She had
him closely confined. No one was allowed to see
him but his two sisters, and they used every means

in their power to overcome his opposition.
But so far from being successful, these good young
ladies became the conquest of their gifted brother.
He spoke to them so touchingly on the contempt
of the world and the beauty and grandeur of virtue that they resolved to imitate his example by
devoting themselves to the practice of Christian
perfection.

Thomas was improving the leisure of his con-
finement by prayer, the study of the Sacred Scriptures, and the perusal of various works on philosophy and theology, when his two brothers, returning home from the army, added new rigors
to his painful situation. On learning of his opposition their wrath was boundless. They rushed
to his apartment, tore the religious habit from his
shoulders, and locked him up in the tower of the
castle.

Nor was this all. These corrupt military officers added crime to cruelty by introducing a
shameless young woman of great beauty into the
Saint's room for the vile purpose of overcoming
his virtue. It was a critical moment. But Thomas
prayed, looked up to heaven, and, snatching a
firebrand, he drove the infamous visitor from his
chamber.

After this signal victory, the young hero
dropped on his knees and, with tears in his
eyes, thanked Almighty God for His mercy and

goodness. He consecrated himself anew to the religious life, and implored the grace of never losing the priceless treasure of chastity. This prayer was followed by a gentle slumber, during which he was visited by two angels, who seemed to gird his waist; and never afterwards was he troubled with any temptation against holy purity.[4] It is no wonder that he is styled the *Angelic Doctor.*

Thomas, after having suffered imprisonment in silence for over a year—some say two years—found relief and liberty in the intervention of Pope Innocent IV. and the Emperor Frederick. His persecutors began to relent.   The Dominicans of Naples being informed of this, and that his mother was disposed to connive at any measures that might be taken to procure his escape, they hastened in disguise to Rocca Secca, where his favorite sister, knowing that the countess no longer opposed the escape of her son, contrived to let him down from the tower in a basket.   Friendly arms clasped him on reaching the ground, and he was carried with joy to Naples.   He made his profession the year following.

---

[4] "It was only a little before his death that he disclosed this incident to Father Reynolds, his confessor, adding that he had received this favor about thirty years before, from which time he had never been annoyed with temptations of the flesh; yet he constantly used the utmost caution and watchfulness against the enemy, and he would otherwise have deserved to forfeit grace —*Butler, Lives of the Saints*, vol. iii.

His mother and brothers, however, renewed their complaints to Innocent IV., and earnestly requested him to interfere in the matter. The Pope called Thomas to Rome, and, in their presence, examined him on the subject of his vocation to the state of religion. The young Dominican gave his reasons with unanswerable force and clearness, and the Holy Father admired his virtue and good sense, and approved his choice. From that time he was allowed to pursue his career in peace unmolested by the schemes of blind and worldly relations.

It was very important to choose an able and saintly teacher to second the genius of the gifted novice. Happily, such a rare man was not far away. It was Albertus Magnus,[5] a Dominican Father of vast intellect, and one of the greatest masters of sience in his age. He taught at Cologne, and there Thomas was sent to pursue his studies.

The Saint studied with intense application. Every moment not employed in devotion and other duties was given to his books. He scarcely allowed himself time to eat or sleep. But this eager pursuit of knowledge sprang from no vain passion or desire of applause. He toiled hard that he might one day be the better able to de

[5] Albert the Great.

fend the Catholic faith and advance the glory of God.

His modest humility, however, made him conceal his progress and intellectual power; and many of his fellow-students thought he learned nothing. His silence was remarkable. Hence they called him the "dumb ox." Even his celebrated master was at first deceived as to the rich mental gifts of his silent genius. But on one occasion he asked Thomas a number of questions on the most knotty and obscure points, and the clear, masterly answers given astonished all present. Albertus Magnus was fairly overjoyed. "We call him," he exclaimed, "the *dumb ox*, but he will one day give a bellow in learning that his voice shall fill the whole world!"

When Albertus Magnus was called to the chair of theology at Paris, in 1245, Thomas accompanied him. It was here that he made a special study of Holy Scripture and the works of St. Augustine. After three years, however, the Saint and his master returned to Cologne. There, at the age of twenty-two, he was appointed assistant to Albertus Magnus. He now began to publish his first works, which consist of comments on Aristotle.

His manners were kind and winning. He was still the same hard student, but said that he learned less in books than before his crucifix or the Blessed Sacrament. It was while at Cologne that he was raised to the priesthood.[6]

He was again sent to Paris in 1252, where his growing reputation attracted a great number of students to his lectures. He accepted the degree of Doctor with much reluctance at the age of thirty-one. Such was his acknowledged ability at this time that the professors of the University of Paris consented to abide by his decision in a point of controversy that had arisen among them in relation to the Blessed Eucharist. Thomas humbly prayed to God for light, and then wrote a treatise on the disputed question. He carried the manuscript to the church and laid it on the altar. Several persons were present. Our Lord appeared visibly and said: " My son, you have written worthily on the Sacrament of My Body."

The illustrious St. Louis, King of France, had a great respect for our Saint, and honored him with his intimate frendship. He often consulted him on affairs of state. It was at the table of this holy monarch that Thomas—whose attention was ab-

[6] St. Thomas converted his worldly relations. "His example and exhortations," says Butler, "induced them to an heroic practice of piety. His elder sister consecrated herself to God in St. Mary's at Capua, and died abbess of that monastery. The younger, Theodora, married the Count of Marscio, and lived and died in great virtue, as did his mother. His two brothers, Landulph and Reynold, became sincere penitents."—*Lives of the Saints.*

sorbed in deep reflections on the subject of his
studies—suddenly exclaimed : " The argument is
conclusive against the Manichees !" His superior,
who was present, told him to remember where he
was. Thomas asked pardon for such an oversight ;
but the king was much edified, and, calling his secretary, said : " Write the argument, as it might be
forgotten."

The meekness of St. Thomas was as remarkable
as his learning and genius. No dispute ever disturbed his habitual calmness. No insult ever ruffled
his temper.

In 1261 Pope Urban IV. called the great Doctor to Rome, where he filled the chair of theology and wrote several of his ablest treatises. As
a preacher our saint has never been surpassed for
force and unction. The people hung on his
words, and often the whole congregation was
melted to tears. Nor were miracles and conversions wanting. On one occasion, while Thomas
was leaving St. Peter's Church, a poor woman, by
touching his dress as he passed, was instantly
cured of dysentery. Two famous Jewish rabbis,
after a conference with him, embraced the faith.
The Pope offered him the archbishopric of
Naples, but the Saint declined all ecclesiastical
dignities.

He consecrated the last period of his life to the
preparation of his incomparable " Summa " which

he began to write about the age of forty. It was while engaged in the composition of this un-rivalled theological masterpiece that a voice from the crucifix addressed him thus: "Thomas, you have written well of Me. What recompense do you desire?" "No other than Thyself, O Lord!" he answered. One of his companions—who was present when this occurred—asserts that he saw the Saint raised from the ground during this wonderful dialogue.

During the last three months of his life, this ex-traordinary man did little less than to prepare for the great end, which he felt was rapidly coming. In obedience, however, to a Papal Brief, he set out for Lyons, in France, where a General Coun-cil was to assemble, May, 1274. His illness in-creased as he journeyed along, and he was finally compelled to stop at Fossa-Nuova, a famous Cis-tercian monastery. The good monks treated him with all tenderness and veneration, but it was in vain they tried to prolong that bright and valuable life.

The great Doctor made a general confession of his whole life, and with tears bewailed frailties that had never amounted to a grave sin.[1] He

---

[1] " His confessor, who knew his life fully, declared that from his birth to his death his mind and heart had never once been sullied. At forty-eight he was as pure as a child of five years old."— *Vaughan.*

then expressed a desire to receive the *Holy Viaticum*, and begged to be laid upon the floor. He was thus prostrate—weak in body, but vigorous in mind—when the abbot and community advanced in solemn procession, carrying the Bread of Angels.

"I firmly believe," began the illustrious Dominican, on seeing the Host in the hands of the priest, "that Jesus Christ, true God and true man, is present in this august Sacrament. I adore Thee, my God and my Redeemer. I receive Thee as the price of my redemption and the viaticum of my pilgrimage—Thee for the love of whom I have studied, labored, preached, and taught. I hope I have never advanced anything as Thy word which I have not learned from Thee. If through ignorance I have done otherwise, I publicly revoke everything of the kind, and I submit all my writings to the judgment of the Holy Roman Church." [8]

[8] Philosophy, theology, piety, and Holy Scripture were the chief subjects on which the Angelic Doctor wrote. His works fill nineteen folio volumes. But the substance of them all is summed up in his great masterpiece, the "Summa Theologiæ."

"What, then, it may be asked," says Archbishop Vaughan, "is this 'Summa Theologiæ'? It is the Christian religion thrown into scientific form, and the orderly exposition of what a man should be. The Angelical had studied the mind of the Church. In as far as it is given to man, he had mastered that divine intelligence."

"He alone," said Pope John XXII., who issued the bull of his

He then received the Holy Viaticum, and made his thanksgiving on the floor. As they all stood about him in tears, he thanked the abbot and his community for their kindness and charity.

His dying words to a monk who asked him how

canonization in 1323, "has cast greater light within the Church than all the other Doctors taken together."

At the Council of Trent two books were placed in the midst of the assembled bishops—the Bible and the "Summa" of St. Thomas.

The famous Balmes spent four years at the University of Cervera studying nothing but the "Summa" of the Angelic Doctor. "Everything," he said, "is to be found in St. Thomas—philosophy, religion, politics. His writings are an inexhaustible mine." In his "European Civilization" Balmes wrote, referring to the vast genius of St. Thomas: "Fortunately, this great man appeared. The first touch of this powerful hand advanced learning two or three centuries." See chap. lxxi. pp. 410–12.

St. Thomas Aquinas is commended as the "prince and master" of Christian philosophers and the great philosophic guide, by our Holy Father Pope Leo XIII., in the famous Encyclical, *Æterni Patris*, dated St. Dominic's Day, 1879.

"Now, as prince and master, Thomas Aquinas," says the illustrious Leo XIII., "far outshines every one of the scholastic doctors; for whilst he had, as Cajetan remarks, the deepest veneration for the holy doctors of antiquity, he shared, so to speak, the intellect of them all. Thomas gathered together their doctrines, scattered about like the members of a body, enlarged them, put them in methodical order, and made such copious additions to them that he may be rightly and deservedly regarded as the glory and matchless defender of the Catholic Church. Of a docile disposition, his memory pliable and retentive, his life perfect, an intense love of truth, very rich in divine and human sciences, he, like the sun, nourished the whole universe by the warmth of virtue and filled it with

we might always live faithful to the grace of God were: "Be assured that he who shall ever walk faithfully in *His Presence*, always ready to give *Him* an account of all his actions, shall never be separated from *Him* by consenting to sin."

To men he spoke no more, but murmured a prayer, and died on the 7th of March, 1274, at the age of forty-eight years. And thus the Angelic

the lustre of his learning. There is no part of philosophy that he has not handled fully and thoroughly. He has treated so clearly of the laws of reasoning, of God and incorporeal substances, of man and the senses, of human acts and their principles, that nothing is wanting under these heads either in his ample store of questions, or in his exquisite arrangement of the parts, or in his choice method of proceeding, or in the solidity of his principles, or in the strength of his arguments, or in the clearness and propriety of his diction, or in his peculiar power of explaining things the most abstruse."

And near the close of this Encyclical the Holy Father, addressing himself to the rulers of the Church, says: "We most earnestly beseech you, venerable Brethren, to restore and extend far and wide the golden wisdom of St. Thomas, for the glory and defence of the Catholic Faith, the good of society, and the improvement of all the sciences."

Thus it has been reserved for our own day to see the crowning glory given to the incomparable St. Thomas Aquinas and his immortal writings.

Those who have neither time nor sufficient familiarity with mediæval Latin and scholastic philosophy to read the "Summa" itself can use some good abridgment. O'Donnell's "Compendium of St. Thomas's Theology" and Lebrethon's "Petite Somme Théologique de Saint Thomas d'Aquin" are the best works of this class in English or French.

Doctor and prince of Christian philosophers passed out of this life to realize away from the twilight of earth the one dream of his magnificent soul—to see God in his glory, and the Blessed adoring before the Everlasting Throne.

SAINT CATHERINE OF GENOA,

MODEL OF CHRISTIAN LOVE AND HEROISM.

DIED. A.D. 1510.

T was in 1447, about a dozen years after the birth of the great Columbus, that another distinguished person was born at Genoa. [1]   At baptism she received the fair name of Catherine. [2]   Her family was illustrious. Giacopo Fieschi, [3] her father, was viceroy of

[1] Genoa, the birthplace of Columbus, and formerly the capital of a republic, is still an important commercial city. It has a population of about 140,000.

[2] Catherine is from the Greek, and signifies *pure.*

[3] The family of the *Fieschi* was for many ages one of the most illustrious in Italy.   Its chiefs were Counts of Lavagna, in the territory of Genoa.   They were for some ages perpetual vicars of the empire in Italy, and afterwards enjoyed very extraordinary privileges in the republic of Genoa, and among others that of coining money.   This house gave to that commonwealth its greatest generals during its long wars both in the East and against the Venetians; and to the Church many cardinals and two popes—Innocent IV. and Adrian V.—*Butler.*

Naples, and her mother, Frances di Negro, belonged to a noble house.

The little one grew up lovely in person, and in ways winning, gentle, and remarkable. She seemed to be exempt from anger and other petty passions of childhood.

Catherine's favored mind early grasped the grandeur of religion. At the time when thought scarcely dawns upon other children she had already penetrated the beauty of piety and virtue. She loved prayer, was a model of obedience, and had a tender devotion to the sacred Passion of Jesus Christ. She despised pride of birth, hated luxury, and practised penance. It should never be forgotten that the most tender age is capable of making great advances on the path of solid virtue.

At thirteen she desired to enter the religious state. She thought that a life of prayer and contemplation was best suited to her inclinations. But in this she was overruled by obedience to her parents, and for other reasons.

Three years after by the advice of her father, she married Julian Adorno, a gay young nobleman of Genoa. He was a person of reckless habits and stubborn temper, and was soon reduced to poverty. Catherine, as became a noble Christian lady, bore her husband's follies and eccentricities with gentle, heroic patience. But it was all an up-hill struggle, and told fearfully on her delicate constitution. To satisfy him she lived alone for a time in a solitary house, never went out except to attend Mass, and then returned as quickly as possible.

By Catherine's prayers and persuasive example her husband, before it was too late, repented of his wild ways. Adorno was visited by a severe illness. He was very impatient. His end was approaching. Our Saint, in deep distress, withdrew to a retired apartment.

"O Love! O Lord," she exclaimed with tears and sobs, "I beg this soul of Thee. I implore Thee to grant my request, for Thou canst do it." Thus she prayed for the space of half an hour, and an interior voice assured her that she was not unheard.

Catherine returned to her husband's chamber and found him calm and completely changed. He was now submissive to the decree of Heaven. He prepared for the end, and soon passed away in holy peace. It was something truly wonderful.

"My son," said our Saint one day to a very dear friend, "Julian is gone. You knew his eccentricities, from which I suffered so much; but before he passed away my sweet Lord assured me of his salvation."

One of her great trials was over. The ten years of her married life were gloomy, sorrowful years, which, however, aided our Saint in the work of her more perfect sanctification. But she was now free to devote herself to good works.

Catherine resolved to serve Christ by ministering to suffering humanity. She took charge of the great hospital of Genoa. Nothing escaped her holy care. She served the sick with incredible tenderness. For them this sweet, high-born lady performed the meanest offices—offices that must have shocked the delicacy of nature and put her virtue to the test. She often dressed the most loathsome ulcers with her own hands. "It is also remarkable," says her biographer, "that she never made the mistake of a single farthing in the accounts of large sums of money which she was obliged to keep; and for her little personal necessities she made use of her own small income."

But her fasts and other austerities were countless. It was her constant study to deny her senses all unnecessary gratification. Her humility and self-denial were admirable. Even while living in the world with her husband she made it a rule never to excuse herself when blamed by others. It was her constant request of God that His pure and holy love alone might reign in her heart. She took as her chief maxim the words of the Lord's Prayer—"*Thy will be done on earth, as it is in heaven.*

"I see," she would say, "that whatever is good in myself, in any other creature, or in the saints, is truly from God; if, on the other hand, I do anything evil, it is I alone who do it—nor can I charge the blame of it upon the devil or upon any other creature. It is purely the work of my own will, inclination, pride, selfishness, sensuality, and other evil dispositions; and without the help of Almighty God I could never do any good action. So sure am I of this that if all the angels of heaven were to tell me I had something good in me I should not believe them."

Catherine often used the word *purity* in her con versation; and from her pure lips it fell with lovely grace. Her language was simple, noble, and beautiful. She wished that every conception and emotion of the mind should issue from it pure, undefil. ed, and without the least complexity. It was im. possible for her to feign a sympathy which she did not feel, or to condole with others out of friendship, except, in so far as it really corresponded with her heart and affections.

In this blessed soul everything was so well ordered and beautiful that wherever she had control or could offer a remedy she could never endure any disorder. She would neither live nor converse with persons who were not very well regulated.

Her love for the Holy Communion was worthy

of an angel. Once when at the point of death, so ill that she was unable to take any kind of nourishment, she said to her confessor: "If you would only give me my Lord three times, I would be cured." It was done, and her health was at once restored.

For nearly nine years before her death Catherine suffered from a malady not understood by the physicians. It was not a bodily infirmity, nor did it seem to herself a spiritual operation. She was very weak. She ate little and suffered much.[4]

Yet her calm, noble countenance was the mirror of happiness. Many persons came from a distance to see her and to recommend themselves to her pray-

[4] "There arrived from England," writes one of the Saint's biographers, "a Genoese named Boerio, who had been for many years physician to the king of that country. He was surprised, when he heard of the fame of this holy lady, that she should speak of her infirmity as not natural and as requiring no medical remedy. Scarcely believing this report to be true, he obtained permission to visit her, and reproved her for the scandal she caused by rejecting medical aid—even accusing her of hypocrisy. To all this she humbly answered: 'It grieves me much to be the cause of scandal to any one, and if a remedy can be found for my disease I am ready to use it.' The physician, availing himself of her consent and obedience, applied various remedies; but at the end of twenty days, finding herself no better, she told him that she had submitted to his treatment in order to remove all scandal from his eyes and from the eyes of others, but that now he must leave the care of her soul to herself. . . . After this Boerio held her in great reverence, calling her 'mother' and visiting her often."

ers。   They beheld a being more divine than human
—a lady with "Heaven in her soul and Purgatory in
her agonized body."

"She saw the condition of the souls in Purgatory," writes her biographer, "in the mirror of her
humanity and of her mind, and therefore spoke of
it so clearly.   She seemed to stand on a wall sep-
arating this life from the other, *that she might relate
in one what she suffered in the other.*"

"So far I can see," says the Saint, "the souls
in Purgatory can have no choice but to be there.
This God has most justly ordained by His divine
decree.   They cannot turn towards themselves and
say:

" '*I have committed such and such sins, for which
I deserve to remain here.*' Nor can they say:

" ' *Would that I had refrained from them, for then
I should this moment be in Paradise.*' Nor again:

" '*This soul shall be released before me, or I shall be
realeased before her.*'

"These souls retain no memory of either good or
evil respecting themselves or others which would
increase their pain.   They are so contented with
the divine dispositions in this regard, and in doing
all that is pleasing to God in the way which He
chooses, that they cannot think of themselves,
though they may strive to do so.

"They see nothing but the operation of the
divine goodness, which is so manifestly bringing

them to God that they can reflect neither on their own profit nor on their own hurt. Could they do so, they would not be in pure charity.

"They see not that they suffer pains in consequence of their sins, nor can they for a moment entertain that thought; for should they do so, it would be an active imperfection, and that cannot exist in a state where there is no longer the posibsility of sin.

"At the moment of leaving this life they see why they are sent to Purgatory, but never again, otherwise they would still retain something private which has no place there. Being established in charity, they can never deviate therefrom by any defect. They have no will or desire except the pure will of pure love, and can swerve from it in nothing. They can neither commit sin nor merit by refraining from it.

"There is no peace to be compared with that of the souls in Purgatory, save that of the saints in Paradise, and this peace is ever increased by the inflowing of God into these souls. It increases in proportion as the impediments to it are removed.

"The rust of sin is the impediment, and this the fire unceasingly consumes, so that the soul in this state is continually opening itself to admit the divine communication. As a covered surface can never reflect the sun, not through any defect in that orb, but simply from the resistance offered

by the covering, so if the covering be gradually removed the surface will, by little and little, be opened to the sun and will more and more reflect the
rays of light.

"It is thus with the rust of sin, which is the
covering of the soul. In Purgatoiy the flames in-
cessantly consume it, and as it disappears the soul reflects more and more perfectly the true Sun, who is
God. As this rust wears away the soul grows in
contentment ; it is laid bare to the divine ray, and
as one increases the other decreases until the time
is accomplished. The pain never diminishes, although the time does; but as to the will, so united
is it to God by pure charity, and so satisfied to be
under His divine appointment, that these souls can
never say their pains are pains.

"On the other hand, it is true that they suffer
torments which no tongue can describe nor any intelligence comprehend, unless it be revealed by such
a special grace as that which God has vouchsafed
to me, but which I am unable to explain. And
this vision which God has revealed to me has never
departed from my memory." [5]

[5] "Treatise on Purgatory," chap i. This is a beautiful work. It
may be found, together with her "Spiritual Dialogues," in the "Life
of St. Catherine of Genoa," published by the Catholic Publication
Society, New York.

"Her 'Spiritual Dialogues' and her ' Treatise on Purgatory,"
writes Father Hecker, C. S. P., in his learned introduction to her
Life, "have been recognized by those competent to judge in such

The Saint's long illness was a tedious martyr-dom. Day and night she was consumed by thirst, but could not swallow a drop of water. [6] For the last two weeks of her life she took nothing except the Holy Communion. Her mind, however, was clear to the last. "Into Thy hands, O Lord! I commend my spirit," she said, and gently expired at the age of sixty-three, on the 14th of September, in the year 1510.

At the final moment her faithful physician was asleep, but awoke just as she departed. A voice whispered to him: " Rest in God. I am now going to Paradise."

It is related of the martyr St. Ignatius that on

matters as masterpieces in spiritual literature. St. Francis of Sales, that great master in spiritual life, was accustomed to read the latter twice a year. Frederick Schlegel, who was the first to translate St. Catherine's 'Dialogues' into German, regarded them as seldom if ever equalled in beauty of style; and such has been the effect of the example of Christian perfection in our Saint that even the American Tract Society could not resist in attraction, and published a short sketch of her life among its tract with the title of her name by marriage; Catherine Adorno."

[6] Only four days previous to the Saint's death ten physicians assembled "in order to ascertain if medical science could invent any remedy for her sufferings. After the most careful investigation of her case, they decided that her condition was wholly produced by supernatural causes and was beyond the reach of medical skill. For all her bodily organs were in good order and showed no sign of infirmity; and they took their leave, lost in wonder and recommending themselves to her prayers."—*Life of St. Catherine.*

opening his heart there was found inscribed on it in letters of gold the adorable name of *Jesus.* The same sweet name ruled the pure heart of St. Catherine, was the inspiring motive of all her actions, and in heaven it was the reward of her bright and beautiful life. [7]

[7] Her body was taken up eighteen months after her death and found without the least sign of putrefaction. From that time it was exposed aloft in a marble monument in the church of the hospital as the body of a saint, and was honored with the title of Blessed, which Pope Benedict XIV. changed into that of Saint, styling her in the martyrology *St. Catherine Fieschi Adorno.—Butler.*

SAINT FRANCIS XAVIER, S. J.,

APOSTLE OF THE INDIES.

DIED A. D. 1552.

———

ST. FRANCIS XAVIER, the prince of modern missionaries and one of the glories of the sixteenth century, was born in 1506, at the castle of Xavier, not far from Pampeluna, in the north of Spain. His parents were pious, wealthy, and noble. The Saint was the youngest of a numerous family.

From infancy Francis[1] was kind and attractive. He was naturally gifted, and early exhibited an intense love of study. Though all his brothers had embraced the profession of arms, he seemed to care only for books and learning.

His parents wisely seconded his inclination, and at the age of eighteen he was sent to the University of Paris. He was a hard-working, ambitious student. He aimed to conquer the world of knowledge; and, on taking the degree of Master of Arts, he began to teach philosophy.

When St. Ignatius came to continue his studies

[1] Francis is from the French, and signifies *free.*

at the French capital, he made the acquaintance of Xavier. He was struck with the generous soul and fine qualities of the young professor, who seemed to have but one failing—his head was full of earthly ambition.

These rare spirits were attracted to each other. Soon they became bosom friends. " What will it profit a man to gain the whole world and lose his own soul?" said Ignatius one day, with gentle force, to his companion. He pointed out that such a noble soul ought not to confine itself to the vain honors of this world. Celestial glory is the only object worthy of ambition. It is even con- trary to reason not to prefer that which is eter- nal to that which vanishes with the fleetness of a dream.

This pointed reasoning made a deep impression on the ardent soul of Xavier; and, after a short interior struggle, grace completed the conquest. He be- came a soldier of the Cross.

In 1534, on the feast of the Assumption, St. Ig- natius and his six companions—one of whom was our Saint—made a vow at Montmartre, Paris, to visit the Holy Land, and unite their labors for the con- version of infidels; but if this should not be found practicable, to cast themselves at the feet of the Vicar of Christ, and offer their services wherever he might wish to give them employment. Xavier was ordained priest in 1537.

The great design, however, of converting the Holy Land had to be abandoned, and the new *Society of Jesus*¹ found a wider sphere for its sublime mission.

¹ St. Ignatius, the glorious founder of the Society of Jesus, was born in 1491, at the castle of Loyola, in the north of Spain. His father was head of one of the most ancient and noble families of that country. Ignatius grew up to manhood a proud and aspiring soldier. He possessed military talents of a high order, and became known as an accomplished commander. In the storming of Pampeluna—which he defended against the French—the young Spanish nobleman received a severe wound that confined him to his sick-room. In this quiet seclusion he read—accidentally read—the lives of the saints. Grace touched his heart. New light flashed on his mind. The invincible soldier at once began to walk the way of the saints. This was just at the period when Luther, the apostate monk of Germany, finally threw off the mask and bade defiance to the Holy See. Ignatius of Loyola was then thirty years of age. His knowledge of books was scant. He could barely read and write. But with unequalled courage he entered on the pursuit of learning and virtue. Taking the degree of Master of Arts, the valiant defender of Pampeluna completed his course of theology, was ordained priest, gathered around him ten choice and learned young men animated by his own master-spirit, and formed them into a religious Order. The services of this company of youthful Christian heroes he placed at the disposal of the Pope. Among them were Francis Xavier, James Laynez, and Peter Faber. Pope Paul III. approved the new Order in 1540 under the title of *The Society of Jesus*—the name given it by St. Ignatius himself. Such, in brief, was the origin of that wonderful religious body, which from its first years assumed the stature of a colossus, which has peopled heaven with saints, and filled the world with the renown of its name and its deeds.—*Popular History of the Catholic Church in the United States*, p. 357

At the request of the King of Portugal, two fathers were ordered to plant the faith in the East Indies. One of these was Francis Xavier. He received the benediction of the Pope, and, with a brief in his hand constituting him Apostolic Nuncio, he stepped with a light heart on board the chief vessel of a squadron that sailed from Lisbon on the 7th of April, 1541. It was on that very day that he had completed his thirty-fifth year.

When asked to accept the aid of a servant, he declined. He said he had the full use of his two hands, and that was enough. But when some one suggested that it was unbecoming to see an Apostolic Legate dressing his own food and washing his linen on deck, the Saint answered that he could give no scandal so long as he did no wrong.

He arrived at the roadstead of Goa[3] in the month of May, 1542, after a long and dangerous voyage, during which he had excited in all the spirit of piety, courage and cheerfulness. It was during this voyage that he first got the name of " Holy Father," which was ever after given him alike by Mohammedans, pagans, and Christians.

Xavier landed, and spent the greater part of the

---

[3] Goa is still the capital of Portuguese India. It is situated on the western coast of Hindostan, and has a population of about five thousand souls.

first night in prayer. He wished to call down the blessing of Heaven on his coming labors.

It was thus braced up with supernatural strength that the next day surveyed the vast, uninviting field. The state of religion in India[4] was truly deplorable. The name of Christian, beautiful and glorious in itself, had been degraded by the crimes of those who claimed to be Christians. Among the Portuguese traders and colonists all virtue seemed to be extinguished by revenge, ambition, avarice, and debauchery. There was a bishop at Goa, but his threats and exhortations were equally despised.

But this moral darkness was soon dispelled. The great Jesuit addressed the merchants before preaching to the savages. "In the name of God," he exclaimed, "do you wish me to ask those people, who have no other fault than their blindness, to become like you, who are full of iniquity?"

After spending the morning in assisting and comforting the unfortunate in the prisons and hospitals, he walked through the streets of Goa with a bell in his hand, imploring all masters for the love of God to send their children and slaves

---

[4] India, or the East Indies, is the finest part of Asia.   It stretches from the Indus River in the west to the Cambodia River in the east, and from the Himalaya Mountains in the north to the Indian Ocean at the south.   The larger part is embraced in what is now known as Hindostan.   India has a vast population.

to catechism. The little ones gathered about him in crowds, and the man of God led them to the church. He began every instruction with the *Lord's prayer*, and ended it with the *Hail Mary*. He taught them the *Creed* and various practices of devotion, and impressed on their tender minds the beauty of piety and religion.

The modesty and devotion of the youth by degrees changed the aspect of the whole town. The stifled voice of conscience began to be heard once more, and the most abandoned sinners sought the confessional. The Saint preached in public and visited private houses. His kindness and charity were irresistible, and in six months he accomplished the conversion of Goa.   It was more than a miracle.[1]

Xavier was soon at Cape Comorin,[2] and entered Paravao by a miracle. A dying woman was cured by the mere touch of his crucifix, and thousands of the natives gathered around him, "listening to his signs," understanding his unknown language.

He had presaged the magic of the Cross, and he now saw its prodigies. His crucifix preached for

---

[1] "To convert a Portuguese trading station in the Indies was more difficult—so contemporaries deemed it—than to conquer all barbarous India for the faith."—*Féval's Jesuits*. In this sketch of the Saint we draw freely on Féval's brilliant litte work.

[2] Cape Comorin is the extreme southern joint of Hindostan.

him while he was learning the Malabar tongue,
and many a day after he had acquired the language,
when overcome by fatigue and incessant
preaching, he would sound his famous little bell
with one hand and raise the image of Christ in
the other, and would thus be surrounded with the
people of the entire villages, who bent their
heads under the saving waters of Baptism.

It frequently happened to him—so great was his
fatigue—that he could no longer raise his arm to
pour the blessed water on the multitudes that came
at the close of his rich day's toil.

The pure heart of the great missionary swam in
torrents of joy, and from his lips broke songs of
gladness. He endured cold, heat, hunger, disease. On the roads his naked feet were torn by
thorns and briars, but he never complained. He
enjoyed suffering. He kept on his way, tireless
and resolute. On earth he walked as if already in
heaven.

His food was merely rice and water. His labors
were incredible. It was a rare thing for him to
sleep three hours at night, and a rarer thing to
use a bed. His couch was the hard ground. Instead of resting at night, he spent the time instructing those who were to be his helpers, and
sometimes a sudden stillness would come upon
his simple audience. Every one held his breath.
A merry, good-natured sign would be made from

one to another, as much as to say: "Keep quiet, don't waken him !"

This was because the "Holy Father," overcome by fatigue, had closed his eyes in spite of himself; and his sympathizing class—young savages who were learning to be martyrs—lengthened as much as they could the chance moments that relieved their beloved master from his unceasing round of labor.

" The dangers to which I am exposed,' he writes to St. Ignatius from the Isle del Moro, " and the pains I take for the interest of God alone, are the inexhaustible springs of my spiritual joy. These islands, bare of all worldly necessaries, are the places in the world for a man to lose his sight with excess of weeping. But they are tears of joy. I never remember to have tasted such interior delights; and these consolations of the soul are so pure, so exquisite, and so constant that they take from me all sense of my bodily suffering." Truly, to be a saint it is something beautiful !

In our short sketch, we have no space to give even a summary of the wonders that marked the footsteps of St. Francis Xavier. He worked countless miracles. He raised many dead persons to life. We have room only for one instance. As the great Jesuit was one day preaching at Coulon, a village near Cape Comorin, he saw that his words fell on hearts of stone. He stopped and prayed that God would honor the name of His beloved Son. He then requested some of his obdurate hearers to open the grave of a man who had been buried the day before, near the spot where he preached. The body was beginning to putrefy, and gave forth a most disgusting smell—a fact which the Saint requested the bystanders to observe. He then fell on his knees and commanded the dead person, in the name of Almighty God, to arise. The man arose, and appeared not only living but vigorous and in perfect health. All present were so struck with this wonder that they threw themselves at the Saint's feet and demanded baptism.

His missions grew with marvellous rapidity. He labored, and God blessed his labors. At the end of two years the crop of helpers that he had planted was almost ripe. At Goa, which was his headquarters, he founded a seminary. His first priests were now ready. To-day he can attempt what seemed impossible yesterday; and now he penetrates still further and further, for he is no longer alone. At one place he baptized ten thousand persons with his own hands in a month.'

' When this holy man first penetrated into the island provinces of the Indians, being wholly ignorant of the language of the people, he could only baptize children and serve the sick, who, by signs, could signify what they wanted. Whilst he exercised his

He establishes the faith at Malacca. He con‹ verts two kings in Ceylon. To him a journey of a thousand miles is nothing.

Nor could his zeal be confined by the boundless regions of India. A mysterious finger points to Ja‹ pan, and he hastens there, accompanied only by three missionaries. It was nine years since he had left Europe, and he had not rested a day.

He learned the language of Japan, and miracles opened the way for the new doctrine. But slow was the progress of truth. The good seed fell on rocks ; and even the dauntless Xavier for a mo‑ ment seemed disconcerted. He regretted having left India. It required all the valor of his resigna‑ tion to harden himself for a work that seemed im‑ possible.

But where the saints pass, God passes with them. The great Apostle redoubled his efforts. Heaven listened to his sighs and tears and prayers, and, after two years of suffering that cost him his life, Xavier was master of Japan.

Will he stop there ? No. He will never stop. He changed his route. He turned his eyes towards

zeal in Travancor, God first communicated to him *the gift of tongues,* according to the relation of a young Portuguese of Coimbra, named Vaz, who attended him in many of his journeys. He spoke very well the language of those barbarians without having learned it, and had no need or an interpreter when he instructed them. He some‑ times preached to five or six thousand persons together in some spacious plain.—*Butler.*

that great unknown—China. But before entering on this gigantic enterprise, he returned to Goa, where he found that India numbered half a million of Christians. Well might he exclaim: "Glory be to God! this is a fine harvest. Let us sow in the fields." And he embarked for China.

But God was pleased to accept his will in this good work, and took him to Himself. He foretold his death. The voyage was a sorrowful one. The Saint labored hard, but at last he was overcome. After suffering great pain he was put ashore, in a dying condition, in a land that was not China. The blessed hero was surrounded by his weeping companions. Tears filled his eyes, he pressed his crucifix to his breast, and, with the light of heaven shining from his countenance, he passed to everlasting glory on December 2, 1552, saying: "In Thee, O Lord! have I hoped ; I shall never be confounded."* He was canonized in 1662.

"Though he was only forty-six years old," Writes Butler, 'of which he had passed ten and a half in the Indies, his continual labors had made him gray betimes; in the last year of his life he was grizzled almost to whiteness. His corpse was interred on Sunday, being laid, after the Chinese fashion, in a large chest which was filled up with unslaked lime, to the end that, the flesh being consumed, the bones might be carried to Goa. On the 17th of February, 1553, the grave was opened to see if the flesh was consumed, but the lime being taken off the face, it was found ruddy and fresh-colored—like that of a man who is in a sweet re-

The heroic labors of St. Francis Xavier in India
pose; the body in like manner whole, and the natural moisture
uncorrupted; and the flesh being a little cut in the thigh, near
the knee, the blood was seen to run from the wound.   The sacerdotal habits in which the Saint was buried were no way damaged
by the lime; and the holy corpse exhaled an odor so fragrant
and   delightful   that the most exquisite perfumes came nothing
near it.   The   sacred remains were carried into the ship, and
brought to Malacca on the 22d of March, where it was received with
great honor.   The pestilence which for some weeks had laid waste
the town, on a sudden ceased.   The body was interred in a damp
churchyard, yet in August was found entire, fresh, and still exhal-
ing a sweet odor; and, being honorably put into a ship,was translated to Goa, where it was received and placed in the church of the College of St. Paul, on the 15th of March, 1554, upon which occasion several blind persons recovered sight, and others, sick of palsies and
other diseases, their health and the use of their limbs."—*Lives of the
Saints*, vol. xii.

In 1744 the Archbishop of Goa, attended by the viceroy, visited
the relics of St. Francis Xavier. No disagreeable odor came
from the body, and it seemed to be surrounded by a sort of illumi-
nation.

After Pontifical High Mass on the 3d of December, 1878, the
body of St. Francis Xavier was taken from its rich shrine and
exposed to public veneration in the presence of the Archbishop of
Goa, three bishops, and an immense multitude of people. "I stood
for a long time," says Bishop Meurin, "gazing at the head, the hands,
the feet, for they alone were uncovered—a rich chasuble embroidered with gold and pearls covering the rest of the body. I looked
at him as others did three centuries ago, and stood convinced that
this was the same body once the tabernacle of that noble and holy
soul chosen by God for the salvation of millions and millions of
souls.   I kissed most reverently the feet of him who preached the
Gospel of peace. . . . *Nowhere any signs of decay.*" (See the *Ave
Maria* of February 1, 1879.

and Japan were a repetition of the marvellous preaching of the first Apostles of Jesus Christ. His words were powerful. Each of his steps was a victory over the prince of darkness. In the short space of ten years he extended the Gospel over an area of nine thousand square miles, penetrated to regions never reached by the legions of Alexander, saved countless souls, and filled the world with the wonder of his miracles and the sublimity of his apostleship.

[9] There are three colleges and numerous churches in the United States bearing the name of St. Francis Xavier.

SAINT TERESA,

FOUNDRESS OF THE REFORMED CARMELITES.

DIED A.D. 1582.

"Oh thou undaunted daughter of desires !
By all thy dower of lights and fires,
By all of God we have in thee,
Leave nothing to myself in me.
Let me so read thy life that I
Unto all life of mine may die."
                              —*Crashaw.*

ST. TERESA,[1] one of the most noble wom-
en and beautiful characters of modern
times, was born at Avila, in Spain, on
the 28th of March, 1515. Alphonsus Sanchez, her
father, was a gentleman of great virtue, purity of
heart, and high respectability; and her mother,
Beatrice Ahumada, who suffered much from sickness, was a lady of uncommon goodness.

At seven years of age Teresa found pleasure in
reading the lives of the saints. Her mind was
greatly impressed by the word *eternity*. "For
ever, for ever, for ever," the sweet child would re-

---

[1] Teresa is from the Greek, and signifies *carrying ears of corn.*

peat, in thinking of the everlasting glory of the blessed. She would often retire to a secluded spot, and say her beads or some other prayers. She gave her little alms to the poor, and loved to do all the good in her power.

When the Saint was only twelve years old, her mother died. It was a great blow. Grief crushed the heart of the tender girl. She threw herself on her knees, and, with bitter tears streaming down her face, she looked up to heaven, and besought the Immaculate Virgin to be to her a mother.

The reading of romances[2] was the first ob-

[2] The old romances were simply extravagant works of fiction in which love-stories and the daring deeds of the heroes of chivalry were magnified to absurdity. Such works substituted falsehood for true history, a childish, idle amusement instead of solid instruction, and tended to destroy in the mind that beautiful thirst after truth imprinted in it by the great Author of nature. In short they inspired an unhappy love of trifles, folly, vanity, and nonsense.

The vast multiplication of bad or useless works of fiction is one of the curses of our own age. "The greater part of the fiction now published and read," says an eminent writer, "has no other object than mere pleasure, and that of a very low kind. Novels of this sort have a debasing effect on the public mind. The reading of them is mere mental dissipation, unfitting the reader both for reading of a more elevated kind and for the acting duties of life. I give it, too, as my opinion—the result of a long course of observation in a profession peculiarly fitted for such a purpose —that much and indiscriminate novel-reading has a most disastrous effect upon the memory. Indeed, I am not sure that the debilitating effect upon the mental faculties is not a more serious

stacle that seriously retarded Teresa's spiritual progress. "This fault," she writes, "failed not to cool
my good desires, and was the cause of my falling
insensibly into other defects—so enchanted was I
with the extreme pleasure which I took in it that
I thought I could not be contented if I had not some
new romance in my hands. I began to imitate the
fashion, to take delight in being well dressed, to
take great care of my hands, to make use of perfumes, and to effect all the vain trimmings which my
condition in life permitted.

"There was nothing bad in my intention. I
would not for the world, in the immoderate passion which I had to be decent, give any one an occasion of offending God. But I now acknowledge
how far these things—which for several years appeared to me innocent—are effectually and really
criminal."

evil even than its relaxing influence upon the conscience and the
moral sensibilities."

It need scarcely be added, however, that there are *good* works
of fiction—works written in the interest of religion and sound
morality. Some of the best and brightest Catholic minds of the
age have enriched this department of literature. But in the se-
lection of all such works we cannot be too choice. Care and
judgment are very necessary guides. Reading of this kind may,
indeed, be quite proper on an occasional amusement, but as soon
as it interferes with other duties, or becomes an occupation, it
immediately assumes the form of an evil. Life is very short. The
misspent hour never returns. Time is too precious to be wasted on
trifles.

There is danger in worldly companions. This
our Saint experienced. She laments her familiarity
with a vain young lady, a first cousin of her own,
whose manners and conversation had anything but a happy influence on the blossoming soul of Teresa.

" Were I to give counsel to parents," says the
Saint, "I would warn them to be well advised as
to what persons are the companions of their children of that age, because the bent of our fallen
nature inclines us rather to evil than to virtue. I
found this myself. I profited nothing by the
great virtue of one of my sisters, who was much
older than I; but I retained all the bad example
given me by a relation who haunted our house."

It is the mature opinion of the Saint herself that, only for romances and idle company, her
early favor would never have diminished, but,
on the contrary, that she would have gone on
increasing in the bright way of virtue. What
a precious jewel is piety in the young heart!
How easily lost! How carefully to be guarded!

After finishing her studies at a convent, and
suffering much from sickness, Teresa resolved to
embrace the religious state. She entered the
house of the Carmelite Nuns near Avila, and
made her profession with great fervor at the age
of twenty. For the next three years, however, her
life was one ceaseless conflict with a complication

of diseases which baffled all remedies.   Her mind was oppressed with sadness. She was several times on the verge of the tomb.   But a happy change came.   The young nun was restored to perfect health through the intercession of St. Joseph, as she learned afterwards.

Two years later her good father took sick, and this tender, affectionate daughter did all in her power to soothe his last days.   She left her convent.   She stood by his bed like a ministering angel, and, when death closed his eyes, Teresa prayed that the light of heaven might shine on his spirit.

After over a quarter of a century spent in the religious state, the Saint was inspired by the Almighty to begin the work of reforming her Order. The Carmelite rule which had been drawn up by Albert, Patriarch of Jerusalem, early in the thirteenth century, was very austere.   But after a time several relaxations were introduced.   A mitigation of the rule was approved by Pope Eugenius in 1431.

At the convent near Avila, in which Teresa lived, other relaxations were tolerated. The visits of secular friends to the parlor were too frequent.   This led to the loss of much precious time, and was often the cause of dissipation of mind and spiritual mischief, as the Saint herself experienced.

At first, the project of reform met with much opposition, and the Saint was slandered and persecuted. During the erection of the new convent at Avila—built by funds given by her relatives—a little nephew of the Saint, named Gonzales, was accidentally crushed by a falling wall. Teresa took him in her arms, prayed to God, and in a few moments restored him in perfect health to his mother.

The boy would often tell his holy aunt afterwards that it was her duty to secure his salvation by her prayers and instruction, as it was owing to her intervention that he was not long ago in heaven. He lived a pious life, and died happily soon after the Saint herself.

In 1562 Teresa and four fervent nuns from the old house entered the new convent. The establishment was confirmed by a papal brief from Rome. Much against her own will, the Saint was obliged to take the charge of governing.

The restored rule was marked by an austere poverty. The nuns wore habits of coarse serge, sandals instead of shoes, lay on straw, and never ate flesh-meat. They fasted eight months in the year, recited the Canonical Office, and offered up their prayers and other good works for the benefit of souls, and particularly for those who labored in the vineyard of Christ.

Despite great opposition, houses of the reformed

Order arose in various cities. The Saint began a new edifice at Toledo, with only four or five ducats in her pocket. " Teresa and this money," she said, " are indeed nothing ; but *God*, Teresa, and these ducats suffice for the accomplishment of the undertaking."

It was in the same city that a young lady of high reputation asked to be admitted to the Order. " I will bring my Bible with me," she added. " What !" exclaimed our great Saint, " your Bible ? Do not come to us. We are poor women who know nothing but how to spin and to do what we are told." This was meant as a rebuke to the vanity and wrangling disposition of the applicant. It exhibits the keenness and happy penetration of St. Teresa, for the woman afterwards fell into many extravagances.

The saint tells us that during her own early religious life she gave up mental prayer for a time. But she adds: " It was the worst and greatest temptation I ever had." [3]

[3] St. Teresa wrote her own life in obedience to her confessor. It is a remarkable work. Among the books of its class it holds the first place after the " Confessions" of St. Augustine. She also wrote " Book of Foundations," the " Interior Castle of the Soul," the " Way of Perfection," and other works. Those named have been translated into English. She also wrote many letters, that exhibit her virtue, prudence, wit, and excellent judgment. " She discovers in her writings," says Baillet, a very reserved critic, " the most impenetrable secrets of true wisdom in what

By mental prayer we learn truly to understand the way of heaven. It is the gate through which God reaches our souls. It is a treaty of friendship with the Almighty. An eminent spirit of prayer, founded in deep humility and perfect self-denial, was the sublime means by which God raised this holy Virgin to such an heroic degree of sanctity. Following the advice of a wise and learned Jesuit father, she made a meditation every day on some part of the sacred Passion of Jesus Christ.

" I do not see how God can come to us, or enrich us with His graces," says the Saint, " if we shut the door against him. Though He is infinitely desirous to communicate all His gifts,

we call mystical theology, the key of which God has given to a very small number of His favored servants. This may somewhat diminish our surprise that a woman without learning should have expounded what the greatest doctors never attained. God in his wonders employs what instruments He pleases, and we may say that the Holy Ghost had the principal share in the works of St. Teresa.

" It is authentically related," writes Butler, " that one night, whilst she was writing her meditation, a nun came into her cell, and sat by her a good while in great admiration, beholding her, as it were, in an enraptured state, holding a pen in her hand, but often interrupting her writing, laying down her pen, and fetching deep sighs; her eyes appeared full of fire, and her face shone with a bright light, so that the nun trembled with awe and respect, and went out again without being perceived by the Saint.'

He will have our hearts to be found alone, and burning with a desire to receive Him. O Joy of the angels! My Lord and my God! I cannot think of conversing with Thee without desiring to melt like wax in the fire of Thy divine love, and to consume all that is earthly in me by loving Thee.

"How infinite is Thy goodness to bear with, and even to caress, those who are imperfect and bad; to recompense the short time they spend with Thee, and, upon their repentance, to blot out their faults! This I experienced in myself. I do not see why all men do not approach Thee, to share in Thy friend‑ship." [4]

Though superior and foundress, St. Teresa chose the greatest humiliations that could be practised in her Order. If she pronounced a word with a false accent in reciting the divine office, she at once prostrated herself in penance. For the least fault she humbled herself. It was her pleasure after the office to steal into the choir and fold up the cloaks of the sisters. She served at table. She performed the lowest offices in the kit‑chen. She carefully swept the most filthy places in the yard.

---

[4] "Without meditation," says that great Doctor of the Church, St. Alphonsus Liguori, "it is impossible to remain a long time in the grace of God." And again: "If you make meditation daily, you will certainly be saved."

But in these exterior employments, the eyes of her pure soul were fixed on heaven. To her every place was a sanctuary. All her actions were offered to God as a continual sacrifice of love and praise and humility.

For years and years she mourned over the slight faults of her girlhood with the compunction of a Magdalen. She remembered them with floods of tears. She set no bounds to her mortifications. She chastised her delicate body by austere fasts, long prayers, hair-shirts, and severe disciplines. It was this lofty spirit of penance that moved her to restore the Carmelite rule in all its original rigor.

This noble woman suffered every kind of persecution. At one period her very friends avoided her as one possessed by the devil. Others went so far as to call her a devil. But when assailed with the most outrageous slanders, she would say with a smile: "No music is so agreeable to my ears."

" Do you think," said Christ to her in a vision, "that merit consists in enjoying? No. It is in working and suffering and loving. He is most beloved on whom My Father lays the heaviest crosses—if these are borne and accepted with love. By what can I better show My love for you than by choosing for you what I chose for Myself?"

Her charity was tender and beautiful. She was the very soul of goodness. She had an extreme horror of detraction. She hated its very shadow. In her presence no one dared to make the least reflection on the faults of another. She always observed the golden rule of speaking of others in the same kind way that she would desire others to speak of herself.

Nor was her great love of truth less admirable. If she heard one of her nuns repeat anything—be it ever so trifling—with the least alteration, she at once severely reprimanded the offender. She often said that no person could arrive at perfection who was not a scrupulous lover of truth and simplicity.

The Saint was singularly devout to the Blessed Sacrament. She used to say that *one* Communion properly made is enough to enrich the soul with all the treasures of grace and virtue. Her ardor in approaching the holy table was inexpressible.

If God often tried His servant in order to purify her virtue, He no less frequently favored her with celestial communications, which added new lustre to her glory. She was favored with visions and raptures. The soul sometimes raised the body into the air during these raptures.

"When I had a mind to resist these raptures," writes the lovely Saint, "there seemed something of a mighty force under my feet. It raised me up.

I know not with what to compare it. All my resistance was of little use, for when our Lord wishes to do a thing no power is able to withstand it.

"The effects of the rapture are great. The mighty power of God is thus made manifest. . . . We must acknowledge that we have a superior, that these favors come from Him, and that of ourselves we can do nothing. The soul is greatly impressed with humility.

"I confess it also produced great fear in me—which at first was extreme—to see that a massy body should be thus raised up from the earth. For though it be the Spirit that draws it up, and though it be done with great sweetness and delight—if not resisted—yet our senses are not thereby lost. At least I was so perfectly in my senses that I understood I was then elevated.

"There also seems so great a majesty in Him who can do this that it even makes the hair of the head stand on end, and there remains in the soul a mighty fear of offending a God so powerful. But this fear is wrapped up in a boundless love. . . . Such a favor also leaves in the soul a wonderful disengagement from all the things of this world." [4]

---

[4] Bannes, a very learned theologian of the Order of St. Dominic, whose name is famous in the schools, and who was for some time confessor of St. Teresa, testified that the Saint one day in public, as she was raised in the air in the choir, held herself by

This great lady was ever simple as as a child. "Do you see Teresa of Jesus?" said her confessor, Father Alvarez, S. J. "What sublime graces has she not received of God! Yet she is like the most tractable little child in relation to everything I can say to her." She obeyed her confessor as she would have done God Himself.

The enchanting modesty of this holy virgin's countenance was a silent sermon on the beauty of purity—a virtue which she preserved spotless from the cradle to the grave. When once asked for advice about impure temptations, she answered that she knew not what they meant.

The Saint's noble and generous soul made her deeply grateful to all who did her the least service. Though the wonderful success of her enterprises was owing to the blessing of God, and to the divine light which she drew down upon her actions by the sublime spirit of prayer, still she was doubtless a woman of rare natural gifts.

some rails and prayed thus: "Lord, suffer not by such a favor a wicked woman to pass for virtuous." He mentions other instances in the public choir, but says that at her earnest request this never happened to her in public during the last fifteen years of her life. Richard of St. Victor teaches that raptures arise from a vehement fire of divine love in the will, or from excessive spiritual joy, or from a beam of heavenly light darting upon the understanding.—*Butler.*

The Saint sometimes saw the adorable mystery of one God in three Persons in a manner amazingly clear.

Her temper was sweet and amiable. Her pure heart throbbed with the most tender affection. In early life the quickness of her wit and the richness of her imagination, poised by an uncommon maturity of judgment, gained her the love and esteem of all her acquaintances. Nor did this charm of person and manners desert her in old age. To the end her prudence and address were admirable. Her gravity, modesty, graceful ways, and wise words were the delight of all with whom she conversed. She lived to see sixteen nunneries of her reformed Order established.

When her last hour came, she kept repeating, until speech failed: "A contrite and humble heart, O God! Thou wilt not despise." And with these words on her lips the dear St. Teresa passed on the 15th of October, 1582, at the age of sixty-seven years, forty-seven of which were entirely consecrated to Heaven. She was canonized in 1621.[6]

---

[6] There are churches in New York City, Brooklyn, Boston, St. Louis, Philadelphia, New Orleans, and various other places in our country bearing the name of St. Teresa.

We have the holy daughters of St. Teresa in this Republic The Carmelite Nuns were the *first* female religious who established themselves within the limits of the thirteen original States. In 1790 Father Charles Neale brought with him from Belgium to our shores four Carmelites, three of whom were Americans, the fourth an English lady. Thus one of the most austere orders in the Church was the earliest to naturalize itself in the young Republic.   The three American ladies were natives of Maryland, members of the Matthews family.   They had made their religious profession in Belgium, with the hope of eventually establishing the Order in this country.   Happily their hope was realized. They took possession of their humble convent in Charles County, Maryland, on October 15, 1790.   In 1831 the nuns removed to Baltimore.   At present they have two houses, one in Maryland, the other in Missouri, with thirty-one religious.   A branch of the Baltimore establishment has lately been founded at Rimouski, Canada.   The number of nuns in each convent is limited to twenty-one. See our "Popular History of the Catholic Church in the United States," pp. 398–9.

SAINT ALOYSIUS OF GONZAGA, S. J.,

THE ILLUSTRIOUS PATRON OF YOUTH.

DIED. A.D. 1591.

UST eight years before the birth of St. Vin cent de Paul, and while St. Francis de Sales was but a sweet little babe of seven months old, and the lovely St. Teresa was yet on earth. leading her nuns on the narrow path to heaven, there was born at the princely castle of Castiglione,[1] on the 9th of March, 1568, a child who was destined to be a brilliant mirror of purity and innocence, and the wonder of all succeeding ages. It was Aloysius Gonzaga.[2]

His father, the Marquis Gonzaga, was a Spanish

---

[1] Situated in Lombardy, in the north of Italy.

[2] It is worthy of remark that a host of great saints was produced by the Catholic Church at the very period of the so-called Reformation. This alone is a solid refutation of the false charge of corruption which Protestants bring against the dear old Church —the mother of saints. The tree is known by its fruit. *Twenty canonized saints adorned the period of Luther's own lifetime.* Among these were St. Catherine of Genoa, St. Francis Xavier, and St. Teresa. The short life of St. Aloysius cast a gleam of pure glory on the same century.

prince, and his mother belonged to a noble **and** distinguished family.   It is said that the child—her first-born—was the fruit of his mother's pious pray- ers.   She besought the Almighty to grant her a son who would consecrate his life to the service of his Creator.   God was pleased at the request of the good lady.   Aloysius was the answer to her tender petition.

As may easily be supposed, the marchioness watched over the education of little Aloysius and her other children with a motherly and religious solicitude.   The first words he was taught to utter were the holy names of Jesus and Mary; and the first action that he learned was to make the Sign of the Cross.   His infant soul was thus early impress- ed with pious sentiments.

Nor was the boy's wealth of goodness a hidden jewel which it took a long time to discover. From the first his compassion for the poor was extraordinary.   He gave away all his pocket- money to beggars.   His manners were kind and amiable, and in praying he seemed like a little seraph.   Thus in Aloysius age and grace grew together.   Such bright and happy inclinations at the very dawn of life gave hopes that its meridian would be still more brilliant, and it was well argued that the bud which promised so well would not fail to produce in due season rare and admirable fruit.

His father—ignorant of the designs of Providence
—desired to train up Aloysius for the military profession. He furnished the child with little guns,
pikes, and swords. The marquis even carried him,
while but four years of age, to Cascal, where he had
assembled a division of the army. Here he was delighted to see the boy carry a little pike and march
before the ranks.

It was during his stay at Cascal that Aloysius,
thrown amid the rude, vicious society of army officers, picked up some unbecoming words, which,
of course, he did not understand. On making use
of them in the hearing of his tutor, he was at once
rebuked. The child, however, must be excused
from all blame, as he wanted both age and knowledge; but to the last day of his life he bewailed
this fault as a subject of deep sorrow and humiliation.[3] Nor could he ever after endure the presence
of any one who cursed or used improper or profane
language.

When he had reached the age of seven years,
reason came to the boy's aid in forming pious habits.
He began to recite the Office of the Blessed Virgin
every day. He said the Seven Penitential Psalms
on his knees—a custom which he observed to

[3] " Cardinal Bellarmine, three other confessors, and all who were
best acquainted with his interior," says Butler, " declared after his
death their firm persuasion that he never offended God mortally in
his whole life."—*Lives of the Saints,* vol. vi.

the end. Thus, at a time when other children
are scarcely able to distinguish between good
and evil, our young Saint began to lay the founda·
tions of that spiritual edifice which grew daily,
and finally received its crowning glory beyond the
stars.

At the age of eight, Aloysius and his younger
brother, Ralph, were placed at the court of the
Grand Duke of Tuscany, that they might learn
Latin, Italian, and various accomplishments suited
to their rank. But none of these things interfered
with his steady progress in virtue. He became exceedingly devout to the Blessed Virgin ; and his
desire to imitate her celestial chastity induced him
to make a vow of chastity. He kept it with mar·
vellous fidelity. To such a degree did Heaven
bestow upon him the perfection of this beautiful
virtue that never in his whole life did he feel the
least temptation against holy purity. This we have
from the testimony of his confessors, the learned
Father Platus, S. J., and the celebrated Cardinal
Bellarmine, S. J.

But Aloysius cultivated this extraordinary
grace by ceaseless prayer and mortification. His
modesty was proverbial. He did not even know
the faces of many ladies among his own relations
with whom he frequently conversed. The language of this noble boy was the mirror of a
spotless mind; and from his very action there

shone forth the grace and beauty that reigned within.

He was the very soul of kindness and courtesy. Never did he speak to his servants in words of command. " Please do this," he would say; or, " You may do this"; or, " If it be no trouble, you may do this." To his governor he was obe· dient as a novice, and towards all he was affable and gentle.

At the age of eleven his father removed him from Florence to Mantua. It was here that he first experienced the ravishing delight of a soul engaged in pious meditation. He found "how sweet is the Lord to those who love Him." He spent whole hours before a crucifix. Often he was so deeply absorbed in heavenly thought that his governor and attendants would enter the apartment and make a considerable noise, in order to attract his attention, without, however, causing him to make the smallest sign to show that he was at all aware of their presence.

When the great St. Charles Borromeo paid a visit to Brescia, Aloysius went to receive his bless· ing. The cardinal was delighted with the young marquis, whom he advised to prepare for First Communion. He prepared with inexpressible diligence for this great and happy act. The day came. Aloysius received the Bread of Angels as one who shone with the beauty and brilliancy of another world.　He was now twelve years of age.

After several years of study, piety, and the practice of severe mortification, he resolved to consecrate his life entirely to Heaven. It was his desire to enter the Society of Jesus. When he told his mother, the good lady smiled with pleasure, but his father was indignant. From all sides came difficulties. But the Saint prayed and confided in Heaven. He finally conquered, by his kindness, firmness, and humility, where he would have been defeated by an intemperate opposition.

The old marquis at length gave his consent. "My dear son," said he, "your choice is a deep wound in my heart. I ever loved you, as you always deserved. In you I had found the hopes of my family; but you tell me that God calls you another way. Go, then, in His name, wherever you please, and may his blessings everywhere attend you."

Aloysius now made over all his estates and lordly titles to his brother Ralph, and the affair was ratified by the emperor in 1585. When the day of departure came, his subjects crowded around, and sorrow was expressed in every countenance. The Saint bade them all farewell, saying: "I seek nothing but the salvation of my soul; may you all do the same."

On arriving at Rome he paid his respects to

the pope, and at once sought the novitiate. He was scarcely eighteen years of age. When he was conducted to his cell he entered it as a paradise. "This is my rest forever," he exclaimed in the words of the prophet; "here will I dwell, for I have chosen it."

He was now hidden amid that silence and retirement peculiar to a religious life. He was daily preparing for himself a crown of glory both here and hereafter. But, like a brilliant diamond in the dark he shone not the less brightly in his new solitude and obscurity.

The bud which had opened with such early prom ise did not fail, as we have seen, to produce fruit in due season; and as its opening had been in advance of its fellows, so it maintained the start which it had obtained, until it gave rich indications of a premature but full and perfect growth.

The angelic life which St. Aloysius led among men rendered him worthy to be called away at an early age to the mansions of the blessed. It was revealed to him one day, while saying his morning prayers, that in a year from that time the call would come. He was then finishing his studies in theology.

Not long after this a deadly pestilence swept over Rome. The Saint devoted himself to the service of the sick and dying. Like a ministering angel he passed through the wards of the hospital.

He exhorted the poor patients, washed their feet, made their beds, changed their clothes, and performed the most loathsome offices with inexpressible tenderness.   But he soon fell sick himself, and joy shone over his youthful countenance. The promised hour was coming.   He received the last Sacraments, and, after murmuring the holy name of Jesus, the beautiful soul of Aloysius Gonzaga winged its flight to that heavenly home where—

> "From every eye is wiped the tear,
>   All sighs and sorrows cease;
> No more alternate hope and fear,
>   But everlasting peace."

His happy death took place on the 21st of June, 1591, in the twenty-fourth year of his age.   He was canonized by Benedict XIII. in 1726.[4]

---

[4] About two years before his conversion to the Catholic faith, the celebrated Father Faber was at Rome.   An incident of the visit is thus recounted by his biographer :   "Again, after praying at the shrine of St. Aloysius on the feast of that Saint, he (Faber) left the church as if speechless, and not knowing where he was going. He said afterwards that he saw then that he must within three years either be a Catholic or loose his mind.   After his reception he told Dr. Grant that on the 21st of June, St. Aloysius had always knocked very heard at his heart."—*Bowden, Life and Letters of Frederick William Faber, D.D.*

There is scarcely a single diocese in the United States that has not a number of churches or religious institutions bearing the name of St. Aloysius.   He is the patron of Gonzaga College, Washington, D. C.

SAINT FRANCIS DE SALES,

BISHOP OF GENEVA, AND DOCTOR OF THE CHURCH.

DIED A. D. 1622.

FRANCIS[1] DE SALES, the light of his age, and the favorite saint of modern times, was born on the 21st of August, 1567, at the castle of Sales, in Savoy.[2] His father was a nobleman of wealth and high rank, and his mother a lady of uncommon virtue. Francis was the eldest of a numerous family.

Under his mother's tender care he grew up a beautiful boy, with a countenance of exquisite sweetness. She taught him to pray, to visit the poor, and to read the lives of the saints. Even at that early age he was the soul of Christian honor. It is said that in such horror did he hold a lie that he would suffer any punishment rather than be guilty of such a disgraceful offence.

Francis was first sent to the college of La Roche,

[1] Francis is from the French, and signifies *free*.
[2] Savoy is now a part of France ; it was formerly a division of the kingdom of Sardinia.

and afterwards to that of Annecy. He was an early riser and a hard student. Among his young companions he was noted for superior manliness and kind, graceful deportment. At the age of eleven he obtained permission from his father to receive tonsure, having at that early period decided to enter the sacred ministry.

In 1580 he was sent to pursue his studies at Paris. He entered the college of the Jesuits, and for five years, under some of the most famous Fathers of that time, he stored his mind with the treasures of learning and literature. But in the pursuit of knowledge, Francis never lost sight of piety and virtue. He prayed much, visited the churches, practised many austerities, and never failed to carry about him his favorite book, "The Spiritual Combat."

It was during his studious career in the gay capital of France that the young Saint was assailed by a terrible temptation. Suddenly a cloud of darkness overspread his soul. He grew melancholy. Something seemed to whisper that he was no longer in the state of grace, and that he would be lost for ever. A feeling of dread crept over him. The evil one said : "In vain are all the good works of De Sales. He is already a child of perdition !"

Francis struggled manfully. He ceased not to pray, but the temptation still remained. He could neither eat nor sleep, and soon wasted away to a mere skeleton. But at length the great cross vanished as suddenly as it came. One day he entered the church of St. Stephen and knelt down before an image of the Blessed Virgin. Near by, on a tablet, was inscribed the famous prayer of St Bernard, the "Memorare." The noble and sorely-tried student repeated it with great emotion. He tearfully implored that it might please God to restore his peace of mind through the intercession of the Immaculate Mary. He then made a vow of perpetual chastity, and all at once he was surrounded by the brightness of celestial joy. He left the church with his mind in a state of sweet calmness. He had received that peace which the world cannot give, and to the last day of his life it never again deserted him. [3]

The young nobleman was now eighteen years of age. His father recalled him from Paris and sent him to the University of Padua to study law.

[3] "No man," says A Kempis, " is so perfect and holy as not sometimes to have temptations, and we cannot be wholly without them. Temptations are often very profitable to a man, although they be troublesome and grievous; for by them a man is humbled, purified, and instructed. All the saints have passed through many tribulations and temptations, and have profited by them; and they who could not support temptations have become reprobates and fell off There is not any Order so holy nor place so retired where there are not temptations or adversities."—*Imitation of Christ*.

It was while here that he placed himself under the spiritual direction of the famous Jesuit, Father Possevinus. Francis completed his studies with brilliant distinction. The degree of Doctor of Laws was conferred upon him with such unusual ceremony as to show that he was looked upon as the very brightest ornament of the university. This took place on September 5, 1591, when he was twenty-four years of age.

After a visit to Rome and the Holy House of Loretto, Francis returned to the family mansion. He was now a finished gentleman and one of the most learned jurists in Europe, and at his father's urgent desire he allowed himself to be called to the bar. He was appointed advocate in the supreme court of Savoy. It was not his own choice. The highest honors of the state lay open before him, but he desired them not. He wisely wished, however, to overcome difficulties by degrees. He prayed for light and waited for some favorable opportunity.

It came. He gently and firmly made his decision known in relation to his entering the sacred ministry. His father was deeply grieved, but finally yielded with the best grace possible ; and the kind-hearted old noble gave his blessing to that richly-gifted son who wished to live only for Heaven, and who was destined to confer an immortal renown on the house of De Sales.

Francis was raised to the dignity of the priest hood on the 18th of December, 1593. It was a day of joy in the city of Annecy. He was then twenty-six years of age. From the first he led a most active missionary life. The Bishop of Geneva sent him to preach in the neighboring towns and villages, and great was the success that attended his sermons. The word of God fell from his lips with inexpressible modesty and majesty.

His father thought that the young priest preached too often. "I had the best father in the world," said the great Saint many years after to the Bishop of Bellay, "but he had passed a great part of his life at court and in military service, the maxims of which he knew better than theology. While I was provost I preached on every occasion in the cathedral as well as in the parish churches, and even in the humblest confraternities. I knew not how to refuse, so dear to me was that word of our Lord, 'Give to every one that asketh of thee.'

"My good father, hearing the bell ring for the sermon, asked who preached. They replied: 'Who should it be but your son?' One day he took me aside and said: 'Provost, you preach too often. Even on working days I hear the bell ringing for the sermon, and they always say to me, *It is the Provost, the Provost.* It was not so in my time. Sermons were much more rare; but what sermons they were ! God knows they were learned and well studied. The preachers spoke wonders. They quoted more Latin and Greek in one sermon than you do in ten. Everybody was delighted and edified. People ran to them in crowds, and you would have said they were going to gather manna. Nowadays you make this exercise so common that nobody regards it and no value is set on you.'

"Do you see," continued the Saint, "this good father spoke as he understood, and with all freedom. He spoke according to the maxims of the world, in which he had been brought up, but of another stamp altogether are the evangelical maxims. Jesus Christ, the mirror of perfection and the model of preachers, did not use all these circumspections any more than the Apostles who followed in His footsteps. Believe me. we can never preach enough." [*]

At this time Geneva was the head-centre of Calvinism. This grim heresy had spread widely, and, among other neighboring districts, it had taken violent possession of the duchy of Chablais. After a time, however, Duke Charles of Savoy, a Catholic, recovered the territory. He desired to re-establish the ancient faith, and for that purpose wrote to the Bishop of Geneva.

---

[*] The holy Doctor, however, did not approve of *long* sermons.

But nobody wished to undertake the perilous mission to such a land of fanatics. All seemed terrified at the difficulties. Francis alone offered himself for the work, and he was soon joined by his first cousin, Louis de Sales.

The Saint and his companion, amid great opposition, set out on the 9th of September, 1594. They traveled on foot. Except two Breviaries, a Bible, and Bellarmine's "Controversies," no books were carried. On coming to the new field of toil and danger they beheld a beautiful land covered with ruins. The rude, destroying hand of the so-called Reformation had passed over church and castle and monastery.

The mission was opened at the town of Thonon. But seven Catholic families were found at that place. Fanaticism soon grew alarmed, and the ministers even clamored to have the missionaries publicly whipped. It was all up-hill work —slow, dreary, and dangerous. The Saint's sermons were often attended by only three or four Calvinists. But day after day he continued to labor, with manly energy and angelic sweetness.

There was everything to contend against. The people were stupid, indifferent, and superstitious. The ministers tried to impress their blinded flocks with the idea that the priests were wizzards. On one occasion a fanatic—afterwards converted

—made three attempts to shoot the Saint, **but** failed.

In spite, however, of want, hunger, opposition from home, and various attempts at assassination, he continued his apostolic mission.   After a time the Jesuits, Franciscans, and others came to his aid, and in a few years the religious conquest of this charming region was complete.   The ancient faith was restored.   It is computed that Francis de Sales thus brought seventy-two thousand souls into the Catholic Church.

"I think I can confute the Calvinists," said the famous Cardinal Perron, "but to persuade and con. vert them you must bring them to the Coadjutor of Geneva."[b]

On the death of the good old bishop of Geneva, our Saint prepared for his consecration by a retreat of twenty days.   He made a general confession.   The ceremony took place in the presence of his mother and a vast concourse of distinguished people, on the 8th of December, the Feast of the Immaculate Conception, 1602.

St Francis now entered on that career which makes him such an illustrious figure in the history of the Church.   His plan of life was simple.   He never wore silks.   He made his visits on foot. Everything in his household was plain but ele

[b]Our Saint.

gant. He kept for himself a little, dark, poorly-furnished apartment, which he playfully called the room of "Francis"—the others being the rooms of "the Bishop."

Ceaseless was his watch over the flock committed to his charge. He took care to place only good priests in his parishes. He gave an impulse to sound education, the study of catechism, and simplicity in preaching. He corrected abuses, reformed convents, and guided many in the path of virtue. He shone like a great light. In short, he was a Bishop of bishops.

The Saint was meek and kind to all, but his affection for the members of his own family was something truly beautiful. Never was this more touchingly shown than at the death of his youngest sister, Jane—a sweet girl who passed to a better world at the age of fifteen.

"You may think," he writes to a friend, "how heartily I loved this little girl. I had begotten her for her Saviour, for I had baptized her with my own hand over fourteen years ago. She was the first creature on whom I exercised my priestly office. I was her spiritual father, and I promised myself much to make something good of her one day."

The holy bishop was soon called to his mother's deathbed. She was a lady whose pure, lofty character shone out to the last. In her trembling hands she held a crucifix, and kissed it even when her eyesight had gone.   When Francis arrived at the couch of his dying parent, she knew him at once, although oppressed with blindness.   She caressed him, saying: "This is my son and my father—this one."

All her family knelt around.   She breathed her soul to God.   "The great prelate then had courage," writes his brother, Charles A. de Sales, "after having given her his holy benediction, to close her lips and eyes, and to give her the last kiss of peace.   After that his heart swelled very much; and he wept over that mother more than ever he had done since he became a churchman. But it was without spiritual bitterness, as he afterwards protested.   He rendered her the funeral honors and duties, and her body was placed to rest in the tomb of Sales at the church of Thorens."

Only another year passed away, and the Saint mourned the loss of his good old preceptor, the Abbé Deage, whose declining years he had soothed with truly filial tenderness.   The first time he said Mass for the repose of the abbé's soul, on reaching the "Our Father" he was so overcome by the recollection that it was the old priest who had first taught him to say the same prayer, that he was unable to proceed for some time.

With the aid of St. Jane Francis de Chantal, a gifted lady whom he had long directed in the way of virtue, the holy Doctor founded the Order of Visitation Nuns in 1610. Eight years later it became a regular monastic body by virtue of a bull from Pope Paul V. [6]

His famous "Introduction to a Devout Life" was published in 1608, and his great "Treatise on the Love of God" in 1616. [7]

We have but space to glance at the apostolic labors in his last years. Popes and monarchs

[6] Teaching is the great object of the pious and accomplished Nuns of the Visitation. At the present time they have eighteen academies for young ladies in the United States. See "Popular History of the Catholic Church in the United States," pp. 399-401.

[7] Taken with his " Letters," these are his chief works. The " Introduction to a Devout Life " is an unrivalled manual of instruction for all who are endeavoring to lead a pious life in the world. Though a small book, it omits nothing, and is filled with the sweet, cheerful, and beautiful spirit of the holy Doctor

The "Treatise on the Love of God " is his greatest work. It seems to have been written during periods of inspiration. It is a mine of thoughts, rich, sublime, and beautiful. " In it," says Butler, " he paints his own soul. He describes the feeling sentiments of divine love, its state of fervor, of dryness, of trials, suffering, and darkness—in explaining which he calls in philosophy to his assistance. He writes on this sublime subject what he had learned by his own experience. Some parts of his book are only to be understood by those souls who have gone through these states.

His " Letters" form a treasury of piety and practical wisdom.

sought his advice. His light shone far beyond the limits of his own diocese. In 1618 he visited Paris, and all regarded him with admiration. It was here that he made the personal acquaintance of St. Vincent de Paul, whom the holy Doctor was in the habit of styling "the worthiest priest he had ever known," and under whose direction he placed the community of the Visitation, which he established in the capital of France.

Not long before his death the Saint made a journey to Avignon. While at Lyons an incident occurred that is worthy of recounting as an example of his kind and gentle manners. As he was boarding a vessel the boatman refused to receive him without his passport. His attendants grew angry, but the Bishop remarked : Let him alone. He knows his business as boatman, and fulfils it. We don't know that of travelers."

Exposed to a bitter cold wind—it was in November—he had to wait an hour for the passport, but he showed a calmness which diffused itself over his irritated followers. At last they got on board. The Bishop went and sat near the boatman who had been tiresome, saying :" I wish to make friends with this good man, and to talk to him a little about our Lord."

But the end was rapidly coming. The great Doctor suffered from weakness of the chest and violent pains in the head and stomach. Still, he never rested. He was an intrepid laborer. The energy of his soul rose superior to the decay of his body. In his last hours he was attended by some Jesuit Fathers under whom he had studied at Paris. "You find me in a condition," he whispered to his Confessor, Father Possevinus, "in which I stand in need of nothing but the mercy of God. Obtain it for me by your prayers." He sank gradually. All present knelt down. The prayers for the dying were recited, and as "All ye Holy Innocents pray for him" was repeated, the grand and innocent souls of the illustrious St. Francis de Sales bade adieu to the scenes of this world. It was the Feast of the Holy Innocents, December 28, 1622.[8]

Many are the anecdotes related of the sweetness, charity, simplicity, and wonderful judgment of this great Bishop.[9] A young man was once brought to him for the purpose of receiving a severe reprimand; but the Saint spoke to him with his habitual kindness. Seeing the youth's hardness, however, he shed tears, remarking that

[8] He was canonized in 1665 by Pope Alexander VII., who assigned the 29th of January for his festival. Many miracles were wrought at his tomb, among others the raising of two dead persons to life.

[9] A full and most charming picture of the Saint and his conversations is to be found in the "Spirit of St. Francis de Sales," by Bishop Camus, of Bellay, It is one of the most entertaining works in the whole range of biography.

such a hard, unyielding heart would bring him to a bad end.

He was told that the young man had been cursed by his mother. "Oh! this is sad indeed," he exclaimed. "If the poor woman is taken at her word, in vain will she afterwards curse her own curse. Unhappy mother of a still more wretched son!"

It was a true prophecy. Not long after the wayward youth perished in a duel, and his mother died of grief.

Some found fault with the Saint for having been too gentle in his reproof on this occasion. "What would you have me do?" he asked. "I did my best to arm myself with an anger free from sin. I took my heart in both my hands, and I had not the resolution to throw it at his head. But, indeed, I was afraid of letting that little drop of meekness—which has cost me the toil of twenty-two years to store up like dew in my heart—to run off in a quarter of an hour. The bees are several months in making a little honey which a man will swallow down at a mouthful.

"Besides," he continued, "what is the use of speaking when we are not listened to? This young man was blind to remonstrances, for the light of his eyes—I mean his judgment—was not with him. I should have done him no good, and myself, perhaps, much harm—like one who is drowned in his attempt to save another. Charity must be wise and prudent." But it was seldom indeed that the heart of the sinner was proof against the gentleness of Francis de Sales.

" Disputes on religious matters," says Bishop Camus, " were very disagreeable to him, especially at table and after dinner. These were not, he said *bottle topics*. I replied one day, taking up his expression, that if a bottle of that kind was occasionally broken it would give forth the lamp of truth, which is all fire and flame. 'Yes, indeed,' he answered, 'fire and flames of anger and altercation, which yield only smoke and blackness, and very little light.' "

When in society, if the Saint heard any one throwing ridicule on another, his countenance immediately testified to his dislike of the conversation. He would introduce another topic to create a diversion, and, when he could not succeed by this method, he would rise and say:

"This is tampering too much on the good man. It passes all reasonable bounds. Who gives us the right to amuse ourselves in this way at the expense of others ? Should we like to be treated thus, and have all our foibles dissected by the razor of the tongue ? To bear with our neighbor and his imperfection is a great perfection, and it is a great imperfection to cut him up in this way by ridicule."

One day a young lady, in his hearing, was amusing herself by quizzing another's want of beauty, and was laughing at some natural blemishes with which she had been born. The great Doctor quietly observed that it was God who had made us, and not we ourselves; and that His works were perfect. But the lady was so foolish as to laugh still more at his saying that all God's works were perfect. " Believe me," he said, "her soul is most upright, beautiful, and well proportioned. Be satisfied that *I know this for certain.*" The fair quizzer grew silent.

He disliked complaining. " One day," writes Bishop Camus, "I was complaining to our Saint of some grievous wrong that had been done me. The thing was so very manifest that he agreed to the truth of what I said. Finding myself so strongly supported, I felt triumphant, and grew very eloquent in dwelling upon the justice of my cause. The Saint, to put a stop to all this superfluous discourse, observed:

" ' It is true that they were in every way to blame for treating you in this manner. Such conduct was quite unworthy of them, particularly towards a man of your position. I see but one circumstance in the whole affair of your disadvantage.'

" ' What is that ?' I asked.

" ' That you have but to show your superior

wisdom by holding your tongue,' said the great Saint.

"This answer so struck me that I was silent at once, and had not a word to offer in reply."

On a certain occasion a person, more talkative than discreet, expressed surprise that a distinguished lady of great piety, who was under the holy Bishop's direction, had not even left off wearing ear-rings.

"I assure you," he replied, "I not so much as know whether she has any ears; for she comes to confession with her head so completely covered up, or with a great scarf so tnrown over it, that I do not know how she is dressed. Besides, I believe that the holy woman Rebecca who was quite as virtuous as she is, lost nothing of her holiness by wearing the ear-rings which Eliezer presented her on the part of Isaac."

He disapproved of unwise austerities. He was once consulted on the introduction of bare feet into a religious house. "Why don't they leave their shoes and stockings alone?" replied the great Saint. "It is the head that wants reforming not the feet!"

He was an ardent lover of simplicity, often saying that he "would at any time give a hundred serpents for one dove." "He labored," writes Bishop Camus, "not only to banish the pest of singularity from religious houses, but also to lead those persons who make a profession of devotion in the world to avoid it.   He said that this defect rendered their piety not only offensive but ridiculous.

"He wished people to conform externally, as much as possible, to the mode of life of those who follow the same profession, without affecting to make themselves remarkable by any singularity. He pointed to the example of our Saviour, who in the days of His mortal life was pleased to make Himself in all things like his brethren, sin only excepted.

"The Saint was most careful to practise this lesson in his own person; and during the fourteen years that I was under his guidance, and studiously observed his behavior, and even his most trifling gestures as well as his words, I never perceived anything in him the least approaching to singularity.

"He often told me that our outward demeanor ought to resemble water, which, the better it is, the clearer, the purer from admixture, and the more devoid of taste it is.   Nevertheless, although there was nothing of singularity in him, he appeared to me so singular in this very thing of having no singularity in him, that everything in him was in my eyes singular."

Though St. Francis was "meek and humble of heart," it was not his habit to use expressions of humility in speaking of himself. He avoided such language. He regarded it as one of the gulfs in which that virtue is apt to suffer shipwreck. He so strictly adhered to this practice that nothing but stringent necessity ever led him to say good or evil of himself, even in the most indifferent matters.

He sometimes said that it was as difficult a feat to speak of one's self as to walk along a tight-rope; and that a strong balance as well as a wonderful circumspection was requisite to avoid a fall. He did not like to hear people talking very humbly of themselves, unless their words proceeded from a thoroughly sincere inward feeling. He said that such words were the quintessence, the cream, the elixir of the most subtle pride. The truly humble man does not desire *to appear* humble, but *to be* humble.

"I have known," says Bishop Camus, "great servants of God whom nothing could have induced to allow any one to take their portrait, believing that such an act would imply some sort of vanity or dangerous complaisance. Our Saint, who made himself all things to all men, made no difficulty about the matter. His reason was this: that as the law of charity obliges us to communicate to our neighbor the picture of our mind, imparting to him frankly and without grudging all that we have learned with respect to the science

of salvation, we ought not to make any greater ob-
jection to give our friends the satisfaction they desire of having before their eyes, through the medium
of painting, the picture of our outward man.   If
we see, not only without annoyance, but even with
pleasure, our books, which are the portraits of our
minds, why grudge them the features of our face,
if the possession of them will contribute anything
to their pleasure?

"These are his own words, writing on the subject to a friend: 'Here, at any rate, is the portrait of this earthly man, so little am I able to refuse you anything you desire.   I am told that it is
the best likeness that was ever taken of me, but I
think that matters very little.   *In imagine pertran-
sit homo, sed et frustra conturbatur.*[10]   I had to borrow it in order to give it to you, for I have none of
my own.   Would that the likeness of my Creator
did but shine forth in my mind—with what pleasure would you behold it!'"

The following are some of the sayings of this
gentle and deep-thinking Saint:

"Truth must always be charitable, for bitter zeal
does harm instead of good."

"A wise silence is better than a truth spoken
without charity."

"I know of no other perfection than loving

[10] "Man passeth as an image, and is disquieted in vain."—
Psalms.

God with all our hearts, and our neighbor as ourselves."

"As physicians discover the health or sickness of a man by looking at his tongue, so our words are true indications of the qualities of our souls."

"In dress keep yourself always, as much as possible, on the side of plainness and modesty, which, without doubt, is the greatest ornament of beauty, and the best excuse for the want of it."

His unsurpassed love of purity could not bear the least act or word that might tarnish its beauty. He called it "the beautiful and white virtue of a soul." "See that lily," he once said; "it is the symbol of purity. It preserves its whiteness and sweetness even amid briars and thorns; but touch it ever so little, and *it will fade.*"

[11] There is a splendid seminary near Milwaukee under the patronage of St. Francis De Sales, and the countless churches bearing his name are scattered throughout every diocese in the United States. He is the Patron of Catholic journalists.

ST. VINCENT DE PAUL,

THE APOSTLE OF CHARITY.

DIED A. D. 1660.

HAT land has not been blessed by the labors, what person has not heard of the Sister of Charity?—

> "Who once was a lady of honor and wealth;
> Bright glowed on her features the roses of health;
> Her vesture was blended of silk and of gold,
> And her motion shook perfume from every fold;
> Joy revelled around her, love shone at her side,
> And gay was her smile as the glance of a bride,
> And light was her step in the mirth-sounding hall,
> When she heard of the *Daughters of St. Vincent de Paul*."

But now—

> "Unshrinking where pestilence scatters his breath,
> Like an angel she moves 'mid the vapor of death;
> Where rings the loud musket and flashes the sword,
> Unfearing she walks for she follows the Lord.
> How sweetly she bends o'er each plague-tainted face
> With looks that are lighted with holiest grace!
> How kindly she dresses each suffering limb,
> For she sees in the wounded the image of *Him!*"

The noble woman, the Daughter of Charity

whose heroism is thus pictured by the poet's pen, honors Vincent [1] de Paul as the father and founder of her society. Let us glance at the career of that immortal benefactor of humanity.

He was born at a little village in the south of France, not far from the shadow of the famous Pyrenees Mountains, in the year of 1576. His parents were good, simple, country people, who owned a small farm. Vincent was the third of a family of four sons and two daughters, who were brought up in innocence and inured to hard labor. He was a bright, thoughtful boy, and gave such early promise of greatness that his father, at much sacrifice, determined to give him a superior education.

But after some time he resolved to be no longer a burden to his poor parents, and, with that manly energy which usually accompanies true genius, he took the matter into his own hands. At twenty years of age we find Vincent entering the University of Toulouse, where, after a long course of study, he graduated Bachelor of Theology. He was raised to the dignity of priesthood in 1600.

The young priest was already a man of virtue and learning ; but he had not yet finished his studies. He was shortly to become well vers-

* Vincent is from the Latin, and signifies *conquering*.

ed in a new science.   By a very rugged road he was soon to reach the mountain-heights of virtue. As gold through a furnace, so Vincent was to pass through the fire of affliction.

In 1605 the Saint was called to Marseilles on business, and while crossing the Gulf of Lyons on his way back the boat was captured by African pirates. A few of the prisoners were killed; the others were put in chains. Vincent and some companions were carried to Tunis, and placed for sale in the slave market.

Mahometan merchants came to look at the unfortunate captives as they would at oxen or horses. They examined who could eat well, looked at their teeth, felt their sides, probed their wounds, forced them to lift burdens and wrestle, and made them run up and down a given space— all to judge of their strength.

Vincent was bought by a fisherman, who soon sold him to an old physician, at whose death he again changed masters. The poor priest finally fell into the hands of a renegade Christian, whom he converted after a time. They made their escape together, crossed the Mediterranean Sea in a little boat, and, after many adventures, landed near Marseilles in the Summer of 1607. The converted apostate became a true penitent, and passed the remainder of his days in a severe monastery at Rome.

Paris was now to be the chief field of our Saint's labors—a field where his zeal was to be blessed with the glory of marvellous success. The slave was to become the counsellor of bishops and princes. But the holy toiler began to labor in an obscure corner. Near the gay capital of France there was a parish so miserably poor that for years no pastor could be found to take charge of it. It was Clichy. At his own request Vincent was placed over this forsaken district. Soon there was a great change. We are told that under his rule the people of Clichy "lived like angels." He built a new church, and left everything in a flourishing condition when, at the advice of Cardinal De Berulle, he became preceptor to the noble family of De Gondi.

It was while in this position that an incident is related of the Saint's firmness and Christian charity. A quarrel had arisen between Count De Gondi and a nobleman of the court. It could only be settled by blood. The morning came. After De Gondi had finished a prayer in the family chapel, Vincent approached and said :

"I know on good authority that you are going to fight a duel. I declare to you in the name of my Saviour, whom you have just adored, that if you do not relinquish this wicked design He will exercise His justice upon you and all your posterity." These words were uttered with such force and kindly earnestness that they had the desired effect. **No** duel was fought.

The Saint now began to devote his services to the instruction of the people in various country villages. And greatly they stood in need of it. It was chiefly to carry on this sublime work that he founded the Priests of the Congregation of the Mis‹ sion. The new congregation was approved by Pope Urban VIII. in 1632. St. Vincent lived to see twenty-five houses established.[2]

Boundless was the zeal of this apostolic man. His kind heart went out to suffering humanity in every form. He was one day returning from a mission, as he noticed in a retired spot near the walls of Paris one of those fiendish vagrants who have recourse to the most wicked schemes in order to excite compassion. The wretch was in the act of mutilating the tender limbs of an unfortunate foundling. Filled with horror and indignation, the great priest rushed towards the heartless vagabond and tore the child from his grasp. "Barbarian !" he exclaimed, "at a distance I took you for a man, but I was grievously mistaken." He then bore away the little creature in

[2] The Priests of the Congregation of the Mission first entered the United States in 1816. At present they conduct six colleges and seminaries in our country and have charge of numerous churches. — *See our Popular History of the Catholic Church in the United States,* pp. 370—72.

his arms to one of those asylums which he had established for the reception of abandoned and helpless infancy.

He founded the Sisters of Charity,[2] established hospitals for little orphans, poor old men, and galley-slaves; and he settled all these homes of mercy under such excellent regulations that they had abundant means of support.

At one time, however, the foundling asylum at Paris was about to be discontinued through want

[2] The Sisters of Charity were established in 1633 by the noble Madame Le Gras under the direction of St. Vincent de Paul. Their object—as wide as the world of human misery—was to bestow every possible care on the poor, the sick, the insane, the prisoner, the orphan, the foundling, and the afflicted of every description. Few and simple were their rules. "You shall have no other monastery," said St. Vincent, "than the dwellings of the poor, no other cloisters than the streets of cities and the wards of hospitals, no other law of seclusion than obedience to your superiors, no other veil than Christian modesty. It is my wish that you should treat every sick person as an affectionate mother cares for her only son."

The services of these devoted women were universally sought after. Before the French Revolution they counted no less than 426 establishments in Europe.

In 1809 the saintly Mother Seton and four companions originated the Sisters of Charity in the United States. The Sisters Charity consist of two distinct organizations in this country—one having the mother-house at Emmittsburg, Md., and the other at Mount St. Vincent, New York. Together they have about 200 houses with over 1,800 Sisters.—*See our Popular History of the Catholic Church in the United States*, pp. 401-*0*

of funds. The Saint called together the charitable ladies who had hitherto kept it alive by their
liberal contributions. Standing near were five
hundred little orphans, born in the arms of the
Sisters of Charity. It was a sight truly touching.

"Remember, ladies," said Vincent, "that
compassion and charity have caused you to
adopt these little creatures as your children.
You have been their mothers according to grace,
since they were abandoned by their natural mothers. Now, decide whether you also will abandon them. Cease to be their mothers, that you
may be their judges; in your hands are their life
and death. I am going to take the votes. The
time has come to pronounce their sentence and to
know whether you will no longer have pity on them.
If you continue your charitable care of them, they
will live; if, on the contrary, you abandon them,
they will surely die. Experience does not allow
you to doubt it."

This beautiful appeal—one of the most eloquent
in the annals of oratory—was answered by tears and
sobs. It gained a great victory. The good work
was not abandoned.

Our Saint assisted Louis XIII. at his death,
which was marked by piety and resignation. The
queen regent nominated him a member of the
young king's council, and consulted him on all

ecclesiastical affairs. The history of the Church in France bears witness to his great and holy influence.

He made some enemies, however, in the discharge of his duties, and they basely undertook to injure him by calumny. It was maliciously whispered around that he had, in exchange for a library and a sum of money, procured a benifice for an ambitious man. The story finally came to Vincent's ears. He was deeply affected on hearing the atrocious falsehood. His first impulse was to seize a pen in order to repel the base attack. But he threw it down, exclaiming:

"Ah! unhappy man that I am. What was I about to do? What! I desire to justify myself, and I have only now heard that a Christian—falsely accused at Tunis—passed three days in torments, and at last died without a word of complaint! And I would excuse myself! No, no; it shall not be."

He allowed the calumny to take its course, and soon it spent itself and went the way of all iniquity. Public opinion was in his favor. And, last of all, the untimely death of the slanderer was a solemn hint that God punishes the calumniator and vindicates the character of His servants sooner or later.

Under the Saint's fatherly guidance the Priests

of the Congregation of the Mission grew in number and usefulness. He was especially careful to
insist on a deep, sincere humility. When two
persons, famous for gifts and learning, presented
themselves to be admitted into his Congregation,
he gave a refusal, saying:

"Your abilities raise you above our low state.
Your talents may be of good service in some
other place. As for us, our highest ambition is to
instruct the ignorant, to bring sinners to a spirit
of penance, and to plant the Gospel-spirit of charity, humility, meekness, and simplicity in the
hearts of all Christians."

He laid it down as a rule of humility that, if
possible, a man should never speak of himself—as
all such references usually proceed from vanity and
self-love.

The hardy frame and intrepid energy of St.
Vincent carried him to a ripe old age. In his
eightieth year, however, he was seized by a violent intermittent fever. But he still bore up for
a time, and to the end he was active. His last
thoughts turned to his dear spiritual children, and
his last words referred to them—"He who hath
begun will complete the good work." And when
he gently passed away on the 27th of September,
1660, at the age of eighty-five years, the world
and religion felt that a truly great man was gone
—that the apostle of charity, the friend of the or-

phan, the cripple, the foundling, the helpless, and galley-slave was no more on this earth.[4]

[4] St. Vincent was canonized by Pope Clement XII. in 1742. Three colleges in the United States honor him as their patron, and churches in Scranton City, Mobile, Louisville, Detroit, Baltimore, Buffalo, New Orleans, Chicago, Brooklyn, St. Louis, Boston, Cincinnati, Philadelphia, New York, and countless other places bear his venerable name. In fact, after the Most Blessed Virgin, St. Joseph, and St. Patrick, St. Vincent is one of the great servants of God most honored in this Republic.

SAINT ALPHONSUS LIGUORI,

BISHOP OF ST. AGATHA, DOCTOR OF THE CHURCH, AND FOUNDER OF THE GONGREGATION OF THE MOST HOLY REDEEMER,

DIED A. D. 1787.

ALPHONSUS LIOGURI, whose name is one of the most illustrious in the history of the Church and in the annals of Christian science and literature, was born at the country-seat of his family, near Naples,[1] on the 27th of September, 1696.

His father, Count Joseph Liguori, was a most worthy gentleman and a good Catholic, while his mother, Lady Catherine Cavalieri, was a model of discreet virtue. Alphonsus was their first-born, and was immediately placed under the protection of the Most Blessed Virgin.

When St. Francis Jerome visited the happy countess, she presented her beautiful babe to receive his benediction. "This little one," said the holy Jesuit, "will not die before he is ninety years

---

[1] Naples, the largest city in Italy, is situated on a beautiful bay of the same name. Near by is the volcano of Vesuvius.

478

of age. He will be a bishop, and will do great things for Jesus Christ."

The first teacher of Alphonsus[2] was his noble mother. In the morning she blessed her dear little son and taught him to recite his prayers. The earliest truths impressed on his mind were the sublime truths of religion. Thus was the precious seed wisely sown : nor did it fall on sterile ground.[3]

At nine years of age he was placed in the schools of the Oratorian Fathers, and the boy's progress in learning and virtue excited much admiration. It was at this period that he made his First Communion and began to exhibit marked traits of a noble Christian character.

One day, during play-time, Alphonsus was invited to take a hand at what the scholars called " the game of oranges." At first he refused, saying that he did not know the game ; but as his young companions insisted, he finally yielded. He soon proved skilful, and won thirty times in succession. Jealousy led to anger.

---

[2] Alphonsus signifies *willing*, or *all-ready*. The name is also written *Alphonse*, *Alphonso*, and *Alonzo*.

[3] " If there was anything good in me as a child," said the holy Doctor in old age, " if I kept clear of wickedness, I owe it entirely to my mother." Mothers are the first and greatest teachers. They are the soul-moulders. This truth should be well understood.

" What ! so you did not know the game ?" shouted one of the older boys in a rage, adding some very profane language to this exclamation.

When Alphonsus heard the words he blushed. " How is this?" he said, turning towards the other boys. " Shall God be offended in this way for a few miserable cents ? Take back your money !" And he threw down the few coins he had won, and left the grounds, his boyish face glowing with Christian indignation.

Years after some of his playmates would recount this admirable incident with emotion.

His parents were delighted at the brightness of intellect exhibited by their eldest son. He had a most happy memory and a vigorous understanding, which easily grasped and retained the facts and principles of science, art, and literature. The services of the most distinguished masters were secured to aid the youth in his studies. which embraced Latin, Greek, French, mathematics, the natural sciences, drawing, music,* painting, architecture, and canon and civil law.

Count Liguori intended him for the legal profession, and Alphonsus was so desirous of seconding the wishes of his father that his great genius, backed

---

[4] St. Alphonsus " was an accomplished musician and possessed, even in old age. a voice of such refined culture and marvellous sweetness that when he sang his auditors melted into tears."

by unceasing industry, enabled him to obtain the degree of Doctor of Laws in 1713, by a special dispensation, as he was then but *seventeen* years of age.

The young lawyer was scarcely twenty when he was already famous as a leading advocate. From 1715 to 1723 it is said that he gained all the cases entrusted to him.

In 1723 the tribunals of Naples were occupied with a suit of great importance. It was a contest between the Grand Duke of Tuscany and a powerful nobleman, in which six hundred thousand ducats were involved. The nobleman placed his case in the hands of Alphonsus, who, after long and careful study, said that he believed it could easily be gained. But he had, somehow or other, overlooked *one* document, and that oversight proved disastrous to himself and his client in the courts. The trial came on. The young advocate pleaded with more than usual keenness and brilliancy; but when the adverse party presented the document referred to, Alphonsus was extremely pained and confused. His opponents were right. He himself had been deceived.[5]

---

[5] " Even in old age," says one of the recent biographers of our Saint, " he could never understand how that important paper had escaped him. But Providence had permitted him to overlook it, that it might be an occasion of opening a more direct way for the accomplishment of God's designs on him."

"World, I know you now," he exclaimed. "Courts of law, never more shall you hear my voice !"

"Law is a dangerous profession, and exposes one to an unprovided death," he afterwards said to a friend. "I renounced it because I wished, above all things, to save my soul, and must, under all circumstances, follow the dictates of my conscience."

After many internal trials and external troubles and annoyances, Alphonsus decided to renounce the world and to study for the holy ministry. He had a remarkably firm character, and of course to decide was to execute.

His father's grief and vexation, however, were boundless. Nor did he try to hide his feelings. When Alphonsus first appeared at home clothed in a cassock, the old count " uttered a piercing shriek, and for a year after never addressed a word to his once idolized son."

The Saint now turned his attention to the things of heaven, and bent his rich, well-trained mind to the study of the sacred sciences. He was ordained priest on the 21st of December, 1726, at the age of thirty-one.

"I am a priest," he wrote in his rule of life. "My dignity is above that of the angels. I should then lead a life of angelic purity, and I am obliged to strive for this by all possible means. . . . The

Holy Church has honored me. I must therefore honor myself by sanctity of life and by zeal and labors."

As a preacher his success was immediate. All hearts were touched by his sermons. Among those who went regularly to hear his words of holy eloquence was Capasso, a man whose great powers of satire and vast knowledge had made him celebrated. One day the Saint and the satirist met.

" You always come to hear me," said Father Liguori, adding with a smile, "Should you not like to make me the subject of some new satire?"

"No, no," replied Capasso. "I listen to you with pleasure, *because I see that you forget yourself to preach Christ crucified.*"

But it was especially as a confessor that the ruling passion of his life became manifest—his passion for great sinners. The holy priest put himself in their way. He met them everywhere. He followed the most hardened and wretched. He attracted them. He heard their tales of sin and sorrow, and gave them absolution.

On one occasion a young gentleman sought the Saint's confessional. He accused himself of a number of enormous crimes in a tone of levity and indifference. He then paused. "Anything more?" asked Father Liguori. " No," said the youth.

" What !" returned the priest, " is that all ? Now, do you not see that the only thing required to make you a Turk is the turban ?   Tell me, my son," continued the kind-hearted Saint in accents of touching tenderness, "what evil has Jesus Christ done you ?"

The words fell like the rod of Moses on the parched rock.   They touched the hard heart of the young sinner, and tears of repentance suddenly gushed from his eyes.   His exemplary after-life proved two things—the depth of his contrition, and the priceless blessing of having a Saint for confessor.

" He could not endure those confessors," says Cardinal Wiseman, "who received their penitents with a discouraging, supercilious air, or who, having heard them, sent them off disdainfully as unworthy or incapable of the divine mercy.   His whole life was a protest against proceedings of this nature, and towards the close of his career he could use these magnificent words, which are the confirmation of his glory, and which should be written in letters of diamond: '*I do not remember that I ever sent away a sinner without absolution.*'"

The life of this illustrious man was filled with incessant labors—sermons, retreats, confessions, missions.   In fact, he went so far as to make a vow never to lose a moment of time.   Even the fragments he used to advantage. "I never remember," said one of his companions, "to have seen Alphonsus waste a moment when he lived with us. He was always preaching, or hearing confessions, or at prayer or study."

It was while conducting missions in various parts of his native country that Father Liguori began to feel the want of fellow-laborers. He prayed for light. He took counsel of the wise and learned. And finally he came to the conclusion that it was the will of Heaven that he should found a new congregation of missionary priests for the spiritual aid of those souls which are the most destitute. Thus arose the *Congregation of the Most Holy Redeemer,* which dates its origin from the year 1732.

The first house of the new congregation was founded at Scala. The Saint was joined by twelve companions—ten priests, two candidates for Holy Orders, and one serving lay brother.

---

[6] Commonly called the *Redemptorist Fathers.*

[7] Three priests of the Congregation of the Most Holy Redeemer landed on the shores of the United States in 1832, just one hundred years after the founding of the congregation. At present they have houses and parishes in most of our large cities.— *See our Popular History of the Catholic Church in the United States,* p. 372.

[8] "A gentleman named Vitus Curzius," writes the Saint's American biographer, "whose vocation was evidently miraculous, was the first lay brother. He had been secretary of the

Most austere was the life of Alphonsus and his disciples. The house was small. The beds consisted of a little straw shaken on the floor. Hard, black bread formed about their only nourishment. One religious exercise followed another with the regularity of the clock. Not a moment was lost. From time to time they spread themselves over the country to gather in a precious harvest of souls.

But all good things have their time of trial, and the work of our Saint was soon tested in the crucible. The evil one created dissensions in the new society. The regulations drawn up by Alphonsus proved very offensive to some of the members. The murmurers grew in numbers,

Marquis of Vasto, and was very intimate with Sportelli, of whose vocation, however, he knew nothing. One day he mentioned to him a dream he had the preceding night. 'I thought,' said he, 'that I stood at the foot of a high and steep mountain, which many priests were trying to ascend. I wished to follow them, but at the first step was thrown backwards. Unwilling to give up, I tried several times to ascend; but to my great annoyance I always slid back, till a priest, moved with compassion, reached out his hand and helped me.' Towards noon, as they walked to the Chinese College, they met Alphonsus. Curzius—who had never seen him before—struck with astonishment, exclaimed: 'There is the priest who gave me his hand last night!' Sportelli now understood the dream and mentioned the design of the founder, whereupon—Curzius instantly begged to be admitted among the disciples of the Saint, but in quality of lay brother. His request was granted."

and to such a pitch did the discontentment reach that all his companions deserted the Saint except two—Dr. Sportelli, a layman, and the lay brother Curzius.

It was, in truth, a supreme moment. Friends and foes alike now laughed at the forsaken founder. Even pious and learned ecclesiastics treated him as a visionary. He was made the butt of ridicule. But the dauntless man of God, pursuing the even tenor of his way, continued to work alone ; and at length the dark day of distress passed, and new laborers came to his assistance. The Pope approved the rules of his Congregation. Its life was no longer doubtful.[*] When the members set about to elect a superior-general, their choice fell upon the holy founder, who was unanimously elected for life.

Several years passed away. One day a venerable old gentleman approached a house of the Congregation, and on entering he was penetrated with feelings of devotion. It was Count Joseph Liguori, who had come to visit his great son. He soon grew so delighted with the humble, peaceful life of the Fathers that he even begged to be admit-

---

[*] For a complete history of the great Saint and his countless trials in establishing the Congregation of the Most Holy Redeemer, see the "Life of St. Alphonsus Liguori," by a Sister of Mercy. It is an excellent work, to which we are greatly indebted.

ted as a simple lay brother. But our Saint did not
favor such a step.

"This vocation," said he to his father, "does not
come from God. You must live in the world and
edify it by your example as father of a family, in
which condition God has placed you."

The old nobleman went home, kept up a regular correspondence with Alphonsus, and under
his wise direction he labored to become a saint.
Some time after he died, covered with years and
merits.

While Father Liguori attended with unceasing
care to all his countless duties as superior-general, he gave special attention to the training of
his students for their missionary labors. It was
his great aim to form priests of solid virtue and
extensive knowledge. "A laborer without science,"
he would remark to his students, "even though
he be a man of prayer, is like a soldier without
arms."

He greatly disliked seeing the truths of the
Gospel tricked out in the frippery of gaudy rhetoric. "Puffed-up orators," he said, "give out but
wind. They think more of displaying their own
eloquence than of glorifying Jesus Christ. If they
escape hell, they will at least have to get rid of
their inflation in purgatory."

Throughout all the well-filled years of his life
the Saint continued to add to his labors and merits

by the preparation of matchless works on piety, virtue, and the sacred sciences. [10]   His writings, learning, and sanctity had made him celebrated. Of course he was offered dignities.   He refused the archbishopric of Palermo.   But when the See of St. Agatha became vacant he was appointed Bishop, and the Pope would not hear of a refusal. After his consecration he said: "I was terrified to think of the burden to be imposed on me and the account I was one day to give of it to God."

The Saint reached his episcopal see on the 11th

The works of St. Alphonsus number, we believe, about one hundred.   Besides his justly, renowned treatises on theology (in Latin)," may be mentioned the "Christian Virtues," "Glories of Mary," "Preparation for Death," "The True Spouse of Christ," "Visits to the Blessed Sacrament," "Instructions on the Commandments and Sacraments," and "The History of Heresies," all of which, and many others, have been translated into English. The decree by which the immortal Pius IX., in 1871, elevated the Saint to the rare dignity of *Doctor of the Church* speaks thus of his works : "But what he reduced to practice in his holy life he taught also in word and by writing.   He stands distinguished for dispelling and clearing up the lurking-places of unbelievers and Jansenists, so widely spread.   And, over and above this, he has cleared up questions that were clouded, he has solved what was doubtful, making a safe path through which the directors of Christian souls may tread with harmless feet between the involved opinions of theologians, whether too loose or too rigorous.   And besides this, he has signally cast light on the doctrines of the Immaculate Conception and the Infallibility of the Sovereign Pontiff teaching *ex cathedra,* and he strenuously taught these doctrines, which in our day have been defined as of faith."

of July, 1762.   He was then sixty-six years of
age.   But he immediately began to work like a
young apostle.   He opened his labors by giving
a mission of eight days.   In a short time many
abuses were corrected, many sinners converted,
and the diocese wore a new aspect.

"We have a holy bishop," said the people.   "We
have a saint among us."

" We prayed to God to send us a good bishop,"
remarked a Church dignitary, "and He has heard
us; but Monseigneur will kill himself."

He won the love and confidence of the poor
people during his visitations.   They flocked to
hear him.   " Let us go," they would exclaim as
he entered their villages, "let us go to hear *the
Saint that smooths the way to heaven !*"

Though even great saints cannot reform everybody and everything in a day, still it is marvellous what one of them *can* do.   One of our Saint's
canons had been a scandal-giver of old standing,
and it was in vain that the illustrious Bishop had
again and again besought him to lead a life of
virtue.

" My son," said Alphonsus at last, throwing
himself at the culprit's feet and presenting his
crucifix, "my son, if you will not obey me as your
Bishop, be converted for the sake of Jesus Christ,
who died for you and for me!"

Even this touching appeal failed to produce

any impression; but after a time the unhappy man became a sincere penitent.

Alphonsus was a Bishop of angelic meekness. On a certain occasion, being rudely insulted by a priest from the country, he treated the offender so gently that his archdeacon, who was present, expressed surprise at what he considered to be simply an encouragement of course wickedness.

"I have been laboring," returned the Saint, "for forty years to gain a little patience, and you want me to lose it all in a moment."

"There is nothing," he remarked on another occasion, "more unseemly in a bishop than anger. A bishop who gives way to this passion is no longer the father of his flock. He is an intractable tyrant who draws universal hatred upon himself"

He was the very soul of hospitality. He loved to converse with the poor, the rude, and the illiterate, whom he always kindly received at his episcopal residence. On finding amongst his letters one from a poor person, he exclaimed: "Ah! this pleases me. It is a request for charity."

The holy Doctor was kind to all but himself. He "was as cruel to himself," said one who knew him well, "as he was kind to others. I would make you shudder were I to relate all the particulars of his macerations, his abstinence from food, his daily scourgings to blood— of the hair-shirts and iron chains which kept his body in a continual mortification, his watchings, and in short everything that can afflict the flesh was made use of by Monsignor Liguori."

The Church was passing through a sad period of gloom and storm during the last years of the holy Doctor's life. Pope Clement XIV., pressed as he was on all sides, suppressed the Society of Jesus in 1773. No one bewailed this unhappy event more than St. Alphonsus. "The loss of the Jesuits," he had remarked some time before, "will place the Pope and the Church in a most disastrous situation; the Jansenists [11] aim at them, because through them they will be the more certain of striking at Church and State."

[11] The Jansenists were a sect of gloomy fanatics who owed their name, if not their origin, to Jansenius, Bishop of Ypres, in the early part of the seventeenth century. In their spiritual teaching all was rigor and extreme severity. They wished to make God a tyrant, not a merciful Father. Frequent confession and communion they condemned. They taught that a general council was above the Pope. They tried to banish joy from religion, and to introduce the demon of melancholy. And for many years and in many places, unhappily, they had only too much success. "We know," says a French writer, "what Jansenist education meant. The little children were sternly treated. They must not laugh or jest too loud, or show their pretty little teeth in smiles. They were forced to submit to sacrifices which, to be meritorious, must be free and voluntary." For over two centuries these sanctimonious knaves troubled the Church. St. Alphonsus did much to destroy Jansenism, and the Vatican Council gave it the final death-blow.

A year rolled by. On the 21st of September, 1774, after celebrating Mass, Bishop Liguori, then near the end of his seventy-eighth year, sat down on an arm-chair. He fell into a tranquil slumber. He remained in this motionless state all day and all the following night. He awoke about eight o'clock on the morning of the 22d, and immediately pulled the bell. With tears in their eyes his attendants gathered around. He asked what was the matter, and they replied that he had neither spoken nor eaten for two days.

"That is true," said the Saint, "but do you not know that I have been with the Pope, who has just died?"

News soon reached the town that Clement XIV. had passed to a better world at eight o'clock on the morning of the 22d, the very hour in which St. Alphonsus had come to himself!

Weighed down as he was by age and infirmities, Alphonsus had long sought to be relieved from the burden of the episcopate. When Pius VI. became Pope he again applied for permission to retire. The new pontiff, with much sorrow, accepted his resignation.

"Blessed be God!" he exclaimed, when he heard the welcome intelligence. "A mountain has been removed from my breast."

It was in the summer of 1775 that he bade adieu to his diocese. The scene at the departure of his carriage was truly affecting. Multitudes surrounded him, and not a dry cheek was to be seen. The kind, paternal heart of the illustrious old Saint was touched, and big, round tears filled his eyes as he gave his flock the parting bene-diction.

The venerable man now retired to a house of his Congregation, where he lived the same as the other Fathers. He wrote and preached as of old. But his poor health soon completely broke down. For eight years before his death he was unable to say Mass. In 1786 he wrote to one of his old friends, a Carmelite: "Father Joseph, we shall not meet again next year." It was only too true. The close was coming, and he bore his cross manfully to the last breath. Violent temptation assailed, but he prayed to Christ and His Blessed Mother. When any friend came to his dying-bed for words of advice, he simply said: "*Save your soul.*"

One of his last utterances was: "I believe all the Holy Catholic Church teaches, and thus I have hope." And with this heavenly hope in his heart, and the crucifix and an image of Mary pressed to his bosom, the bright soul of the great Alphonsus Liguori—"the Saint who had smoothed the way to heaven"—passed calmly out of this life as the sound of the Angelus bell sweetly rolled along the air on the 1st of August, in the year

1787. He had reached the ripe age of ninety-two.[12]

[12] St. Alphonsus was canonized by Pope Pius VII. in 1836; and in 1871, Pope Pius IX. conferred upon him the rare and magnificent title of *Doctor of the Church.*

There are churches in Wheeling, Baltimore, New Orleans, Brooklyn, St. Louis, Philadelphia, New York, and many other places dedicated to divine worship under the patronage of St. Alphonsus. How true it is that " the just are held in everlasting remembrance."

OTHER TITLES AVAILABLE

Trustful Surrender to Divine Providence.
A Year with the Saints.
Saint Michael and the Angels.
The Dolorous Passion of Our Lord. Emmerich.
Modern Saints—Their Lives & Faces. Ball.
Our Lady of Fatima's Peace Plan from Heaven.
Divine Favors Granted to St. Joseph. Binet.
St. Joseph Cafasso—Priest of the Gallows. St. John Bosco.
Catechism of the Council of Trent.
The Rosary in Action. Johnson.
Padre Pio—The Stigmatist. Carty.
The Life of Anne Catherine Emmerich. 2 Vols. Schmoger.
Fatima—The Great Sign. Johnston.
Wife, Mother and Mystic. Bessieres.
St. Rose of Lima. Sister Alphonsus.
Charity for the Suffering Souls. Nageleisen.
Devotion to the Sacred Heart of Jesus. Verheylezoon.
Who Is Padre Pio?
The Stigmata and Modern Science. Carty.
The Incorruptibles. Cruz.
The Life of Christ. 4 Vols. Emmerich.
St. Dominic. Dorcy.
Is It a Saint's Name? Dunne.
St. Anthony—The Wonder Worker of Padua. Stoddard.
The Precious Blood. Fr. Faber.
The Holy Shroud & Four Visions. O'Connell.
Clean Love in Courtship. Lovasik.
The Devil. Delaporte.
Too Busy for God? Think Again! D'Angelo.
The Prophecies of St. Malachy. Bander.
St. Martin de Porres. Cavallini.
The Secret of the Rosary. St. Louis De Montfort.
The History of Antichrist. Huchede.
Purgatory Explained. Schouppe.
St. Catherine of Siena. Curtayne.
Where We Got the Bible. Graham.
Imitation of the Sacred Heart of Jesus. Arnoudt.
Alexandrina—The Agony & The Glory. Johnston.
Blessed Margaret of Castello. Bonniwell.
The Ways of Mental Prayer. Lehodey.
The Douay-Rheims Bible. Leatherbound.

At your bookdealer or direct from the Publisher.